# HINDU HOLIDAYS AND CEREMONIALS

# HINDU HOLIDAYS AND CEREMONIALS

## WITH
## DISSERTATIONS ON ORIGIN, FOLKLORE, AND SYMBOLS

RAI BAHADUR B. A. GUPTE, F. Z. S.

WITH EIGHTEEN ILLUSTRATIONS

GYAN

*Published by*

Gyan Publishing House
5, Ansari Road
Daryaganj, New Delhi-110002
Phone: 011-47034999, 9811692060
E-mail: books@gyanbooks.com

*Distribution Network*
gyanbooks.com
India, USA, Canada, UK, Australia, France



ISBN : 978-81-212-9588-8 (PB)
First Published, 1916

2nd Impression 2023

*Printed at:* Gyan Press, Delhi.



**HINDU HOLIDAYS AND CEREMONIALS**
Author: RAI BAHADUR B. A. GUPTE

The Author

*Photo by—* *F. Harrington*

Rai Bahadur B. A. Gupte

# HINDU HOLIDAYS AND CEREMONIALS

WITH

## DISSERTATIONS ON ORIGIN, FOLKLORE, AND SYMBOLS

BY

RAI BAHADUR B. A. GUPTE, F.Z.S.,

*Fellow of the Royal Society of Arts, London, Honorary Member Bombay Art Society, Associate Member Asiatic Society of Bengal, Member Royal Agricultural Society of London,*

*formerly*

*Honorary Assistant Superintendent of Ethnography to the Government of Bombay, Assistant Director of Ethnography for India,*

*retired*

*Deputy Minister, and Member of Council, Indore.*

---

WITH EIGHTEEN ILLUSTRATIONS, SIX IN COLOUR.

---

1916

## LIST OF ILLUSTRATIONS

# PREFACE

THE origin and evolution of this work will form an interesting fascicle of the history of India duiing Lord Curzon's regime, as it was he who succeeded in creating the Ethnographic Survey of India in the face of strong opposition from certain quarters. His Lordship's name will remain in the pages of the future history of India as the greatest patron of the science of Ethnography of the vast continent of India.

Sir Herbert Risley was selected for the important duties of Honorary Director of Ethnography for India. That was a happy choice and through his able and scholarly directions, a tremendous mass of the most fascinating details of the social life of India has been collected. I was first appointed Honorary Assistant Superintendent of Ethnography to the Government of Bombay, and subsequently Assistant Director of Ethnogrophy for India under Sir Herbert. He asked me to write some articles for the Indian Antiquary at Sir Richard Temple's request. This is the beginning of the work I now call the *Hindu Holidays and Ceremonials.*" When Sir Herbert was promoted to the Secretaryship of the Government of India, Sir Edward Gait was appointed Census Commissioner. I continued working under both the officers and in that joint capacity submitted some of my articles to him, as well as to the Honourable Mr. R. Burn, I.C.S. who succeeded him.

On the 1st of July 1903 Sir Edward Gait, the then Census Commissioner and my chief remarked on my note on Ganesh and Gauri that "it would be better" if I "could find time to incorporate these interesting notes in a full discussion of the *Vratās*." I followed this advice but it took me years to collect sufficient materials for this volume. Some of these notes were revised and published by Sir Herbert Risley, some were contributed to the Indian Antiquary and edited by Sir Richard Temple, some were published in the Journal of the Asiatic Society of Bengal and revised by Dr. N. Annandale, and some appeared in the *Bombay Gazette*, the *Statesman*, the *Reis and Rayyet* and other journals. But the originals of all these stories are not in print and attempts had to be made to collect unpublished traditions.

The best course to follow was to take the help of a lady. Indian ladies can collect folklore and traditions with a facility denied to the sterner sex owing to social restrictions on free conversation between members of different sexes. Religious episodes are moreover communicated to ladies by the priests and priestesses without reserve, because they are not supposed to criticise them. Publication or discussion among educated young men involves exposure in several instances, resulting in the loss of sacerdotal influence. I therefore asked my wife to help me in collecting materials and I am thankful to her for valuable help—the result of her indefatigable labour of love. She has collected together quite a library of Sanskrit and Marāthi books and manuscripts bought solely to help me in my task.

I am responsible for the translations and dissertations added in the light of the training I have received as a literary Assistant working under Sir James Campbell, Sir George Birdwood, Sir Edward Gait, Sir William Meyer, Sir Herbert Risley and the Honourable Mr. Enthoven.

I am obliged to so many authors and friends that it is impossible for me to make a complete list, I therefore thank them all. Mrs. Gupte is specially obliged to the wives of Mr. Jogesh Chandra Dutt, J.P., Honorary Magistrate of Calcutta, Rai Bahadur Matilal Ganguli, Mrs. Jogesh Chandra Bose, Mrs. Motilal Bose and Mrs. Mahendra Nath Shome—our old landlady.

Mrs. Alice Elizabeth Dracott rendered very valuable assistance in examining the proofs. She is herself the author of a book styled Simla Village Tales. Her experience and literary attainments have been fully utilized in avoiding unEnglish expressions which often creep in unobserved, in works compiled by an Indian, however experienced he may be.

BELVEDERE, CALCUTTA,
15-5-16

B. A. GUPTE.

# INTRODUCTION

In this Chapter I have strung together the opinions of European scholars on allied matters, to be able to give an idea of what to expect from the study of these pages.

J. Bryant's "System of Analysis of Ancient Mythology" tells us "that like the people of Babylonia and Egypt where the first ray of religion possibly appeared, the people of this country began with devotion to the *unaccountable phenomena of nature.* He says that the Deity which they originally worshipped was the Sun. The worship of Baal was the worship of the Sun, Ham was esteemed the Zeus of Greece and Jupiter of Latium."

The Hindu *Ratha-saptami*, *Sanskrāt* and *Kapilā-shathi*, are examples. Even the *sandhya* of the twice born castes of India has for its chief deity the vedic Savita or the sun. Bryant adds that the ancients soon conferred the titles of the Sun upon some of their ancestors. Of this we have an example in the Mārtand of Jejuri near Poona. There, instead of the glorious orb as its very name Mārtand implies, people worship Khand-oba—which means the swords-man-father from *Khand*, the sword *oba* or *aba* the father. A woman married to the sword of a hero is called *Khandā-Rāni* in Marathi from the same root *Khand*, a sword. But the Khandoba of Jejuri still retains the attributes of the Sun. For instance, he rides a yellow steed (yellow rays), his flag is also yellow (yellow reflected light on the clouds), and he has two wives one fair and one dark. They represent Eos and Eve respectively.

Fergusson says that "the inhabitants of the Valley of the Ganges, before the Aryans reached India, seem to have been Tree and Serpent worshippers, a people without any distinct idea of God, but apparently worshipping their ancestors, and it may be, indulging in human sacrifices." (p 126)

In addition to ancestor worship being thus mixed up with Nature worship there are deified Patriarchs, who may or may not have been the heads of their line. The Bāpdev of Kadāppa or Sāvarsai may be cited as instances. *Bāp* clearly means father. Like Nimrod the son of Cush, he was a hunter. His history is plainly alluded to under the character of Alorus, the first king of Chaldæa, but more frequently under the title Orion, the starry constellation. "This personage is represented by Homer as of a gigantic make and as being continually in persuit of wild beasts." If we look at the celestial chart, what do we see, but hunters and wild beasts! The Orion of the West, is the *Mriga* constellation of this country. Thus it will be seen that the story of the *Mahā-Shivarātra* merely reproduces in a modified form the ancestor- worship and worship of Nature, which originated in Chaldæa the cradle of ancient astronomy. It is said that the Cushite or Cuthite families which went from Chaldæa carried with them memorials of their ancestor. *Nibarhana* says Mr. Waidya in his Sanskrit dictionary means "killing, destruction, annihilation." It is for Philologists to say whether Nimrod the killer or hunter has any connection with this root. Nibros in the Greek language is a fawn which gave occasion to many allusions about that animal, and its skin in the Dionusiaca and other mysteries. Hindu God Shiva, whose origin can easily be traced to the Mithun or third sign of the Zodiac, and who is mentioned in the *Shivarātra* story, has a fawn in his hand. He is associated with a fawn skin in many of his pictures or representations. Ideas thus travel with colonies, they may undergo modifications, but some of the resemblances do remain.

J. Bryant again tells us (p. 7) "that the Amonians call Ham, Amon, and having in process of time raised him to divinity they worshipped him as the sun. The reading therefore of folklore stories is a fascinating study. One has to divest them of fantastic allegory with which they have been obscured. He adds, that " they have been veiled in allegory, and are often renewed under a different system and arrangement. A great part of this ancient lore has been transmitted through poets, who have rendered it still more extravagant and strange ! "

Sir William Jones declares the subject to be " so obscure and so much clouded by the fictions of the Brahmans that we can hope to obtain no system of Indian Chronology to which no objection can be made." " We find the whole, like the grotesque picture blazened high and glaring with colours, and fitted with group of fantastic imaginary. But in the allegorical representations of facts there was always a covert meaning, though it may have escaped the discernment of subsequent writers." My intelligent and well-informed readers have to find out the " *covert meaning* " Sir William thus refers to.

Brennand in his Hindu Astronomy says that " the early religion, indeed, of the Hindus like other religions, had as we know, a close intimacy with *time and seasons* " ( p 25 ). Some of the popular and general Hindu Holidays seem to have been based on changes of the season, and others on natural phenomena. *Ganesh* and *Gauri* for instance represent the death and resurrection of the season, so do *Vatsāvitri*, *Diwāli*, and *Holi*. *Vasant-Panchami* marks the near approach of the summer. *Champā Shashthi* marks the phenomenon of the rising Sun driving or dispersing a fog, *Mahāshivarātra* marks the night on which the *Mrig* constellation or the Orion is seen in its best aspect. *Somavati* represents the absence of *Soma* (the moon) on a Monday, like "Hamlet without Hamlet". *Navānna-pornima* implies, as its name shows, the day on which the first meal of the new corn is to be tasted. These are possibly the most ancient ceremonials and signify the reverence felt at the change of the seasons, by primitive people. The worship of the symbols of creative power represented by *Shiva* and *Pārvati* are more modern as my comments of the *Mahāshivarātra* shows, that Shiva, Pārvati, Nandi the Bull of Shiva, the Lion of Pārvati and even Ganesh of the *shaivite* group are taken from the signs of the Zodiac. Gemini is the sign which suggested the eternal couple the curious origin of everything in nature, and a number of stories gathered round the group. *Pradoshas, Shivarātris, Haritālikas, Kālipujās* and worship of the female power have all emanated from that group. Story after story has been inserted to increase the number of fasts and feasts, to add to the income of the priests, and advice is everywhere given to feed and support them bountifully.

In the third set the holidays are mythological and historical. These are birth-days of different heros or gods such as *Rāma-Navami, Janmāshtami* and the *Jayantis* or birthdays of *Hanumān, Parashurām, Narsinha* etc.

The last class includes special stories compiled for the edification of the weaker sex. Of these there is an endless variety : *Satya Nārāyan, Satya-Vināyak, Siddhi Vināyak.* and *Solā-Somvār,* or sixteen Mondays are examples of this group. Women are the best customers of the priests all over the world, and numerous *vratas* have been invented for their special use, such as *Gopadma, Panch-Deva, Prithvi-Puja,* the *Lamp day, Friday* fasts, *Nāgpanchami, Shilā-Saptami, Pithori, Vasu-bāras,* etc. The *shāstras* suggest only a few ceremonials, the *purānās* add a large number, and traditions supply the largest group. It is this last group which is very difficult to get at for ethnographic purposes as the priests and the women alone are the store houses of the set, and here lies the importance of the assistance of Mrs. Gupte who helped me in collecting folklore stories of this kind in the three, provinces of Bengal, Bombay, and Central India.

Brennand tells us how ancient myths and allegories originated. He says that when Hinduism was overpowered by Buddhism, the success of the revolution which made

Buddhism the state religion is supposed to have been owing to a great increase in the population, and a wide-spread discontent among the lower orders which found in the new Government a relief from the severe discipline of the Brahmanical and other high classes. Caste was abolished and the freedom of the subject asserted. The overthrow of the Aryan (Brahman) rule was therefore, easily accomplished. We can only form conjectures regarding the attitude of the Brahmans in this juncture of their affairs. It may be that some of them temporised with the ruling powers, compelled by circumstances to conform to the spirit of the times, and appeared as converts to the new faith, concealing their opinions to avoid persecution. Others appear to have turned their attention to literary persuits, and *created those allegories, fables, and tales of fiction,* which have since been the amusement and formed the mythology of the country for many centuries", (p 135).

"The knowledge acquired by the Hindu astronomers was guarded with the greatest care, as sacred and was supposed to be so secret that it was not known even to the Gods." It was not to be communicated to the common people, and being regarded as a revelation, to inspire Saints, was only to be divulged to disciples similarly inspired (p. 27). They were to be communicated only as myths and allegories with hidden meanings."

"The astronomical mythology of the Hindus, grotesque and barbarous as some of their stories may appear, had within it *much that was valuable in point of instruction*" (p 323). (The italics are mine.)

Some of these folklore stories will show that they are intended for recording discoveries in astronomical phenomena. When writing was not known or when it was not communicated to the masses, stories were used instead. The folklore of *Kokilā-vrat, Kapilā-Shasthi,* and the tortoise incarnation are examples. The shapes given to the constellations mentioned in them, served as hieroglyphics to fix them into the memory. Mrs. Gupte's *Divlāi* and *Vat-Sāvitri* drawings also serve as hieroglyphics. They have served to transmit from generation to generation the folk-lore of the death and resurrection of the seasons. In this connection Lord Arundell of Wardour records in his book called "Tradition principally with reference to the Mythology and the law of Nations" (page 122), that "what strikes one most forcibly in contemplating these ages, is the contrast between their intellectual knowledge and their mechanical and material contrivances for its application, when paper, parchment, or even the smoothed hides, as adapted for the purposes of writing, were unknown." "This establishes the retentive strength of their memory, and their intellectual familiarity with great truths." According to the Chinese accounts, the works of Confucius were proscribed, after his death, by the Emperor Chi-Hoangti, and all the copies were recovered from the dictation of an old man who had retained them in memory," (like the *Vedas*). In the article in the *Cornhill Magazine*, November 1871, containing a valuable collection of South Indian folk songs, it is said at page 577 that "they are handed down from generation to generation entirely *viva voce*, and from the ministrels have passed into public use." So are these folklore stories and songs about Hindu Holidays and ceremonials. In many instances they possibly record, in addition to natural phenomena a few historical facts intermixed with supernatural fiction. They, moreover, record the manners, customs, and beliefs of the time. Compared with similar stories of the different provinces they yield interesting material for the comparison of manners and customs of different societies at different stages of their existence. Brennand again adds :—

"*With the Hindus, this study became a duty, in as much as the celestial bodies were viewed as Gods, and the worship of them was enjoined by the Vedas.*" (p. 26).

The originators knew the causes of many of the phenomena, as Brennand has recorded that "there is no doubt that the cause of the eclipses, notwithstanding the superstition of the people generally, was well understood by the Hindu astronomers and that even in the Paganism and mythology of the Hindus, *there is substratum of worth so far as they are connected with their system of astronomy*" (p. 320). But he says that to extend further investigation on the subject, many Hindu writings and symbols exist which if translated or interpreted would throw *greater light upon the evolution of myths.* It *was the diligent use which the Hindu astronomers made of astronomy, that gave them their superiority over all other nations.*" (The italics are mine.)

There is every likelihood of many of these mouth-to-mouth stories and *zenāna* ceremonials disappearing in the near future as I have myself noted great changes during the last forty years. The zeal, the enthusiasm, the solemnity, and even the fear of the displeasure of the demi-gods at the slightest mistake in the ceremonials, have undergone great modifications. Many of the *vratas* have become obsolete, and most of them are more tolerated than appreciated. The advance of civilization under the British rule has arrested the growth of superstitious observances, and no new stories are being added. Of the old ceremonials, those that are voluntary are scarcely observed, and those that are compulsary are delegated to the care of priests with a few additional coins as hush money! "*Purohit dvāra*" viz., through the priest I do perform this *puja*" has become a very common formula. Before therefore they disappear altogether, it is important ethnographically that they should be carefully recorded and how far I and Mrs. Gupte have succeeded in achieving this end, I leave it to my readers to decide.

## CONTENTS

# FOLKLORE IN ANIMALS AND PLANTS

In this chapter, I have collected together the folklore in the animals and plants mentioned in this book and arranged them alphabetically. Of course there are many other animate and inanimate things round which similar traditions have grouped themselves, but I feel it advisable to confine my remarks to those only which are required for studying these pages.

## I. FOLKLORE IN ANIMALS

**Antelope,** gazelle's skin is much in use among ascetics. Shiva is supposed to wear it. In some parts of India, antelopes are not killed by Hindus. The Saint, Shring Rishi was born of a nymph transformed into a doe.

**Bear** (p. 63). Jāmbubant was the king of bears, or perhaps of a primitive tribe wearing the mask of a bear. His daughter Jāmbuvanti married Krishna (see Ganesh for folklore).

**Boar.** *Varāh.* In the third incarnation, Vishnu was a boar.

**Bull.** *Nandi,* (pp 56 & 85) is the charger of Shiva. It is worshipped along with that God, or separately as Basāppa by Lingayats in the Kanara District.

W. Brennand in his Hindu Astronomy says: "That the bull should have been held to be a most sacred animal in prehistoric times among the migrating tribes, and afterwards especially revered in Egypt and India, is a circumstance that would appear to have its explanation in the fact that, between the years 2426 B.C. and 266 B.C., the equinox was retrograding through the Constellation TAURUS. The Egyptians undoubtedly worshipped one of these animals at their City of Pharbethus. When the Apis died it was put into a coffin and interred in the temple of Ser-Apis. The Bull's head was esteemed a princely hieroglyphic, and Astarte, it is said, placed the head of a bull upon her head as a royal emblem. Mountains, places and peoples are named "Taurus, Taurica, Taurini, Taurisci, Tauropolis, Tauropolium. The Persian priests of Mithra (Sanskrit "Mitra" the Sun) used to clothe themselves in the skins of lions at the Mysteries called Leonticae, and were called lions because the star Cor Leonis was near the summer solstice and a parallel of declination through it in the year 2305 B.C. might properly be termed the "tropic of Leo." Bulls are always let loose on the 13th day of the obsequies of a member of the twice born or high caste families along with a heifer but the latter is appropriated by the priest and the bull alone let loose. The brand of a trident indicates connection with Shiva and as the origin of Shiva is traced to the third sign of the Zodiac, the sanctity of the Bull may safely be traced to the second sign Taurus. The commencement of this feeling among the priests may be placed between B.C. 2426 and 266 while the equinox was retrograding through it as is testified by corroborative evidence regarding Leo, the Lion.

**Conch.** *Shankh.* The shell of the *Turbinella pyrum,* is worshipped in front of the family gods. *Shankh* is said to be the brother of Laxmi, the goddess of wealth, because both of them were churned out of the ocean. Shankhâsur was the shell-demon which Vishnu killed in his first incarnation (*Matsya*). Vishnu has a conch called *Pānchajanya* and Arguna has one called *Devadatta.*

**Cow.** The sacred nature of the cow is well-known. The earth is repeatedly represented in the *Purānas* as a cow appearing before the gods to lodge her complaints against the sinful actions of the demons.

**Cowries.** Shells, *Cypress monita,* used as coins in India, are supposed in Bengal to represent Laxmi, the Goddess of

Wealth. They are worshipped along with her, or are offered to her. The goddess of Kolhapur wears a wreath of shells and her devotees do the same.

**Crocodile.** (See Gherial).

**Crow.** The crow is considered an inauspicious bird and yet is fed on the *Shrādh* day under the belief that it carries the food it eats to heaven for the *pitris.*

**Cuckoo.** *Eudynamys Orientalis*, represents *Sati* the wife of Shiva (see *Kokila Vrat*). This bird is therefore worshipped. It is said to be the harbinger of spring as its cry indicates the approach of the season. It is considered a good omen to hear the cry of a cuckoo on certain occasions.

**Dog** (p. 19). The dog is considered an unclean animal although there are four dogs in attendance on Dattātreya or Trimurti, this animal is not touched after a bath, and is not allowed in the interior of that part of a house in which the gods are worshipped. (See Trimurti).

**Donkey.** In Bengal, Sitalādevi the goddess of smallpox, rides a donkey, but in Western India she is seated on a lotus. She has a temple at Thana, in Salsette. In the Marātha country, the man who deserves a public disgrace is compelled to ride a donkey .

**Eagle.** Garud is the celestial eagle the charger which carries Vishnu. The Khatris of the Punjab feed eagles on the *Shrādh* days. It is believed that the Great Garud lives on snakes. He is the king of birds. He has a white face, red wings, and golden body.

**Elephant** (p. 55). This animal is considered auspicious and indicates royalty. Its association with Ganesh has made it sacred. It is said that Indra, the king of the gods, has a white elephant and Laxmi has two of them pouring water over her body. It is the charger of Indra (see Gaja Laxmi). It is believed that the heavens are supported by four elephants, one in each direction East, West, North and South.

**Fish.** *Matsya* was the first incarnation. Vishnu was a fish or a merman. A fish is a lucky symbol. It is lucky to meet one carrying fish. It forebodes success.

**Gharial & Crocodile.** Gharial and alligator are both called *Makar* in India. The nymph of the Ganges is said to ride on a Gharial, while Madan, the God of Love, has an alligator on his flag. He is therefore called Makar-dvaj. *Makar* is the 10th sign of the Zodiac. There was once upon a time a big fight between a *Makar* and an elephant and Vishnu had to intervene.

**Horse** (p 20). The horse is much esteemed in the Marātha country. The sun has a seven-headed mythical white horse yoked to his car. Mārtand of Jejuri (p. 20) rides a horse. Horse sacrifice was considered the highest goal of the ambition of an Emperor. Horses are worshipped and wreaths of flowers are put round their necks on the Dasara day.

**Lion.** *Sinha* is the charger of Durga, the wife of Shiva.

**Monkey** (p 82). Anjana was the mother of Hanumān. The red faced monkeys are still claimed by the Kāthodis, a forest tribe, as their ancestors and are not killed or eaten. Rama's monkey army possibly consisted of an aboriginal tribe wearing the mask of monkeys, but that association has produced a feeling of respect for the life of an anthropoid, and it is considered sacred. Hindus therefore do not kill monkeys.

**Mouse** (p. 25). *Mushak.* Is the charger of Ganesh who rides it. (pp 55 & 56).

**Peacock.** Is the charger of Sarasvati in Bombay. It is also the charger of Kumār, the god of war, the six-headed son of Shiva. It is a sacred bird in India. Its feathers are largely used in making *Morchels,* ornaments accepted as signs of royalty. Krishna had his crown or headdress decorated with peacock's feathers. In some countries in the west, it foretells death, but not so in India.

**Rat.** (see Mouse).

**Shells** (see Conch and Cowries).

**Snake.** Snake-worship is one of the most ancient institutions of the aborigines of India. Among the Aryans *Shesh* (p 61) is the thousand-hooded snake on whose coils Vishnu sleeps. *Vāsuki* is the name of the snake Shiva has round his girdle. *Kāliya* (p. 56) was the snake Krishna vanquished. (See Anant, Nāg panchami, and Manasa).

**Sparrow** (p. 40). Sparrows are considered harbingers of harvets and are never killed by high caste Hindus. See Divāli.

## II. FOLKLORE IN PLANTS

**Aghāda.** *Achyranthes aspera* (p. 80) represents Gauri in the absence of balsam (see Gauri). Its twigs are used as tooth-brushes on the Rishipanchmi day. In the *Purān* called the *Chaturmās Mahātmya*, this plant is called the transformation of Budha the 9th incarnation of Vishnu. Its twigs are required for the sacred fire. The leaves are used in *Ganesh* worship according to the *Shrāvan Mahātmya purān.*

**Am** or **Amba** (p. 205). *Mangifera Indica.* Mango inflorescence is held sacred to the Moon, to whom it is offered on the 2nd day of *Māgh.* It is also sacred to Madan—the Indian cupid. Festoons of mango leaves are hung round the halls and bowers in which marriage and other auspicious ceremonies are held. Mangoes are distributed among Brahmans on the *Vat-Sāvitri* day. In the *Chaturmās Mahātmya* (Chap. XX) it is said that this tree is the transformation of the god Prajāpati. Its twigs are ordered to be used as tooth brushes, and its leaves as spoons for pouring libations. On the *Mahāshivarātra* day, Shiva is worshipped with its blossom. (*Smritisār granth*).

**Amlaki.** *Phyllanthus emblica.* Is worshipped and a meal is taken sitting under it (see *Avali Bhojan*). Chips of its wood thrown into water clear it and this property may have induced people to sanctify it in primitive days. Its wood is still used in well-curbs. In the *Kārtik Mahātmya purān* the worship of this tree is recommended, and it is added that a married Brahman couple should be fed under it, whereby all the sins are washed off. The book called *Vrat Kaumudi* also recommends the worship of this tree. It is held sacred for sheltering the gods, when they were turned out of Heaven by the demon Mrudumanya. (p. 44). See *Ekādashi.*

**Apta.** *Bauhinea tomentosa.* Is worshipped and looted on the Dasara day and its leaves over which *mantras* (incantations) are repeated are distributed as gold. In the *Dharma-sindhu puran* it is recommended that in the absence of the *Shami* tree (*Prosopis spicigera*) this tree must be worshipped on the Dasara day. The *Sahyāndri Khand* describes the same process.

**Ashoka.** *Jonesia asoka, syn. Saraca Indica* (p. 204). Is held sacred on account of its association with the abduction of Sita—who was kept in a garden containing groves of this tree. Its buds are eaten by women in Bengal on the *Ashok Shasthi* day. It is supposed to bloom vigorously if kicked by a young lady. *Vrat-rāj* recommends its worship on the 13th day of *Chaitra* (March-April).

**Avali.** See Amlaki.

**Bael or Bel.** *Aegle marmelos* (p. 94). Its trifoliate leaf is sacred to Shiva and no worship of that God is complete without it. The *Chaturmās mahātmya* says that its three leaflets represent the Hindu triad, Brahma, Vishnu, and Shiva. The *Jaimini Aranya Katha* records that Draupadi the wife of the Pāndavas was ordered to offer a hundred thousand of the leaves of this tree to Shiva.

**Balsam.** *Impetiens* (p. 77) represents Gauri in *Bhādrapad.*

**Bena.** See *Khas* (p. 101).

**Chirat.** *Mukia scrabrella.* It represents the giant Narkāsura in Divāli and is crushed as such. Its pulp is then applied to the body, possibly due to some medicinal virtue (see Divāli).

**Dub** (p. 71) *Cynodon dactylon.* Its leaves are sacred to Ganesh who is worshipped with them. The *Chaturmās Mahātmya* says that this plant is the transformation of *Rāhu.* It is worshipped on the 8th day of *Bhādrapad* (August-September). It is there said to be a very fertile and gregarious goddess and her marriage with the *Ficus Indica* is recommended.

**Durva.** See Dub *(Supra).*

**Fig.** The Indian fig. *Ficus Indica* or *Bengalensis* is worshipped on the *Vatsāvitri* day, as it possibly represents eternal life. Its branches give aerial roots which grow like big stems and support them. It never dies and that is why it possibly represents longevity. (See *Vatsāvitri*). It is believed that this tree is haunted by a ghost known as *Khais*, and also by Vetāl the chief of *ghosts*. In the *Chaturmās Mahātmya*, this tree is said to be the transformation of Brahma. Its twigs are used in fire worship. The *Vratrāj* recommends that women should worship the tree on the 15th of *Jestha* (May-June). It grants the survival of husbands and fulfilments of wishes finally ensuring a place in Shiva's heaven. It is further ordained that the performance of the thread ceremony of this tree, and its marriage with *Durva* (*Cynodon dactylon*) ensure good luck and plentiful progeny.

**Fig.** *Ficus religiosa, Pimpal.* This tree is worshipped for its association with the three gods Brahma, Vishnu, and Shiva. It is believed to be haunted by a *munja*, or the ghost of a boy who died during his thread ceremony (*munj*) before it was completed. The *Chaturmās Mahātmya*, however, calls it the transformation of *Guru*, Jupiter. It is frequented by all gods and is therefore very sacred. No one should fell it. Women should worship it, and go round it a thousand times in one day. In the *Shrāvan Mahātmya*, it is ordained that this tree should be worshipped on every Saturday of that month *Shrāvan* (July-August). The *Vrat Kaumudi* orders its worship on the *Somavati* (which please see). Saint Valkhilya tells us that Vishnu becomes *pimpal*. The thread ceremony of this tree is strongly recommended along with its marriage with *Tulsi* (*Ocimum Sanctum*). Its dry twigs are used in the worship of the sacred fire (to feed it).

**Gingelly or Gingly.** See *Til.*

**Halad.** Powdered tubers of the *Curcuma longa*, turmeric form an important item of the worship of all gods.

It is also used as a cosmetic by women whose husbands are alive. No widow is allowed to use it. Mixed with slaked lime its powder (which becomes red) is applied by married women to the fore-head.

**Jack fruit tree.** *Artocarpus integrifolia.* The Nambudri Brahmans of Malabar produce sacred fire by friction of the dry branches of this tree.

**Kārle** *Momordia charantia.* It is considered inauspicious to pass under this creeper and is supposed to have some influence over the lives of children. Mothers and women desirous of children never pass under its shadow (p. 50).

**Khas** or **Khus** (p. 101). *Andropogon muricata syn Veteveria odorata.* Its fragrant roots known as *Khas* are much in use. See Khas Shasthi for folklore.

**Kush-grass.** *Eragrotis cynosuroides* is held sacred and considered necessary as a mat to the *pitris.* The eldest son of Rāma was named *Kush* after this grass. In the *Chaturmās Mahātmya* this *grass* is said to be the transformation of Ketu. The *Shrāvan Purān* directs that on the *Pithori* day (which please see) this grass should be pulled out if required for ceremonial purposes, such as funerals and *Shrādhas.*

**Kushmānd.** *Cucurbita* or *maxima.* This fruit represents the buffalo-demon sacrificed on the Dasara day. It is also considered a great merit to hollow this fruit, fill it up with gold and jewels and to present it to a Brahman as a *gupta-dhan* or secret gift. *Vrat Kaumudi* calls this creeper a goddess and recommends its worship. In the *Padmapuran* Saint Nārad once recommended it to King Chandrasen for worship. King Chandrasen was the chief of the Chāndraseniya Kāyasth Prabhus a twice born caste of Bombay Baroda, and Central Provinces. Dharma recommends it to Krisna in the *Vrat Kaumudi.*

**Nāral.** *Cocos nucifera* Cocoanut. It is considered an auspicious offering to the gods, and is worshipped as

Laxmi in the absence of an image. When placed on the top of the *lota* or water-jug it represents *Varun*—the god of rain. The tradition runs that the cocoanut palm is the *Kalpa-Vriksha,* or wish-granting tree of primitive society. Its stem supplies beams for cottages, or when scooped out it serves as a canoe. The leaves cover huts as roofs, the flower-stocks yield a cool drink, the fruit gives food, oil, and a milk-like juice, the shell of the fruit yields a medicinal oil and serves as fuel. The husk supplies ropes for building huts, etc. In fact everything required for the nourishment and housing of a primitive race is supplied by this tree and therefore perhaps it is called *Kalpa-Vriksha.*

**Neem.** *Melia Azadirachta* (p. 82). Its leaves are eaten on the New Year's day. Its medicinal properties are possibly recorded in the folklore (see Gudhipādva p. 81.) It is said that a certain woman was anxious that her husband should return home soon, when he was preparing to go on a business tour. She sought help from a medical man. He advised her husband to sleep under a tamarind tree on his way out every night during his travels, and to sleep under a neem-tree on his return journey. He did so, and was soon taken ill owing to the unhealthy acid vapours given out by the tamarind. He therefore did not much prolong his journey. He had to turn back. He slept under the *neem* and by the time he reached home he was quite cured! The oil of the *neem* is a well-known remedy for leprosy and other skin diseases. During the epidemic of small pox, festoons of the fresh leaves of this tree are hung on the doors of Hindus' houses.

**Nivadung** (p. 144). (*Panchdhāri*) *Euphorbia pentandra* is worshipped in Bengal as the Goddess Manasa (p. 142). In Bombay during Divali, boys of the Pāthāre Prabhu caste, have great fun with lamps prepared from it. Small pieces of the stem are used as lamps. Boys carry them to the houses of their friends and put them in the verandahs. This act shows the desire of the boy to have a bride from that house. As it is done by very young children not exceeding 10 years of age, it means no mischief and the fun is much enjoyed by the neighbours. Sometimes a boy from the house in which the lamp is placed retaliates by taking it back and putting it in the verandah of the house from which it came to his place. Every one laughs at these pranks.

**Padma,** Lotus (p. 111). It is the seat of Laxmi the goddess of wealth. Brahma was born out of the lotus which issued from the navel of Vishnu.

**Pan.** *Piper betel.* Betel leaf is chewed along with betel nut and spices. Is always offered to idols at the end of the *puja.*

**Parijat** (p. 61). *Nyctanthes arbor tristis.* This is the fragrant flowered tree, which Krishna brought down from heaven, and gave his wife Bhāma. Its fresh flowers are much in demand for *pujas.*

**Patai.** See *Khas* (p. 101).

**Pimpal or pipal.** *Ficus religiosa.* See fig tree.

**Plantain** (p. 94). *Musa paradisiaca.* Some people claim the position of the all-wish-granting tree to plantain (compare cocoanut). In many *pujās,* bowers made up of four plantain trees used as pillars are considered acceptable to gods. Plantains also form an acceptable offering to them. In the *Vrat Rāj* women are advised to worship this tree on the 4th of *Kārtik* (October-November) whereby their husbands are said to survive them, and their lives prolonged. It is also worshipped on the 3rd of *Shrāvan* (July-August). When placed near the entrances of houses, along with its long leaves and laden with fruit, this tree forms an emblem of plenty and fertility.

**Rui** (p. 71). *Calotropis gigantia.* The leaves of this plant are offered to *Mangla Gaur.* A wreath of the same is put round *Hanuman's* neck. At a marriage, a wreath of the flowers of this plant is put round the neck of the bridegroom by the bride. If a man loses his two wives one after another, and has to get himself married a third time, he is married to this plant in the first instance, to ward off early death of the next wife. It is then destroyed. In the *Skandhpurān* as quoted in the *Chaturmās Mahātmya*, this tree is supposed to be the transformation of the sun (*Surya*). The *Smitisār Granth* recommends its twigs as tooth brushes on ceremonial occasions. They are, when dry, offered to the god of fire as *samidha*, *fagots*.

**Shami** (p. 71). *Prosopis spicigera.* This is the tree on which the Pāndavās deposited their arms, while they were serving, King Virāt. It is worshipped on the Dasara day, and its leaves are said to be dear to Ganesh. Its dried twigs are used in feeding the sacrificial fire.

**Til.** *Sesamum orientale* or *indicum* is associated in Bengal with the worship of the goddess of wealth possibly owing to its utility as a commercial product. The souls of the dead ancestors are worshipped with this seed. It is pounded and applied to the body on the *Sankrānt* day. It is coated or mixed with sugar and eaten on the same day. *Tilānjali* or *til* mixed with water is an absolutely necessary offering to *pitris*.

**Tulsi.** *Ocimum sanctum.* This is supposed to be Vrinda who was transformed into a plant by Vishnu. It is held sacred to him and is married to him every year. It is a great purifier of the atmosphere and is said to destroy mosquitoes. The Vaishnavas wear a necklace made of bits of the stem of this plant. [ See *Tulsi's* marriage for folklore ].

**Umbar.** *Ficus glomerata* is the seat of the Trimurti or Dattātraya. It is much worshipped, and women desirous of getting sons go round it a thousand times every morning. Its dry wood is used for producing sacrificial fire.

**Vata.** See fig tree.

## SOME STRIKING RESEMBLANCES

Whether the heavenly bodies are named after the Gods or the Gods after them, is a question which will ever remain undecided. But it cannot be denied that the study of the folklore of these holidays and ceremonials shows curious similarities in their attributes. For instance, the Sun as Vishnu has his early refraction on the horizon to represent the lotus on which Brahma is seated. It comes out of its body just as the lotus does. The long floating clouds and the asterism Draco may together be compared to *Shesha* the snake, and the sky to the ocean of milk to complete the figure. The Sun as an independent God, has his seven-headed horse or seven horses in the seven stars of the Ursa Major and his refraction again as his charioteer, Aruna, but the stars are the seven Rishis or Saints as well. Mārtand is visible in the rising sun, with his yellow steeds (rays), his yellow flag, and he defeating demons (clouds) followed by dogs Cannis Major and Minor, and by his wife Eve. The Moon may be compared to Krishna and the Stars to Gopis or milk-maids. Soma, the Moon, as such has his wife in Venus. The Moon, is again the wanderer who resembles the Nārad of the *Purānās*, wandering from house to house or asterism to asterism. The sixty-four Yoginis or Fairies of the Pithori are possibly the *Vikalās* each representing fourth part of the sixteen *Kalās*, or sixteen parts of the Moon's diameter. Shiva and his wife Pārvati are visible in the third sign of the Zodiac, Jemini. Ganesh the big-bellied head-less trunk resembles half-Gemini half-Cancer with its outstretched legs forming the four hands and two legs of the God of Knowledge. Nandi is certainly Taurus the bull, Pārvati's Sinha is Leo the lion, Sati, the sixth sign Virgo, Budha is Mars, Venus as a male is Shukra. In another aspect the Sun is Indra and his rays the thunderbolt, Guru is Jupiter, Shani is Saturn, and ram-headed Daksha is Aries the ram. Varun is the God of rain. Orion is the Trimurti with his dogs in Cannis Major, and his cow in Lupus. His mother Anusuya, or Anu the sky, is placed at Ardra, and his father Atri at Serius.

The fourteen gems mentioned at page 226 (*infra*) also seem to resemble heavenly bodies. They are:—(1) *Kaustubh*—Saturn, which was just discovered when the list was made, (2) *Dhanvantari*, Sagittarius for *Dhanu*, a bow, (3) *Chandra*, the Moon, (4) *Kāmadhenu*, Tauras the bull or cow, (5) *Airāvat*—the seven snouted elephant of Indra *Ursa major*, with its seven stars, (6) *Rambha*, the celestial maid, *virgo*, (7) *Uchchaishrava* the seven-headed horse of the sun *Ursa Minor*, with its seven stars, (8) *Haridhanu* (*Indra-dhanu*) Rainbow, (9) *Amrit*, possibly the light of the sun visible immediately after the total eclipse of that luminary, (10) *Lakshmi* is the Earth *Bahuratna-Vasundhara*, literally the store-house of jewels, (11) the *Pārijātak* may have been taken from the appearance the Orion when the three stars of the belt stand perpendicularly, to give the idea of a stem. The four terminal stars joined to the three stars of the belt would form a tree, (12) *Sura*, alkohol, the idea possibly emanated from the resemblance of the pot in the *Kumbh* Constellation to a toddy-drawer's jug, (13) the shadow of the moon was the poison, (14) *Shankh*, conch-shell possibly half of Pisces. Like the seven wonders of the world, the immortal poet has linked together these fourteen gems of the universe. I give below the Sanskrit text:—

*Laxmi Kaustubh Parijatak Surah Dhanvantrischhandramah*
*Gavah Kamadughah, Sureshvar Gajau, Rambhadidevangnah*
*Ashvahaptamukho Visham Haridhanuh Shankhamritamchambudheh*
*Ratnani hi chaturdash Pratidinam Kuryuh sada mangalam.*

It is quite possible that when the Tortoise Incarnation was thought of the shape of the Pisces, the last sign of the Zodiac resembled a fish and a conch-shell in juxtaposition instead of two fishes as at present. That may have been the real origin of the *Shankh*, among these gems. In the ancient Zodiac, Pisces is shaped like a merman half-man half-fish. Taking that for Vishnu, the conch-shell near it was possibly the Shankhāsur or Conch-shell giant.

On examining William Peek's map of the sky as seen during October and November, it will be found that nearly all the constellations and planets which gave the idea of these fourteen gems were either visible or known at the time of the historical eclipse of the Sun which occurred on the 25th of October 945 B.C.

Leaving the other minor semblances of heavenly bodies aside, we descend to the terrestrial globe and what do we find? Goddess Prithvi is clearly the Earth, Vāyu the Winds, and Agni is visible in fire. The Ammonite is Vishnu, the oval agate is Shiva, the red agate is Ganesh, the crystal *Suryakānt* is the Sun, and the fossil coral Chandrakānt is the moon. Among the trees again the trifoliate leaf of the Bael symbolizes the three Gods Brahma, Vishnu and Shiva. The *Pimpal*, *Vat*, Jack, and other trees represent the food of the God of fire because it is produced by friction for sacrificial purpose from these trees. Every river, every tank, every spring, every mountain represents a God or Goddess. God in Nature, God everywhere, God as the Sun in his wonderful works. Stories about these Gods and Goddesses containing fanciful, wild and romantic flights of imagination, wonderful myths, and astonishing feats of valour, are the things one can find and enjoy in these pages.

It has been shown in a previous chapter (p. ix) that the sanctity of the bull is due to the retrograding position of the equinox at *Taurus* (the bull) between the years 2426 B.C. and 266 B.C. The half-lion half-woman sphinx of Egypt owes its origin to the transitory position of the equinox between *Leo* and *Virgo*. *Encyclopedis Metropolitana* records that the sphinxes refer to the rise and overflow of the Nile, which lasted during the passage of the sun through the constellations *Leo* and *Virgo*: both these signs are therefore combined in the figure which has the head of a Virgin and the body of a Lion. The position of the equinox is therefore possibly the origin of the Durga and Jagatdhātri of Bengal, a woman riding a lion or one riding a tiger and not symbolized by sharing the body of the Lion—'half and half.' These facts lead one to conclude also that the sanctity of Gemini as Shiva and Pārvati is due to the same cause, that the sanctity of half-Cancer half-Gemini joint figure, shaped into half-man half-elephant,* Ganesh, is due to the same cause, and that the Persian symbol of the sun rising on the back of a lion or tiger is also due to the same cause. The last one is a very significant design as it shows what it means by depicting the rising orb. In consideration of these facts it may be safely surmised that all the stories regarding these constellations were compiled to fix into memory this all important astronomical fact, and that the prominence given to each was so given during the period at which the observation was taken and recorded in each country. These astronomical symbols, it seems, became deified in course of time.

---

* The upper front claw of Cancer can easily be imagined to be the snout of an elephant and its body as the head of that bulky animal. It is easy to modify in imagination the shapes of the constellations. This process is visible in the different representations of the Indian Zodiac as published in different provinces.

The Secretary of the Astronomical Society of India shows by actual calculations that the Equinox was between Gemini and Cancer during the period 6689 B.C. and 6151 B.C. This proves the great antiquity of the evolution of Ganesh out of the combination of half-Gemini and half-Cancer, like the Sphinx of Egypt.

*Photo by*— *F. Harrington*

Mrs. Ramābāi, *alias*, Māi Sāheb Gupte.

## APPENDIX.

### APPRECIATION.

**Sir Richard Temple on Mrs. Gupte's Divāli Drawings.**

Government House, Port Blair, Andaman Islands,
22nd November 1902.

DEAR MR. GUPTE,

I am much obliged for Mrs. Gupte's delightful plate. The point scientifically is whether a picture correctly represents what an ordinary Indian woman would draw in her own house. That is what we want to know and this point, I have so brought out that your wife ought to get credit for faithful reproduction.

Yours truly,
R. TEMPLE.

**Sir George Birdwood on the article on Divāli.**

Dated 28th August 1903.

MY DEAR GUPTE,

If it be all I can,—I am so frail now,—get through for this Indian mail, I must write, however briefly, and gratefully to thank you for your paper from the Indian Antiquary on "Divāli-Folklore" and I must add for Mrs. Gupte's most interesting "Divāli Drawing" in illustration of your paper. You can hardly know how interesting her drawing is in connection with current theories of the evolution and devolution of ornament. Your paper is invaluable. Your theory of the origin of the Divāli is deeply suggestive and will receive grave consideration so soon as it has got into circulation among the specialists interested in such speculations. I hope myself to direct attention to it;—that is to say I am determined to do so if only I am strong enough to sit up a sufficient time at my writing pad for the purpose;—which rarely happens now. To Mrs. Gupte's drawing I shall also I hope be able to draw attention before I can write anything about your paper, as I am under a promise to write something for the Society of Art Journal on Lumholtz's "Unknown Mexico," a long extract from which appears in last Friday's Number of the Journal on Conventionalism in Primitive Art; and Mrs. Gupte's drawing will greatly help me in this. So far you have admirably and beyond all my expectations responded to my pressing advice to you, which I have ever given to all Hindus of literary culture, with a natural turn for antiquarian research to concentrate your efforts on the antiquities of common life. *i.e.* folk customs, observances, ceremonies, superstitions and ritual, and pageantry and the general folklore of India. I was always impressing this on Dr. Bhāu Dāji, but he had already advanced too far in what are erroneously distinguished as the higher,—the strictly historical and philological departments of antiquarian research to be turned into its bye-ways; but the Rāo Sāhib Vishvanāth Nārāyan Mandlik was infected with my views while he was yet young and he adopted them with enthusiasm and his death was a really irremediable loss to the study of the prehistoric sociology of the Mahratta people of the Deccan and the Concans.

Now you, by the good luck which always waits on resolute purpose and steady, patient labour, have in your Divāli "paper" "struck oil,"—as the English of the United States of America say: and I earnestly beg you to continue to work at that under-ground, but fathomless and all illuminating "tap," until paper by paper, you will have at last accumulated in the I.A. materials for a quite original and most fascinating book, at once scientific and popular, on the antiquities of the great religious festivals of India,—

India of the Hindus, as I am always saying, for there is no other India worth a "copper *dām*" nor ever will be.

After the Divāli take up Dasara, and then the Rākhi-pornima and then the Holi. Inspire other Hindus also to pursue the same line of research—for there is work enough for every Argive willing to put his hands to it, and in such work there is no room for petty curryings and jealousies. Only be very careful to go direct to the people—to their folklore, and take nothing from the books of previous workers in the same fields, especially Europeans. The value of your own investigations will be all the greater the more entirely you are ignorant of the theories of experts in these matters who have gone before you, particularly European experts. Set forth in Hinduism only whatsoever things are pure and lovely, and of good report, and of any virtue and praise, and ever think of these things, Raise up before your people their highest ideals, and give them all the glory of them, before all men. In Bombay I was a regular *chābuk Savār* to my erring Hindu friends in *private*, but in public I always honoured them to the highest height. I have observed this rule all my life—all my public writing has been one, heartfelt, glowing praise of India, India of the Hindus—not only of the people of India but of all foreigners. How much more should a Hindu observe it of Hindus; and emphatically of Hinduism.

Do not take this as a flick of my *chābuk.* It is because I know your essential gentleness and calmness of soul, and your loyalty to your great vernacular culture, that I drop this affectionate caution as "a word to the wise." Ah!—if I were only a Brahman, and could speak to Vaisyās and Kshatriyas, and Brahmans as a Brahman! Will you present my most respectful compliments to Mrs. Gupte, and with my best regards

Believe me always your sincere old friend,

GEORGE BIRDWOOD.

Extract from another letter of the same date.

Your delightful and invaluable paper: The cry of "Bravo Gupte" is really what sprang to my lips when I read the paper.

GEORGE BIRDWOOD.

---

**Sir George Birdwood's remarks on Mrs. Gupte's Divāli Drawings.**

Sir George Birdwood has contributed to the "Journal of the Society of Art," a paper on "Conventionalism in Primitive Art," many passages of which will be read with considerable interest by his friends in India. In the course of a learned survey of the early arts of many races, Sir George says:—

This mode of decoration in India is entirely a domestic art, hereditary in Hindu families on the female side only, and the designs used are of a dateless tradition. I never saw any systematic or responsible notice of these tattoo marks, and domestic "drawing" until my young friend, Mr. B. A. Gupte, recently published in the "Indian Antiquary" his papers on "Female Tattoo Designs in India," and on "Divāli Folk-lore;" in the latter of which he reproduces a copy by Mrs. Gupte of the ritual design with which she decorates the threshold of their house at the time of the annual celebration of the Divāli ['*dips*,' a "lamp," of "*dips*" and '*avali*,' a "row"] the Hindu "Feast of Lanterns," held in the new moon of Kārtik [corresponding at present with 20th-30th October] in honour of Lakshmi, the consort of Vishnu, and "Goddess of Good Luck and Prosperity." I reproduce a half-page, which might be extended to half a dozen pages, of these tattoo marks, and the copy of Mrs. Gupte's Divāli "drawing." Mrs. Gupte's draftsmanship with her finger-tips, and a powder dredge, must not be judged by her drawing with a European pen or pencil. The two accomplishments, as every craftsman knows, are quite different. Moreover I, in copying Mrs. Gupte's pen copy of her own Divāli "drawing," have done so with my own touch of fingers, and movement of wrist, for it would have been as fatiguing and unnecessary to reproduce her pen-copy in fac-simile. The study of these tattoo marks and ritualistic devices seems to me to suggest at least two obvious conclusions:—

> "The desire of the moth for the star,
> Of the night for the morrow,
> The devotion to something afar
> From the sphere of our sorrow"

---

**The Hon'ble Mr. Burn.**

Submitted

A paper on "Sāvitri Drawings," supplied by Mrs. Gupte —for favour of being edited.

B. A. GUPTE,

14-7-05.

I have been much interested in reading this paper, and regret I have kept it so long. The following points occur to me:—

(1) The Sun and the Moon almost invariably occur on Sati-pillars in Bundelkhand, and are usually interpreted as symbols of chastity, thus implying the everlasting union of the faithful wife with her husband.

R BURN,

3-9-5.

DEAR MR. GUPTE,

Many thanks for letting me see your note on the Tulsi plant. The custom of marrying the Tulsi plant to the Shāligrām is peculiar. In Sanskrit drama, of course, we often meet with the custom of marrying two shrubs to each other, *e. g. Mādhavi-lata* to *Asoka* &c. The expression *Patta-Rāni*, for Rukmini, the chief queen of Krishna, reminds me of the similar expression (*Patta-Mahādẹvi*), which

I have met in a copper plate inscription of the Bengal king Madana-pāla-deva, who reigned about 1150 A.D.

Yours sincerely,

T. BLOCH.

22nd Sep. 1909.

---

**Sir Louis Dane, on the article on Maha Shivaratra.**

D. O. No. 1138. Barnes Court, Simla, 21st September 1911.

DEAR SIR,

I am desired to acknowledge receipt of your letter dated the 16th instant and the brochure forwarded therewith, and to say that His Honour has read your ingenious theory with much interest.

Yours faithfully,

E. C. BAYLEY, *Major*,

*Private Secretary, Punjab.*

---

**Dr. N. Annandale on the "Dark Monday" Somavati.**

No. 2282. Indian Museum, Natural History Section, Calcutta, 21st Dec. 1910.

DEAR MR. GUPTE,

I am sorry that I have not had time to go through the whole of the paper which you asked me to criticise. If I may make a suggestion as regards it, it seems to me that it would be much more useful to ethnologists if it was somewhat compressed, but the greater part of it seems very interesting. The proofs are herewith returned.

Yours truly,

N. ANNANDALE.

LORD REAY'S appreciation of article on Mriga Nakshatra of the Mahā-Shivaratra, dated March 10th 1911.

DEAR MR. GUPTE,

Your publication is very interesting and illuminating.

6, Great Stanhope Street }
Mayfair W. } REAY.

---

**Sir Edward Gait on the present volume.**

D-O No. 172, Ranchi, the 10th May 1912.

MY DEAR SIR,

I am interested to learn from your letter of the 9th instant that you are writing a book on Hindu holidays and fasts.

The enclosures to your letter are herewith returned.

Yours sincerely,
E. A. GAIT.

---

**The Honourable Mr. Enthoven's Notes.**

The first 75 pages of these proofs are returned herewith corrected. The rest have been retained, and will follow shortly.

Many of the legends would benefit by rewriting in a more coincise form—and the story on p. 40 should be omitted.

I am inclined to think that the work could best be published as a kind of "Dictionary of the Folk Lore of Indian Festivals," and that the different fasts and feasts should be given in alphabetical order for convenience of reference, with a preface describing the sequence of the same during the year, English equivalents being given for the Hindu Months.

For the use of the general public, a kind of "Dictionary" or "Gazetter" would be more suitable, I think—as certain ceremonies occur more frequently than once a year—and it would be very convenient to be able to turn "Dasara," "Nārali Pornima," "Friday Worship," "Monday Worship," etc. in a work modelled on these lines.

I must not conclude without expressing my opinion that these notes contain an immense amount of interesting matter, and should prove useful to students of Indian folklore and ceremonies. I shall be glad to assist Mr. Gupte further, when he has decided on the final form of the work, in seeing it through the press.

The moral on p. 52, and similar reflections such as these quaint folklore stories suggest, should in my opinion be made the subject of an introductory preface—which can form part of the work whichever plan Mr. Gupte adopts for its final ordering.

R. E. ENTHOVEN,

29-6-12.

---

**Lord Curzon's General Appreciation,**

Dated 10th October 1915.

DEAR SIR,

His Excellency desires me to tell you that he knows, what good and useful work you have done under Mr. Risley.

Yours faithfully,

R. NATHAN,

*Private Secretary to the Viceroy.*

**Sir Herbert Risley's General Appreciation,**

S. S. Delhi, 16th February 1910.

DEAR MR. GUPTE,

The rush of the Press Bill was so absorbing and I was so exhausted by the 8 hours day in Council that I had reluctantly to put off writing to you until I got on board ship.

Well, we have worked together for more than 8 years and have seen many things happen in India. And though all that time you have given me most intelligent and loyal assistance and have enabled me to accomplish scientific and literary work which without your help would have been quite impossible. Whatever credit I have gained in Europe in the departments of Ethnology and Archaeology is, I feel, due in large measure to your indefatigable industry and careful judgment in furnishing me with materials and in drawing attention to the points of importance. I trust that my transfer to the India Office will not break off our relations and that you may still find it possible to keep me in touch with the caste and religious movements in India of which you know so much. I have informed Sir Harold Stuart, who is himself an authority on Ethnographic Survey, and I have no doubt that he and Mr. Gait will be ready to give you any assistance that you may need. And I need not say that I shall bring your services in the matter of Anthropometry prominently to the notice of the Anthropological Institute.

With kindest regards from my wife and myself

I am yours sincerely,

H. H. RISLEY.

# Folklore of Hindu Holidays and Ceremonials.

**Adhikmās**—An intercalary month during which Brahmans are feasted and fed. Widows bathe in the nearest river, tank, or creek, take only one meal a day and spend most of their time in listening to stories from the Purānas.

**Adit Rānu Bāi**—Adit means the Sun or the gods collectively. Adit-rānu-bāi the mother of that luminary or of the gods. Adit-dora is the necklace worn only by the Brahman and Prabhu women. *Sunday* is sacred to Adit-rānubāi, who is supposed to be the mother of the sun or the sun as a female; literally Adit, the sun, and Rānubāi the queen. There was a city in which there lived a poor Brahman. He used to go to the jungle to collect *durva* (*cynodon dactylon*) grass and the twigs of certain trees for fagots to ignite his sacred fire for worship. He once met some fairies who were engaged in worship. He asked them to explain to him what the nature of the *puja* was. They said that on the first Sunday of the month of Shrāvan (July-August) one should leave his bed without speaking a word, should bathe himself with his night dress on, should bring water without placing the pot on the floor, should draw the figure of the sun on a betel leaf with red sandalwood paste, should draw a whorl with six volutions, should take a twine formed of six threads, should

**Adit Rānu Bāi,—**

tie six knots in that twine, should offer betel leaves and flowers to the symbol, and worship it. Finally a married Brahman woman should be fed with dainties and offered clothes or cash. The Brahman performed the *puja* in this manner. The Sun was pleased with him. He became rich. The queen of the realm sent for him. The poor Brahman was terrified, he shivered. The queen assured him that there was no ground of fear. He was asked to give his daughters in marriage to the prince and to the son of the prime misinster. So he did. The Brahman retired to his seclusion after the marriage. After twelve years, he came to the city to see his daughters. He first went to the eldest daughter, who had in course of time become herself the queen. She offered him light refreshments, but he could not partake of them because he had to perform the *puja* of the sun and to recite the story. The queen, his daughter, said that she had no time to waste; her husband, the king, was about to start on a *Shikār* expedition. He therefore left the palace, and went to the second daughter. She received him well. She heard his sacred story, she worshipped the Sun as advised, and she prospered. Later on the king left for *Shikār* but lost his way, the queen became very poor, she lost all she had. She had four sons. On a certain Sunday, of the month of Shrāvan, her son was sent to her prosperous sister to obtain some help. His aunt received him well and handed him a calabash * fruit full of gold coins and jewels. On his way home he met the Sun dressed as a gardener, who forcibly took the fruit away. He returned home disappointed. On the second Sunday, the ex-queen sent her second son to her sister. She received him well, and gave him a hollow stick filled with gold coins and jewels. The Sun met him on his way home, dressed as a cowherd, and forcibly took the stick away. On

*See Kushmand

**Adit Rānu Bāi,—**

the third Sunday the third son was deputed. He got a hollowed out cocoanut filled with gems. He was told not to part with the nut until he reached home, but he placed it on the parapet of a well in order to draw water, as he was excessively thirsty through the influence of the Sun. The nut rolled down into the well. On the fourth Sunday, the fourth son got some food from his aunt but the Sun swooped down, shaped as a kite, and took it away. On the Sunday following the poor queen went herself to her opulent sister. She also was well received, but the younger sister explained to her the folly of neglecting the *puja* of the Sun and allowing their father to leave home without listening to the sacred story. She expressed her regret and began worshipping the great luminary as advised. The Sun was pleased, fortune smiled on her again. The lost king returned home safely. She started for her old capital after thanking her younger sister. At the first day's halt she performed the *puja* and asked her attendants to get some one to listen to her story. A poor dealer in fagots was taken to her. He said he had no time to listen to stories as he had to earn his bread. She took out six pearls, gave him three, and held the other three in her hand while she was reciting the story. The result was that his fagots were turned into gold. He promised to perform the *puja* and left. At the second stage, a gardener whose well had dried up was brought to the queen. She offered him three pearls and made him listen to her tale with the result that the well was flooded with water and the garden became fertile. At the third stage, an unhappy old woman was brought to her. She gave her three pearls to induce her to listen to the story and showed her how to perform the *puja.* The result was that her sons, one of whom had been drowned, another who was swallowed by a boa-snake and the third who had lost his way in a forest, all returned alive. She became prosperous. At the

**Adit Rānu Bāi,—**
fourth stage, a man who had lost his limbs was placed before her. She placed three pearls on his chest, held the other three in her hand, and recited the tale. The maimed man recovered his limbs. At the fifth stage she reached home. She became happy and always performed the *puja* with devotion.

**The Necklace.**—There is a necklace called *Adit-dora* worn only by Brahman and Prabhu women. It consist of a tube of gold about an inch long, with twelve rings resembling the elevations at the points of a bamboo or a sugarcane. On each side of this mystic tube are placed beads of gold. The rest of the necklace is made up of minute glass beads. On Sundays of the Shrāvan month women worship this necklace also. The twelve rings possibly represent the twelve months of the year and the six volutions of the whorl, the six Indian seasons, Vasanta, Grishma, Varsa, Sharat, Hémanta, and Shishira.

**Adukkh-Navami.**—A particular lunar day, the ninth of the first fortnight of Bhādrapad (August-September). On this day the Devi (goddess) is worshipped by women, that all evils may be averted during the ensuing year. Men who have lost their wives give dry food and other offerings to a Brahman, and feed a married woman '*in memoriam*' of their deceased consorts. This day is also called AVIDHA-VA-NAVAMI.

**Agrahāyani**—The constellation of Orion or Mrigashirsha. See Mahāshivaratra for its folklore.

**Agrayānam**—Another name for Navānnapornima or the full-moon day on which new rice is tasted for the first time, after it has been offered to the family gods cooked as *kshir* or rice boiled with milk and sugar. It is a harvest day.

**Aheva-Navami**—See Adukkh-navami. The ninth of the second half of the month of Bhādrapad, on which day offerings are made to the manes of women who have died before their husbands.

**Ajepādva**—The first day of Ashvin (September-October) on which those who have lost their maternal grand-fathers worship their manes. See under Navarātra-Dasara.

**Akāsh-Dipa**—The lamp hung aloft upon a pole or tree in the month of Kārtik (October-November). It is believed that it supplies light to the manes of the dead in the celestial world.

**Aksharā-rambh**—The ceremony of setting a child to learn the alphabet from the sand board. See under Dasara.

**Akshaya-Tritiyā**—The third lunar day of the first half of the month of Vaishākha. The special fasts and feasts of the month of Vaishākh begin with *Akshaya tritiya,* On this day oblations are offered to deceased parents. A pot full of water, a fan and a pair of shoes are given to a priest so that they may reach heaven for the use of the dead father during the hot season which begins at this time.

In the Vrat-Rāj a story is told to the effect: that once upon a time there lived a very poor Bania. On this day, he performed the *tarpana* or ceremony of giving offerings to the Brahmans in the name of his dead father, with the result that he was at the next birth born a very rich Kshatriya and performed many *yagnas* or sacrifices. His lavish expenditure on feeding Brahmans, instead of reducing his wealth, tended to increase it by leaps and bounds. He enjoyed life, passed his days happily and ultimately attained salvation. If this day falls on a Wednesday while the

**Akshaya-Tritiyā,—**
moon is in the Rohini or fourth lunar constellation, the day becomes specially sacred.

*Gauri* in the swing which has been worshipped during the month of Chaitra (March-April) has to be finally worshipped and removed to the family altar. All married women with husbands alive and all unmarried girls take part in the *puja*, and distribute sweets, fruits, and germinating gram. It is said that on this day the Treta Yuga had its beginning, and that Parashurām, the sixth incarnation of Vishnu, was born.

**Amāvāsya.**—A day of the conjunction of the Sun and the Moon, the fifteenth day of the dark half of a lunar month. See Somavati-Amāvāsya for its folklore.

**Amlaki.**—Phylanthus emblica. See Avalibhojan for folklore).

**Am-Shasthi.**—(see Shasthi,)

**Ananat**—Dharma, the eldest of the Pāndavas, asked Krishna to tell him of a *vrata* which would grant him a kingdom along with prosperity for life. Krishna mentioned *Ananta vrata* as the one that would fulfil his desires. He was asked to define the word Ananta as it has several meanings. For instance, the chief of the Nāgās or hooded snakes was called Ananta, as well as the enternal God who has no beginning and no end. Krishna replied that he himself was that endless God. Just as the sun is the soul of the solar system, the sun is the maker or producer of the space known as time; just as time is divided into seconds, minutes, hours, days, nights, weeks, months, years and seasons, he is worshipped separately in different places by different people. It is but the maker of divisions of time, so am I the essence of everything. I

**Anant,—**
have no beginning, no middle and no end. I have no birth and no death. I have been given endless names. I am the Creator, the Protector, and the Destroyer, all in one. In me are included all the stars, planets, land, sky, space and sound. This Ananta *vrata* was for the first time in the history of the world performed by a woman named Shila. Listen how."

In the *krit yuga* there lived a Brahman named Sumantu. He married Diksha, the charming daughter of Bhrigu. Their daughter was named Shila. Diksha, the wife of the Brahman, died of fever. Sumantu married another woman. Her name was Karkasha. This second wife was irritable, quarrelsome and troublesome. Shila was a good girl. She lived in her father's house. She used to draw pictures of various kinds on the walls and doors, and worship those which were sacred. She became marriageable. Her father was in search of a suitable husband but he could find none to his liking. At this time saint Kaudinya came to him as a guest. He was looking out for a girl for wife. Kaudinya proposed and was accepted. He was married to Shila. When he was about to go home, Sumanta remarked to his wife that he had a mind to give some nice present to his son-in-law. The wife became very angry and, like a shrew, she destroyed or dispersed even the flags and pennons raised for the auspicious ceremony. She locked up all the jewellery in the house and told the son-in-law to leave the place at once. She told him that she had no money left, and gave him the crumbs and other remnants of food for his breakfast. Sumantu, the father of the girl, was very sorry, but he kept quiet. Kaudinya, the son-in-law, started with his new wife in a bullock cart. He had to cross the Jamna. In order to give the animals some rest, he unyoked them. He and his wife went to the river to bathe. There she saw, on the bank of the river a large number of women in red garments. It was the 14th day of

**Anant,—**

the month of Bhādrapad, and therefore these red dressed women were performing the *puja* of the endless God, Ananta.

She modestly approached the women and begged of them to explain to her the sacred *puja* and the *vrata* they were performing. It was called Ananta *vrata*. Shila then enquired as to how the *puja* had to be performed and they told her all the details. The newly married bride Shila performed the *puja* as directed. She gave to Brahmans half of her scanty supply of food received from her stepmother, and shared the other half with her husband. She then started again in her bullock cart. It was not long before she attained the fruit of her devotion to Ananta, for her house was soon filled with provisions, her farmyard was full of cattle. Many guests were always entertained by the favoured Shila. She got gems such as diamonds and rubies, a large quantity of jewellery and her ward-robe was full. She felt herself supremely happy. One day her husband saw the fourteen-knotted thread round her arm. He asked her what it was. "Is this a charm for subduing me? Tell me the truth. Why have you worn this thread? She replied that it was Ananta who granted all desires. Her husband Kaudinya would not believe it. He cut it out, and shouted 'What is Ananta?' and the sinner threw the thread into the fire! His wife ran up to the fire, took the thread out and put it in a pot full of milk. But, for this disrespectful defiance, he lost all his wealth. His cows were lifted by thieves, his house was burnt to ashes, and his money was looted by *dakāits*. Everything disappeared as fast as it came. Quarrels sprang up between him and his relations. They beat him. He became a beggar. No one would even speak to him. His body suffered from pain, his mind was tortured by distressing thoughts. He became despondent, and

**Anant—**

asked his wife why he was so persecuted by Fate and asked her advice as to what to do. The good faithful wife said that she was afraid it was the result of the gross insult he had offered to the endless God Anant. He repented. He prayed unto the endless Lord for forgiveness. He performed severe austerities in the forest and thought of nothing but Lord Anant. "Where shall I see," said the poor penitent—"that Great Lord who had granted wealth to me, and taken it away as fast?" He wandered like a maniac—into the thickest part of the jungle. There, he saw a fine old mango tree, but it had no feathered resident in its umbrageous branches. On the contrary, it was full of vermin of all sorts. Kaudinya stood before this tree and asked it whether he had seen Lord Anant, saying "I have been longing to see Him." The tree replied, "Oh Brahman! I have not seen Him." He left the tree, wandered further on, and came across a cow followed by a calf. He asked the animal whether she had seen Lord Anant. She said that she did not know Him. Going still further, Kaudinya met a bull standing on a green pasture. The mad Brahman asked him the same question. He was given a similar reply. Further on he saw two tanks, one near the other, so much so that the gentle ripples on the surface of the one met those of the other. They were both full of lotuses, lilies and other water-plants. Among the foliage of these beautiful flowering plants were seen groups of lovely gambolling birds, and swarms of blue singing beetles. The Brahman stopped, gazed at the tanks with admiration, and asked them whether they had seen Lord Anant—the Endless. The tanks replied: "Oh Brahman! we have not seen Him." Proceeding onwards, Kaudinya met a donkey and an elephant. He again put his oft repeated question and got similar replies. Exhausted, fatigued, parched, distressed, the poor penitent pilgrim became desperate and tied a rope to an

**Anant—**
adjacent tree to hang himself. As he was putting the noose round his neck, there appeared Lord Anant dressed as an old Brahman. He called out to him to desist, caught him by the hand, took him to his cave. There he showed him a beatiful, prosperous city, in the midst of which was his palace, where he sat on a bejewelled throne, with his four emblems—conch, wheel, mace, and lotus. The celestial falcon Garud was standing with folded hands. The Lord then showed him his all pervading form. It was full of innumerable individuals and very bright, like the great gem Kaustubha. It was full of all sorts of vegetation. Seeing this omnipresent and omnipotent Existence, the pilgrim prayed with folded hands. He said, " Oh invincible, God of Gods, Oh Anant! I bow unto thee. I am a great sinner, I am full of sin, Oh Anant! protect me and destroy my sins. Oh Lord! By placing on thy lotus-like feet—my humble head—I have this day gained the fruition of a life and have secured the essential, the true vital goal of mortal existence." The omnipotent Lord replied, " Oh Chief of Brahmans, do not be afraid. Tell me what you want." He replied, " Oh Lord, I grew very arrogant with the wealth you had bestowed on me, and destroyed the *anant*-thread my wife was wearing. I, through that sin, lost every thing I possessed. Dissensions and quarrels sprang up in my family. Everybody refused to speak to me. I therefore became desperate, and went into the jungle to find you. You are kind enough to grant me the boon of an audience and have just revealed to me your all-pervading self. I therefore feel that all my desires have been fulfilled. Only tell me how to wash off the sin." The Lord replied, " Go home and worship the thread—*anant*—for fourteen years. It will wash off all your sins and you will get all your desires fulfilled. You will get sons and grandsons and all the happiness possible on earth. In the end, you will

**Anant—**

return to me. Moreover I grant you a blessing. Listen, he or she who performs the Anant *puja* and attentively listens to the history of your wife Shila's devotion to me, will get the same blessings which will be showered on you." The Brahman further asked the Lord of Lords to explain to him what was the mango tree he saw, what were the cow and the bullock he met, what were the two tanks, what was the donkey and what the elephant. The God replied: " The mango tree was a Brahman learned in the Vedas. He did not teach his pupils well and was turned into a tree. The cow is the Earth. She swallowed the seeds of the medicinal plants I created, and was turned into a brute. The bull is personified " goodness " (*dharma*), the two tanks represent the confluence of alms and sins. They were sisters born in a Brahman family and loved each other tenderly. They gave all alms to themselves, monopolised all charities, never gave anything to other Brahmans or poor people. They have, owing to that sin, been turned into tanks. You see how their waters mingle with each other. Not a drop goes out. The donkey you saw is " anger " personified, the elephant you met was " arrogance " personified, and the old man you met was myself. This cave (*guha*) is the personification of moral life on earth." Saying this God Anant disappeared.

Kaudinya, the Brahman, returned home, and per formed the *puja*. He got all that he wanted, and full of years and honors he returned to Heaven. The Brahman took fourteen years to acquire the full blessing of the *puja*. But if a devotee listens to this story or performs but only once this *vrata* he gets all that at once. Krishna added "Oh Dharma! I told you how to regain your kingdom. You will get it and all your sins will be washed off. Do not doubt. If any one but reads this story, a seat in Heaven—Vaikunth—is assured to him. If one but ties that thread round his arm, that one

**Anant**—
will most assuredly obtain all wordly pleasures and obtain *moksha*, Salvation.

**Annapurna worship**—Annapurna literally means the "supplier of food." It is one of the manifestations of Shiva's wife. She is seated on a throne, and holds a ladle like the Græcian horn of plenty.

Among the Chāndraseni Kāyasth Prabhus she is worshipped by the bride, when the bride-groom is expected to arrive. She sits pouring coloured yellow rice on the image and repeating "Oh Goddess! give me home by protecting the honoured guest who has just arrived" (meaning the bridegroom).

**Āshādhi-Ekādashi**—The eleventh day of the month of Āshadh (June-July) It is considered specially sacred. (See Ekdāashi).

**Ashvath**—*Ficus religiosa* tree. (See Somavati for its folklore).

**Avali-Bhojan**—See under *Vaikunth chaturdashi.* It is a dinner taken under the *Phylhanthuz emblica* tree on the 14th day of Kārtik. (October-November).

**Avidhavā-Navami**—See Adhukkh-navami.

**Bāras.**—The twelfth day of a lunar month. For folklore see Vasu-bāras, and Birthday of Vāman (Vāman Dvādashi)

**Bhadrakāli**—In the third chapter of *Shivalilāmrit,* a section of the *Brahmottarkhand* of the *Skandhapurāna,* the origin of the Bhadra Kāli of Gokarna-Mahabaleshwar in the Bombay Presidency has been described. This

**Bhădrăklăi—**

Bhadra-Kāli is cousidered very sacred, because she represents the entire body of Uma, the wife of Shiva, as compared with Kāmākshi, Kāli, and others who symbolize only the limbs or parts of her body as thrown in all directions by her infuriated husband. Moreover, she lives there with her husband and not alone. It is that place where Rāvan, Kumbhakarna and Bibhishana performed austerities. It is that spot where Rāvan brought the *atma-lingam* from Kailās, and Ganesh laid it perpetually.

The story runs :—Rāvan's mother was in the habit of worshipping a *lingam* for ensuring prosperity to her son. But Indra took it stealthily away out of spite and threw it into the sea. Rāvan's mother thereupon refused to take even a morsel of food as her devotions were interrupted. Rāvan promised to his devoted mother, that he would bring the chief *atma-lingam* down from Kailās, and left for that mountain, the home of Shiva. There, he performed the most severe austerities. He had a melodious voice and sang so well that Shiva was pleased at hearing his own praise in verse. The King of Ceylon chopped off his own head, made strings out of its skin, and with the harp prepared from those strings played to the satisfaction of the God of Kailās, who asked him to name his desires. Rāvan thereupon asked for the *atma-lingam* and a wife as beautiful as Uma herself. Shiva took out from his own heart the luminous *amta-lingam* as bright as a crore ot suns and handed it over to the demon, with the injunction that it should never be placed on the earth except where it had to be located for ever. Holding the gem in his hand, Rāvan repeated his request for a beautiful wife—as charming as the Goddess. Shiva replied that his wife Uma had no equal in beauty all over the universe, and therefore he could only offer her as she was. Infatuated Rāvan

**Bhādrākāli—**

accepted her—blinded as he was by unholy lust for the mother of the Creation. He placed her on his shoulder and walked off—with the mother of the God of War, Skandh! He was going to the south. When he was seen taking away the *atma-lingam* and the Goddess, all the Gods were alarmed. Her sons Ganesh, Skandh and and Virabhadra, as well as Nandikeshwar were all astonished. They went to Shiva and complained how he could part with their mother. Lord Shiva smiled, and added that her great champion Vishnu, the Lord of Vaikunth, will release her. Bhavāni *alias* Uma also began praying. She was and is herself a great power, but when ordered by her husband to go, she, as a dutiful wife, would not disobey. She therefore invoked the help of Vishnu. Lord Vishnu appeared before Rāvan in the garb of an old Brahman and asked him where he got so charming a wife from? The demon replied, that she was given to him by Sadāshiva, the Lord or Kailas, and elated with the praise walked a pace. "Do look at her," said the *pseudo* Brahman. Here the power of Vishnu made him forget himself and he took her down to gaze at her beauteous face. But alas! The all-powertul goddess had turned herself into an old hag. Dirty, hideous, with frightful eye-brows, sunken cheeks, and toothless mouth she stood—a horrid repulsive figure! The Brahman laughed a cynical satanic laugh and chided: "Oh, Rāvan' what a beauty, for a wife of the Emperor of Ceylon!" Rāvan felt humiliated and disgusted and left her on the spot. As soon as he turned away, Lord Vishnu, the husband of the goddess of wealth, established her there as Mother Bhadra-Kāli where she still lives. The demon returned to Kailās and complained to Shiva for giving him such a dirty hag. "Yes you speak the truth my friend said he, "she is a witch, a bad lot. She prevades the 'innumerable universes,' and she is invincible, you

**Bhādrākāli—**

cannot rule her. She is uncontrollable." God Vishnu then created a charming girl and assured Rāvan that she would be born as Mandodari, the daughter of giant Mayāsura, that she would marry him and be a faithful wife. Rāvan was satisfied at this assurance and proceeded with the journey still holding the *atma-lingam* in his hand. But as soon as he came to the same spot where he had left Uma, he met Ganesh in the garb of a cowherd. The great God of Success, was requested by the other gods to save the *atma-lingam*, and that was why he waylaid Rāvan. At this moment, Rāvan felt an uncontrollable call of nature. So painful was it that he had to request Ganesh to hold the *lingam* in his hand for a few minutes. Ganesh said that he had charge of the cows and could not wait long. He could only stay for an hour and a half at the longest. "Quite sufficient," thought Rāvan and went aside, but he could not return quickly. Half an hour passed and cowherd Ganesh shouted, "Beware Rāvan, one *ghanta* has passed." Another half an hour and another warning from Ganesh followed. But Rāvan could not move. He made signs. He made violent gestures begging him to stay! It may be noted here that in India speech is prohibited during the relief of nature. The third *ghanta* or half an hour passed and Ganesh shouted "Off I go, Sir. My cows have strayed. I cannot stay." He then placed the *lingam* on the earth. At this very juncture Rāvan felt free to move and ran after the cowherd (Ganesh), but he was gone. He disappeared. His cows also disappeared, but Rāvan just-reached one of them as she was sinking in the bowels of Mother Earth. He caught the beast by her ear, but the whole of the body was gone. This ear now seen petrified or fossilized is the relic that has given the spot its name Gokarna, or cow's ear, from *go*, *gau*, a cow, and *karna* an ear. Taken with the name of the God Mahā-

**Bhādrākāli—**

baleshwar or the all-powerful, it is called Gokarna-Mahābaleshwar, and the chief Goddess there is called Bhadra Kāli. Rāvan, the king of demons, the ten-headed and twenty-handed giant, tried his best to lift the *lingam* up·but it was eternally fixed. He who could shake Mount Kailās with his powerful and plentiful arms, failed to uproot it and that is why it is called Mahābaleshwar, the all-powerful God. He then turned once more to the ear of the cow and tried to pull the beast out of the bowels of the Earth, but he had not the power. The ear of the cow, the *lingam* of Shiva, and Goddess Bhadra Kāli are all there still, as Three in One. All the Gods worship them. Rāvan's mother and brothers had to come there to worship. Once Bibhishana came to the temple unexpectedly, while a Brahman named Hemādpant was worshipping the God. He got frightened at the sight of the giant and hid himself in the *nirmal* or wastebin containing the rejected leaves of the *Bel* tree, (*Æagle marmelos*) dear to Shiva. Devout Bibhishana bowed to the *lingam*, took a pinch of the *bel* leaves and placed it in his turban. Poor Hemādnant was carried in that pinch unnoticed by the giant. He went to Ceylon and there learnt the script known as Modi or modified Nāgari. He again hid himself in the turban of the giant and as soon as he returned to the temple to pay his homage to Mahābaleshwar he escaped. He had thus been able to import a new script into the Maratha-speaking territory. Such is the tradition but the fact remains that Shivāji introduced it in Government correspondence, through his Secretary or Chitnis Bālāji Avaji. It is therefore known as *Chitnisi valan*. Gokarna Mahābaleshwar, the seat of Bhadra Kāli, is reached from Bombay by coasting steamers, and is visited by thousands of pilgrims who have faith in this *purān*. Many of them prefer it to all other seats of Kāli, owing as is related above, to the fact of the entire Goddess being present there.

**Bhādva.**—Bhādrapad, the name of the month of the Hindu year (August-September). Gannesh-worship is the chief-festival of the first half of this month. See Ganesh for folkore. The second half is sacred for the worship of the manes of the ancestors, when feasts are given to Brahmans. See Shrāddh.

**Bhāu Bij,**—The second day of *Kārtik* is reserved for friendly greetings between brothers and sisters. It is said that Yamuna often asked her brother Yama, the God of Death, to her house to dine, but he evaded. At last, moved by repeated importunities, he went to her on this day and was bathed and sumptuously treated. He was pleased, and bid his sister to ask for a blessing. She said, that he should come to her to dine every year on this day and should grant happiness to all those who respond to their sister's calls and accept this day's feast. He granted this request, and that is why all brothers are well treated on this day.

**Bhaumavār.**—Tuesday. *For Folklore,* see Mangla Gaur.

**Bhishma-Panchak-Vrat.**—On the 11th of *Kārtik* General Bhishma of the Kaurava's army, was laid on his death-bed on the battle field: but as he had the power of fixing the time of his death, he lived till the sun had crossed the vernal equinox. During the period he lay on the bed of arrows erected by Arjuna, he was advising the Pāndvas, how to rule justly and fairly and how to attain heaven in the end, and therefore some people fast on these days and spend their time in reading that advice.

**Birth-day of Dattātraya,** (see Datta Jayanti).
**Birth-day of Hanumān,** (see Hanumān Jayanti).
**Birth-day of Krishna,** (see Janmāshtami).

| | |
|---|---|
| **Birth-day of Kurma,** | (see Kurma Jayanti). |
| **Birth-day of Mārtand,** | (see Champā Shasthi). |
| **Birth-day of Narsingha,** | (see Narsingha Jayanti). |
| **Birth-day of Parashurām,** | (see Parashurām Jayanti). |
| **Birth-day of Rāma** | (see Rāma Navami). |

**Bodana.**—Curd, fried pulse-cakes called *vada* etc. mixed up together & presented in oblation to Mahā-Laxmi or the tutelary goddess of a family by a company of five married women. For folkore see Mahā-Laxmi.

**Bodhini.**—The eleventh day of the first half of *Kārtik* when Vishnu awakes from sleep. See *Ekādasi* for folklore.

**Brihaspati.**—The planet Jupiter the *Guru* or Preceptor of the Gods. For folklore, see under Wednesday and Thursday worships.

**Budh.**—The planet Mercury or Regent thereof. For folkore see Wednesday worshp.

**Chaitra Gauri** :—(March-April) Gauri or the wife of Shiva is worshipped in this month by every married woman whose husband is alive. On the 3rd of the month a brass *dola* or swing containing the images of Shiva and his family is placed on a raised dais, and the images are worshipped every morning. A fresh wreath of flowers has to be added every day. If flowers be not available, spun cotton is shaped like a wreath and put on. During the whole period, each family holds a ladies' meeting on select-ed days. All the married ladies and unmarried girls, that is all women excluding widows, are invited to attend. The image of Gauri is dressed with clothes and the best orna-ments and jewellery are put on the figure. All the curiosi-ties and nice things in the house are arranged in

**Chaitra Gauri,—**
front of the figure on tiers or stepped platforms. Fruits, parched grains, sweets, and flowers are freely distributed among the visitors. Germinating gram seeds form an important item. The room is lighted in the best possible style, and young newly married couples are specially entertained. It is in fact a gala day for all ladies except widows. There are generally many invitations on one day, and women and girls are seen going from house to house in the best of spirits, and in full dress. A very happy month indeed. This gathering is called *Halad-Kunku* literally "turmeric and saffron" ceremony.

**Champa Shashthi** :—The sixth day of the bright half of Mrigasirsha. At Jejuri, near Poona, there is a large temple dedicated to Mārtand, known also as Malhāri and Khanderāo or Khandoba. The Pauranic origin of this place of pilgrimage is given in the Kshetra Khand of the Brahmapurān. It is said that Malhāri or Mārtand was an incarnation of Shiva for destroying two demons named Mani and Mall. Once upon a time the seven Rishis represented by the seven stars of the Ursa Major went to the Manichurna mountain to perform austerities. They had their families with them. Demon Mall came there for chase with Mani and a large army. He destroyed the cottages of the Rishis and defiled their sacred fires. The Rishis removed their families to another mountain, and went by turn to Indra, Vishnu and Shiva for protection. It was Brahma who had blessed these demons with power to conquer the world, and even the gods. They became uncontrollable and annoyed the gods. They drank hard and committed excesses. When all these complaints reached Shiva, he promised to destroy them. Shiva became Mārtand Bhairav, and accompanied by two young female attendants, dogs, seven *crore ganas*, and a vast army of ghosts, and all the gods joining him, went to the Manichurna mountain.

**Champa Shashthi,—**

Mall was assisted by Chandrakopāsur, Sindhunad, Gomukh, Dhumra-Vaktra, Shurpa-karna, etc. All the Daitya soldiers were killed by the army of the gods. When Shiva placed his foot on the head of Mani, he prayed for mercy and asked the boon that he who reads the description of his fight with god Shiva might have all his wishes fulfilled. He was then sent to heaven ('Kailās'). Mall, the second brother, was also defeated and killed. Then came his five sons, Lohargal, Shulakhar, Devha-Gandharva, Kunbhir and Mahābāhu. They were cursed and became mountains. The Rishis then asked Shiva to remain on the mountain in their midst and he did so as a double-'lingam' of the *Svayambhu* or self-evolved type, that is, not being shaped by human hand. This battle took place on the 6th day of the first half or *Champā-Shashthi* of 'Margashirsha,' the 9th Hindu (lunar) month, when the mountain was under the influence of the Shata-tāraka or the 24th lunar mansion containing a hundred stars. A large city soon grew on the spot. It was named Prema-puri or the town of love. The image of Mārtand or Mārtand Bhairav there, is also called Mairāl. Its local name is Khanderāo, he is the family god of many Marāthas. His consort Mhālsābāi is riding and seated behind him, and is attended by a dog. Khanderao is supposed to be riding a yellow horse, his flag is yellow, and the demons he killed were also yellow.

The most curious circumstance about this god remains to be told. To him are vows offered for being favoured with children, on condition that the first born shall be left in the temple for the service of the deity. A large number of men and women have thus gathered round the temple and are fed by the pilgrims. Tbe men are called Vāghias (tigers) and the girls Muralis (flutes?). They lead an immoral life. They have no caste, as they admit infants of all castes and tribes into their fold.

**Champa Shashthi,—**

Khāndoba literally means the swordsman. He is the guardian deity of the Deccan. At Jejuri he is shown as a *lingam.* He uses turmeric powder which is called *Bhandār* and is carried in bags made of tiger's skin by the *Vaghias,* who apply them to the foreheads of the devotes. *Bel* (*Aegle marmeloe*) leaves and *Bhandār,* the turmeric powder, held in hand like the Koran or the Bible and sworn upon, form the most binding oath for a Deccan Marātha. Nothing will compel him to swerve from the promise so made. Sumer Singh who murdered Peshwa Nārāyan Rāo, was thus made to swear by Anandibāi the jealous aunt of the prince, and the wife of Raghunāth Rāo Peshva. So sacred is the *bel* and *bhandār* of Khandoba.

Khāndoba had a mistress named Bānāi (literally, a quiver from *bān* an arrow and *ai* the mother or one that holds the arrows). She was of the Dhangar or shepherd caste. It is said that he once went to a Dhangar hamlet and saw this girl. They both fell in love and he abducted her. The Dhangars are his most attached worshippers. They offer stone sheep to Bānāi and ask for flocks and herds. But 'Mārtand' is one of the names of the Sun, the great luminary. it is therefore difficult to reconcile the theory of the incarnation of Shiva, the God of destruction, with the power attributed to Khandoba. He is supposed to protect people from epidemics. It is suggested that the whole story is but a a sun-myth, in which its yellow rays have destroyed the yellowish or pea fog of the Northern mountains, where the Aryans lived before they came down to India. The story of the hunter fits in, when Mrigshirsha, the fifth mansion, resembles the head of an antelope, Shatatāraka, the hundred star mansion, the Bānāi the quiver holding 100 arrows, the Ursa Major, the 7 Rishis; and cannis the dog of the astronomical chart. The arrival of the sun therefore at this particular point, indicated the defeat and death of the demons.

**Chandi.**—Havish Mangal Chandi is observed in April-May in Bengal. Chandi is one of the manifestations of Kāli. Havish (Sanskrit, Havishya) is a fast observed during the day and broken on nightfall with a preparation of *Mug* (*Phaseolus mungo*). Mangal indicates Tuesday and also means luck or fortune. Havish-Mangal-Chandi therefore means, the good-luck-giving-Chandi-fast observed on Tuesdays.

The story runs that the milk-maid friend of a Brahman woman saw her observing this fast with the result that she was always happy and had no occasion to shed tears. She asked her Brahman friend to explain to her the nature and fruition of the fast and was told that it should be observed on Tuesdays in the month of *Vaishākh* (April-May) and added that " one who observes this fast remains always happy and will have no occasion to shed tears. Her whole life will be one round of pleasures and happiness". The milk-maid said that she would like to perform the *Vrat*, but her Brahman friend tried to dissuade her from doing so, as it is a difficult and complicated ceremony. She however made up her mind and the Brahman woman was obliged to teach the details, inspite of her unwillingness to let the secret out. The month of *Vaishākh* came in due course, and the milk-maid began observing the fast. The result was as expected. Goddess Mangal Chandi was pleased with her. She began to prosper, she became very rich and happy. Reaching the climax of happiness all of a sudden, she now got a craving to cry and weep. She went to the Brahman lady and said " As I have already enjoyed too much of pleasure, I am now inclined to weep ". Her friend was astounded and advised her to give up such an idea, explaining to her that one who performs the *Vrata* of Mangal-Chandi shall never have to weep. She will

**Chandi,—**

always be happy, and that is why the fast is called *Havish-Mangal-Chandi*". But seeing that she was determined to find out an excuse for weeping, the Brahman woman instructed her " Go to the yonder field, cut down the pumpkin creeper growing there, and take it home. When the owners will learn about the mischief, they will abuse you. Cry then to your heart's content". She did so, but she was protected by the goddess. As soon as she touched the creeper it began to grow more vigorously than before. The owners thought she was a superhuman being, and out of respect, sent leaves of the pnmpkin creeper for her to cook and eat. There, the plan to cause her to weep, failed. She explained this to her friend who said " there lies a dead elephant belonging to the king, go there and weep for it." She did so, but as soon as she touched the elephant, it came to life again. When the king heard of this miracle he sent her valuable presents. This scheme also failed. The milk-maid could not weep. She went again to her friend for advice, and was told " As you are bent on weeping, do one thing. Prepare some sweets, mix deadly poison with them, and send them to your daughter. She did so, and sent the sweets with her son. He ate a portion. But by the merit of the *Vrat* the stuff was turned into nector. The boy took the sweet balls to his sister and presented them to her. The milk-maid's daughter and son-in-law and the other members of their family ate the balls and were much delighted. They found them very sweet and delicious. On the other hand the milk-maid was waiting for the return of her son with evil tidings. He came and explained to his mother that every-one in her daughter's house was exceedingly delighted, and that they have requested her, to supply some more. She was sadly disappointed. She was very angry, she went to her friend and told her what happened.

Chandi,—

The Brahman woman was also much annoyed. At last, she advised her not to perform the *Vrata*. That blunder caused the displeasure of the vindictive goddess, and all her men, elephants, horses, sons and daughters died. She then cried in despair. She repented, and went to her friend, for advice. Her friend taunted her, that as she was anxious to weep, she should do so with all her heart! But the poor milk-maid said that she had enough of it. She was then told "Wait till the next Tuesday and perform the *Vrat* as before. Do not send the dead bodies for cremation until that day. In the mean time sing the praises of goddess Mangal-Chandi and pray unto her. She did so; on the Tuesday following she observed fast and was still crying ; holding in her hand the pot of water required for the worship. Then she heard a voice saying. "Sprinkle the water of this pot on the dead bodies." She obeyed, and all her people and beasts came to life again. Her neighbours learnt of the fruition of the *Vrat* and adopted it. Who ever performs this *Vrat* lives a happy life. She will never have to shed tears. Even they who tell or listen to the story live eontented.

**Chandra.**—The Moon. On the Ganesh day Hindus do not look at the Moon. If any one accidentally happens to see him he expiates the sin by fasting on certain days sacred to Ganesh and called *Sankasthi chaturthi* or the fourth of the latter half a month, which if observed as a fast, wards off impending calamities or *Sankasht*. So firm is the belief in some quarters, that the man or woman who happens to see our satellite on that auspicious day, thinks that unless he or she gets himself or herself abused by some one on the next day he or she has no escape! The police all over India has to remain alert, because these offenders against the curse of Ganesh throw stones on the roofs of their neighbours' houses simply to annoy them and provoke them to use abusive language! A single abuse naturally produces irritation and provocation, but on this night a shower of filthy words is accepted with a sigh of relief that the danger prognosticated by the evil sight of the moon would be warded off!

The origin of this belief is given in the Skandh Puran. It says that once upon a time while elephant-headed Ganesh was riding his mouse and passing from Satyalok (Brahman's abode) through the moon's abode (Chandralok) he fell down. The moon who is very proud of his (the moon is a male in Indian mythology) good looks laughed at him. Ganesh cursed him and said: "Oh! you sinner, Oh you antelope-shaped nibus-faced fellow! Those who look at your face hereafter shall be falsely accused of offences against the law." This curse produced consternation all over the universe. The moon hid himself in a lotus flower. When he could not be seen, gods, Rishis, Gandharvās, all were very sorry. Headed by Indra, they went to Brahma for advice. He said that God Ganesh was alone able to remove the baneful influence of his curse, and advised an appeal to him. Brihaspati, the preceptor of Gods, was then deputed to the Moon to direct how he should propitiate God Ganesh. Lord Ganesh was pleased, and appeared before him in all his glory attended by the eight Goddesses of success (*ashtsiddhi*). The moon begged to be pardoned. He was asked to name the favour he sought. He naturally begged that the terrible curse be wiped off. Ganesh refused. He said he would give him anything but that. The gods interceded. Ganesh revoked the curse. He said: "On the fourth day of the month of Bhādrapad (Ganesh day) those who will see you, shall suffer from the curse in the course of the following year: there is no gain-saying that. But sin will not touch those who will bow unto thee on every second day each month." At the further importunities of the repentant moon, Ganesh directed that "If by accident any one happned to see the moon on the special Ganesh day, he should fast on the fourth day of the second half of a month, worship me, and worship the moon with his consort Rohini as soon as they rise above the horizon. He should give to a priest a gold image of myself. He shall, if he does so, be protected from calamities."

**Charpota or Chapra Shashthi.**—Charpota are cakes made of the fresh husk of the palmyra fruit with its yellowish pulp and covered with bamboo leaves. *Chapra* is the corruption of the same word. This day falls on the 6th moon of Bhādrapad (August-September), and the *puja* is performed in Bengal. The story runs that there was a Bania with three sons and three daughters-in-law. The youngest had some children, of whom the grandfather was specially fond. The grandmother of these children had to go to some tank for performing the *Puja* of the Chapra Shashthi; but it was an inconvenient place and the owners of the tank were not very civil. She therefore proposed to her lord that a new tank be excavated on their own property. Her husband, who was a wealthy merchant, readily granted her request. The tank was ready, but there was no water in it. Even during the monsoon, no water accumulated. It remained all dry! The merchant and his family were sadly disappointed. He was despondent. At this juncture, Shashthi appeared in his dream and advised him to sacrifice one of his grandsons to propitiate herself. It was a horrible rite! The Bania got frightened at the dream and was in tears. His wife, when she learnt of the dream was also overtaken with grief. They cried, they sobbed, they tried to console each other. They argued among themselves; they shivered at the very idea, they shuddered to think of the spectacle and the crime of murdering their own child! At last, overcome by the fear of the terrible Goddess, they planned the sacrifice without the knowledge of the mother of the child, and Oh God! the grandfather actually cut the throat of the babe and sprinkled its innocent blood over the spot. He could not look at the spectacle! He shut his eyes, but on hearing the sound of a rush of waves he looked out only to see the tank full up to the brim! This happened on the morning of the Chapra Shashthi day! He hastened home and quickly got together materials for the worship of the Shashthi. The whole family gathered near the Ghāt, the *Puja* was quickly performed, the mother of the child was so busy that she had not noticed the absence of her dear little mite. Her turn to let the cradle in, came. She did so, but was astonished to find it floating with her own child inside it! The whole family ran up the Ghāt to lift up their little hopeful!

Town people came to see the miracle. The result was that at the advice of the priests, all women held plantains in their aprons over their laps, and listened to the story of the Chapra Shashthi. The *Puja*, henceforward, became very popular among mothers and is performed every year.

*Chaturmās Pujās.*—During the four months of the Indian monsoon, from the 10th of Ashādh to the 10th of Kārtik, there are certain *vratās* which ladies are advised to observe. It is said that Vishnu goes to sleep on the coils of the great snake Vāsuki on the 10th of Ashādh. After two months, that is, on the 11th of Bhādrapad he turns to the right side and after the 10th of Kārtik he wakes up. In the Kārtik-Mahātmya, it is said that when the giant Shankhāsura (conch-shell) carried away the Vedas to the bottom of the sea, Vishnu took four months to recover them in the Matchch or merman incarnation. The eleventh of

Ashādh is called Shayani-Ekādashi owing to this association. The Vratrāj tells us that during the *Satya Yug* or Gold age there lived a king named Māndhāta. His territory was once much in distress owing to a famine extending over three years. He asked Saint Angira to explain to him why his kingdom suffered, who said that the visitation was due to a *Shudra* performing religious penances ! He advised the king to destory the offender. The King expressed his unwillingness to kill a man engaged in the service of God, to whatsoever caste he may belong. His Majesty was thereupon asked to observe this fast instead. He did so, and the famine disappeared. Another ceremony observed is the *Worship of Cows' Foot Prints.* Once upon a time the Gods found that their musical instruments produced discordant notes, the wires were broken, the leather was cut open and there could be no harmony. They directed that enquiry be made of the sinful woman or beast that had not been performing *pujas* and stopped the concert. It was ordained that the offender should have her skin removed to make new 'strings.', At this Krishna got alarmed as he thought his sister Subhadra might not have performed any *puja.* He ran up to her and asked her if it was so. She confessed that she had not. Krishna told her to begin at once on the 10th *Ashādh* by drawing three foot-prints of cows in front of any temple, in front of a Brahman's house, under the *ashvath* (*Ficus riligiosa*) tree, or on the bank of a tank. These symbols should, he said, be worshipped every morning until the 10th of Kārtik and the process repeated for five years. At the end of the first monsoon an unmarried girl should be invited to dinner and offered betel. At the end of the second year (or monsoon) a similar girl should be well fed and given bangles, on the third occasion plantain fruit should be offered her after dinner, on the fourth a bundle of sugarcanes, and on the fifth a dress. Subhadra thus escaped the punishment, but there lay a cow-elephant sleeping with her legs to the south and her head to the north. The emissaries of the gods removed from the back of the animal a strip of skin from head to tail. It was made into thin thongs to replace those broken. Those, who perform this worship, will escape the divine punishment meted out to the erring elephant! The third *vrata* observed is the worship of *The Five Gods* which is an all round alliance with them. On one occasion, Shiva and Pārvati went round the world. They halted at one place. Pārvati was shampooing her husband's feet. He found that her hands were too rough and advised her to serve a Brahman woman as a midwife or a *dāi*. Goddess though she is, she did serve a Brahman woman as a menial and regained soft hands! The Brahman woman asked her to show her the way to propitiate all gods to ensure a happy life. Pārvati told her to worship from the 10th Ashādh to the 10th Kārtik gods, Ganesh, Vishnu, Nandi, Mahādev and Pārvati (herself) offering them their favourite flowers and food. She added, that Brahmans should be fed from time to time. The woman did so. She became rich. One day Pārvati went to her house incognito, dressed in rags. The woman could not recognize her, Goddess Pārvati was very angry, she went to Ganesh, her son, and asked him to take revenge. He declined to do so because he was devoutly worshipped by that woman. She went to all the other gods. They all refused to take revenge on a woman who had worshipped them. Pārvati was disappointed, Shiva appeased her wrath by explaining to her that inability to recognize a person incognito, was no crime. She was advised to go again in her usual dress. She did so, and was most hospitably received. She was satisfied and blessed the Brahman woman. The fourth *vrata* observed is the *puja of The Earth*—If Goddess Earth be worshipped from the 10th of Ashādh to the 10th of Kārtik or from the 3rd of Shrāvan to the 3rd of Māgh by a woman, she will, it is said, get all happiness: sons, daughters, grandsons, wealth and every mortal thing she wants. She should draw a hexagonal symbol of the moon and one of the sun. Added to these, there should be drawn six foot-prints of the cow. These symbols should be worshipped every morning. The daughter-in-law of a prosperous family should be invited to dinner, and offered a dress with toilet requisites. The fifth observance is a fast on the *Chaturthi* or the fourth day of the dark half of every month. It is called Sankashthi from *Sankashth,* trouble, distress, difficulty, and *Chaturthi* the fourth, that is the fourth day which, if observed as a fast, removes all difficulties. It is sacred to Ganesh the God of success. After fasting all the day, the worshipper has to wait until the moon rises above the horizon and then to perform the *puja* of the God. People in distress, people who desire sons, and mothers who wish their sons to succeed in their educational course, chiefly observe this fast.

**Dark night, the,—**

The dark night of each lunar month is called *Amāvasāy.* The story runs in Bengal, that there lived a poor Brahman, a devotee of the sun. He had a son whom he got married at the age of 16, but on the day of the nuptials he disappeared. The Brahman died in grief. His wife and daughter-in-law were living miserably together. One day the sun appeared as a guest and asked for a tub of warm water to bathe. Then he, as an honored guest, wanted the clothes of the old lady's dead son. They were given to him. When rice was ready, he claimed the plate which was used by the son. The daughter-in-law felt annoyed but the mother granted the request. The climax came when he claimed the daughter-in-law as his wife. The mother, like the mother of the Tichbourne claimant, believed that he was her lost son and even that request was granted. Satisfied at the devotion and faith of the poor woman, he disclosed himself and said that he was the great luminary, the sun, and that her son was no other than himself incarnate. He thus visited the ladies but always disappeared at dawn. One day when he was returning, the mother secretly followed him. He noticed it, and asked her not to do so. She explained to him that he ought to look after his mother and wife, who were practically starved. At this, he gave her about two pounds of pearls and told her that they would relieve them both from poverty for sometime. The mother gave them to the daughter-in-law who was so ignorant that finding that they were not eatable, and that they could neither be cooked nor pounded into pulp, threw them away. After sometime, the son appeared again but found that the two women were still very poor. He inquired and learnt how the wealth was lost. He inspected the place where they were thrown, and found that trees had grown there and were laden with pearls. He plucked them all, and gave them to the mother. He then explained to them both, their use. A few of them were sold in the market for thousands. The mother built a house, consecrated a temple, and a tank and bequeathed the whole lot to Surya, the Sun. When the Sun again came and entered the room, the mother locked him up and did not allow him to go. He begged to be set free but, it was all in vain. The result was that there was no sunrise and the universe was all in dark. Brahma, Vishnu, and Mahesh went to the house and asked the mother to let her son go. At their importunities he was brought out of the room. The sun then explained to the mother who the three visitors were, and added that his confinement was due to a curse. She was not to blame. At the request of Brahma, Vishnu, and Mahesh he took his mother and wife with him in his celestial chariot. But before leaving the world they distributed everything to Brahmans. The mother and daughter-in-law went to heaven with their son and husband, on an Amāvāshya day. The citizens were astounded. They therefore began to adore the sun and to fast on the Amāvāshya day, adding the worship of the sun. From that time the *puja* came to be introduced in this country, (Bengal,) and is repeated on every dark day all the year round, (*i.e., Bāramās,* twelve months.)

**Dashahāra,—**

In Jeshtha (May-June) the second month of the Hindu calendar there are only two fasts and no feasts. The first one begins on the first day of the first half and ends on the tenth. Dashaharā is an epithet of the Ganges, and this is supposed to be the celebration of the birth of the nymph of that river, or her descent from heaven at the request of Bhagirath, the ancestor of Rāma. Some people living on the banks of the Ganges as well as those of other rivers, go to the stream to bathe and to offer oblations. On the 10th day however, every Hindu family living on the banks of the Ganges sends offerings of fruit and flowers to the river, which are taken by the priests as their perquisites.

**Datta Jayanti,—**

This celebration falls on the tenth of Mārgshirsha, (November-December) means the birthday of Dattātreya the embodiment of the Hindu Trinity—Brahma the Creator, Vishnu the Protector and Shiva, the Destroyer —all the three in one. The story runs:—Once upon a time saint Nārad discovered that the wives of the three chief gods had become so conceited that they vaunted they were the models of *pativratās.* A *pativratā* is a devoted and faithful wife who has not even dreamt of another mate. Nārad began his joke with Pārvati by praising in her presence the virtues of Anasuya—the wife of Saint Atri: "So holy, so pious a wife, did not exist."

That remark raised the jealousy of the wife of Shiva and she induced her husband to so persecute the wife of the saint as to deprive her of her chastity! Nārad then went to his father Brahma and in the presence of his own mother Sāvitri he repeated the same high praise. Sāvitri insisted on Brahma's persecuting the woman. Finally going to Vishnu, he sowed the same seed of discord with equal success. At the instigation of their wives the three gods started for the hermitage of Saint Atri and simultaneously reached it.

They shouted for alms, the lady Anasuya came out with a handful of corn. They refused to accept and said that they wanted an *ichchā-bhojan*, dinner with wished for dainties. She consented. They were asked to bathe themselves in the adjoining river. By the time they returned, the dinner was ready. They took their seats. The hostess came out with the first plate. They refused to accept it and added an impossible condition. They said that she must come out nude! Revolting though the very thought was, she reflected for a moment and through her virtuous eye could see the motive of the guests. She recognized them at once although they were dressed like mendicants! She took a cupful of water, washed her husband's feet with the liquid and sprinkled the washings over the guests. Wonderful to behold! They became little babies! She then threw away her *sari* and lifted up each to suckle! But the gods lost all power. They could not resume their original full grown shapes! They were all put in a cradle and lulled to sleep! Their wives missed them, they waited for their return, but were disappointed. They prayed, they cried—all in vain. Distracted, they started in search. Where the three roads to the three heavens meet, Nārad met them! They asked him if he knew where their husbands were, as he was the living embodiment of all n-e-w-s (North, East, West and South), and as he had access everywhere. He of course knew every thing, but he merely told them that they were seen going to Saint Atri's hermitage.

All the three goddesses went to that house. They enquired of Anasuya, if she knew where their husbands the greatest of gods were. She replied in the affirmative and pointed to the cradle! Oh lord! husbands in cradles, nude, all dumb! What could they do! Anasuya put all the three babies on a carpet and asked each goddess to pick up her own lord! Vishnu the most knowing and the most jocular of them winked at Brahma, and Brahma at Shiva. They thus conspired not to reveal themselves. The goddesses looked, looked again, looked once more, to see if they could with any mark, make out who was who in that little group. At last, Laxmi put her hands forward to lift up Shiva and every one laughed! Shiva was not her husband! Seeing Laxmi's discomfiture the other two goddesses withdrew and begged of Anasuya to restore their husbands to them. She was very willing to do them a good turn, but she added that as she had nursed the three gods as her babies they should, in return, induce them to stay with her as her children in some form or other. After due consideration of all the pros and cons it was decided that the three gods should assume a combination-shape. The hostess then again took a cupful of water, washed her husband's feet with it and sprinkled the washings containing the dust of the Brahman's feet over the bodies. They regained their original shapes, blessed Anasuya and left with their crest-fallen wives! Dattātreya, this child so born has three heads, and six hands. The central one is Vishnu, the right hand one of the figure is Shiva, and the left hand one is Brahma.

**Dāvāchi chauth,—**

This is the fourth day of the first half of the month of Shrāvan (July-August). It is sacred to Ganesh and his mother Gauri. Yellow and red silk threads are taken. To the former are given 16 knots, and to the latter 21. Each such thread is then worshipped. The yellow ones represent Gauri, and the red ones Ganesh. The number of the amulets thus prepared corresponds with the number of girls and boys in the family. Sweets of sorts are prepared, and a feast takes place. The red silk amulets are tied to the arms of the boys and the yellow ones to those of the girls. Pastry and sweets are distributed among the families of relations and caste people.

**Dev-Divāli,**—The fifteenth or full-moon day of Kārtik, called also Tripuri Pornima, which please see for folklore.

**Dava-Guru,**—Brihaspati, Jupiter; for folklore see Thursday worship.

**Devakārya,**—The worship of the Penates: business connected with it. Annual worship of the family Gods. See Champā-Shati for folklore.

**Dhan-Teras,**—(Dhantrayòdashi) The thirteenth day of the waxing moon in the month of Ashwin. On this day Shroffs &c worship money. See Divāli for folklore.

**Dhanurmās,**—Period during which the sun is in Sagittarius. The offerings to idols, and the feastings at early hour.

**Dhond-Mās,**—Dhond Mahina. An incalary month formed of the aggregate days omitted in reckoning the lunar year. See Adhik-Mās.

**Dhulavad,**—The day of throwing dust *(Dhul)* after the burning of the Holi. It usually occurs on the first day after the full moon of Phālgun, (February-March). See Holi for folklore.

**Dhvajāropan,**—Raising the flag or standard. New year's day *(Varsh Pratipada)*, see Gudhicha Pādva for folklore.

**Divāli,**—

(I) Vishnu apportioned four chief holidays between the four *varnas* or castes. The Brahmans of the alms-receiving class have to observe the *rākhi-purnima*, or the full-moon day of the month of Shrāvan, (July-August) and to collect money by tying the well-known *raksha* or protecting charm to the wrists of their masters; and every employer will testify that they have not neglected this opportunity. To the Kshatriya or warrior caste, Vishnu gave the Dasara holiday, to the Vaisyas or trader caste, the Divāli when they are expected to worship goddess Lakshmi who presides over wealth, and to the Sudras or servile class, Phālgun or Holi, the Saturnalia of the last month of the Hindu Calendar.

(II) The second idea claims Divāli as the day on which Rāja Bali was deprived of his empire on earth. In Maharashtra, women prepare effigies of King Bali, either in rice-flour or cow-dung according to grade, worship them and repeat the blessing "May all evils disappear, and Rāja Bali's Empire be restored."

There is no such worship in Bengal.

(III) It is believed that Vishnu killed Narkāsur or the giant of filth on the 14th day of the second Ashvin. (September-October.) On this day, all Hindus bathe very early before sunrise after anointing their bodies with many perfumed unguents and oils. There are two baths taken, one after the other, just as is done on the death of a near relation. After the first bath, a lamp made of rice-flour and an oval piece of the same stuff called *mutke* are waved round each male by some girl or married woman, and the fruit of the cucurbitous plant, *chirāt*, is placed in front of him. He then crushes the fruit under his left foot, extinguishes the lamp with the toe of his left leg, and takes the second bath. He wears a new dress and partakes, with his freinds and relations, of the numerous dainties prepared for the occasion. This, it is said, is in celebration of the victory of Vishnu over the giant.

(IV.) The fourth explanation is but a variation of Lakshmi-worship in which Bengalis bring home clay figures of their dreadful Kāli and worship it in the place of the charming consort of Vishnu, represented by heaps of Rupees placed in trays. They say, that Kāli is Lakshmi (Goddess of wealth), is Saraswati (Goddess of Learning), and the procreative female power as well!

(V.) The fifth idea has a historical basis. It is that King Vikrāmaditya of Ujjain, a scion of the Gupta race, was crowned on this day, the 16th of Ashvin, and counted his era accordingly. This is thus a new year's day.

(VI.) It is asserted that after his return from Lanka, (Ceylon) Rāma was crowned on this day!

Taking, however, into consideration the season or the time of the year, one is led to suspect that the primitive origin of *Divali* has connection with the movement of the earth round the sun. That luminary passes the *tula,* the *libra* or the 'balance', about this time and marks the beginning of the second half of its course. 'He' is then seen going farther and farther from the Northern hemisphere, the nights become longer in proportion, snow begins to fall on the peaks of the Meru or Himalaya mountains. At this time the desire to wish him (the sun) speedy return to enliven the North is natural and is possibly expressed in the quotation given above. The sign of the zodiac, *libra* or balance, may have influenced belief in the weighing of the harvest-products followed by "counting" the cash realized. Hence the joy felt by the Banias.

We have thus (1) the desire to see the sun return to the land of the Aryans, and (2) the destruction of the giant of filth or farm-yard and other manure-heap, which have to be removed or taken away from the house, heaped together, worshipped, topped by a burning lamp and offered a coin. This is done before the early bath is taken and has possibly some connection with the sowing of wheat, gram and oil seeds. The crushing of the cucurbitous fruit and the extinguishing of the lamp waved round the face of the bather, perhaps, indicate the death not only of the giant of filth or manure, but that of the first season, producing rice. It is said that this Narkāsur (night-soil giant) was born of the Goddess, Earth ! So he (filth) always is !

The third stage of evolution may be preceived in the fact that the *bhādvi* crop is sold about this time, and the ubiquitous Bania has reason to be proud of the wealth it brings to his coffers. He therefore worships Lakshmi, or his accumulations heaped in trays.

Rāma's accession is a Pauranic embellishment of the natural religion, and the Kāli-puja is an innovation of the Aryans, who have systematically been cheating the non-aryan races of the East of India, in spite of their admission* into the sacred religion, in order to counteract the numerical strength of the Buddhists. Aryan Brahmans took the assistance of the non-Aryans when needed, but carefully kept them on the lower rung of the ladder by thrusting down ·their throats such irregular beliefs. They thus preserved a distinct line of demarcation and sank the 'converted' Bengalis deeper in their follies about the worship of their local non-Aryan hideous deities.

In Bengal, it is likewise believed that the night of the *pitris* (ancestors) begins at this time, and that the lamps are lighted on the tops of poles to serve as a guide to these benighted souls. The *shrādhas*, or offerings to ancestors, are also performed on this day, the 30th or dark night of Ashvin. It is this fact of the ancestors' souls being over taken by a night, which extends over six months, that gives life in Bengal to a great feast on their account, to serve them for half the year.

---

*Vide Adisur's mention of five "Kulin Brahmans sent out from Kanauj" (in Ballal Sen's Charitra) to convert Bengal to Hinduism.

The latest stage of the evolution need not surprise any one. It was quite possible to have selected for the celebration of Vikramāditya's coronation, a day hallowed by the sacred memory of a similar grand ceremeny ascribed to Rāma, whose glorious career has been the ever-enchanting and ever-inspiring theme of all Hindu poets.

I solicit the attention of ethnographists to the chief points I have thus been able to disclose out of the multiplicity of accounts of the origin of *Divāli*, viz., the change of the season; (2) the death of the rice-crop harvest; (3) the time of manuring the soil for the second crop (4) the sun reaching Libra, the seventh sign of the Zodiac; (5) the coronation of Rāma; (6) the selection of this coronation day for the conventional coronation and era-making day of Vikramāditya, the last of the Guptas ; and I invite further details with comments. Crooke's *Popular Religion and Folklore of Northern India* gives the legend of a king who was visited by his fate in the form of a snake that saved him from death by forging the figure '70' in the place of the '0' fouud in Yama's account-books, but as the lamps are not kept burning all the night, and as nobody keeps up all the night, corroborative evidence is wanting. The return of the spirit of the dead king sounds like the story of Vatasāvitri, whose husband, Satyavān, was restored to life at the devoted worship of his proverbially chaste wife.

As a help to the elucidation of this interesting subject I add a note on some peculiarities of the Divāli Worship. There are many interesting details in this worship which are likely to reveal peculiar phases in the social strata of the Hindu society. For instance, the Chāndraseni Prabhus of Bombay mould their effigies of Bali Rāja out of cooked flour, while the *mālis* or gardeners of Indore, who are Sudras, use cow-dung. In the houses of the former, the figure of the king and that of his consort are mounted on horseback, followed by a mounted minister, and saluted by four footmen, who stand like a guard of honour in a row. The whole scene is placed in a silver or brass tray, while the Sudras mould a figure on the bare floor lying flat with its face upwards. The former draw from the 8th day of the second half of *Ashvin* to *Divāli*, a set of symbols in rice-flour or powdered calspcar on the floor of their compounds or verandahs and in front of the main entrance, *vide* plate drawn by my wife, Mrs Gupte, specially in the native women's style. She has, however, reproduced only those designs, which are considered absolutely necessary, omitting the more elaborate and complicated ones.

The central temple (1) is ascribed to Lakshmi-Nārāyan. In this compound name, the precedence given to this Goddess over her husband may be noted. Besides (2) the usual sun, (3 and 4) the moon, and (5) the hanging lamps, (6) the *shankh*, (6) shell, (8) the mace, (9) the lotus, (7) the wheel, (11) the *svastika*, (10) the *shesha* or thousand-hooded cobra, and (18) the cow's footprints, there are (16) sparrows, (17) the mango, (14) the *bael* (wood-apple) tree (*Aegle marmelos*), and (19) the footprints of Lakshmi.

The second part of the temple contains the usual figure of Garuda and (15) the turtle is an accessory of the structure placed just below the bells. No. 12 is called *āthavinda* and No. 13 *pāthavinda* but I do not quite understand what they mean. The first may mean "reminder" from *āthav*, to remember and the second "send off" from *pāthav*, to despatch. Some interest attaches to these symbols, because they are considered necessary in this group, and may signify the "reception" of the new season and the "bidding good-bye" to the old one.

In further explanation of the Plate, I would add that it is purposely drawn in native women's fashion without correction, to show how the subject is habitually represented. It is not intended to be a specimen of art. The three figures in the niches of the temple are,

( 1 ) Vishnu with four hands holdinga *sankha, chakra, gada and padma*, ( 2 ) Lakshmi with her arms at her side and her hands pointing downwards, ( 3 ) Garuda facing them with folded hands.

**Divāli Ceremonials (September-October)**—on the 13th day of the second half of Ashwin, women bathe, after applying unguents and fragrant oils. The image of the Goddess Lakshmi is washed with milk and worshipped for three days commencing on this day. All family members are fed with special dainties.

On the 14th day of the dark half baths are taken before sunrise, to mark the death of the demon Narkāsur at the the hands of Vishnu and the same process is repeated for three days.

On the 30th or last day of the month which is also the last day of the Samvat year, Banias hold a great *puja*.

The first day of Kārtik (October-November) is therefore the New Year's Day, and also the day on which king Bali was made to give the universe to Vishnu and abdicate himself. Before the birth of Krishna, the cowherds of Gokul used to worship Indra on this day. On one occasion Indra got annoyed and showered heavy rain. Krishna therefore stopped his worship and substituted that of mount Govardhan. It has since been called the 'Ankot' day. Cows and bulls are decorated, worshipped and well fed on this day.

Gambling is considered auspicious on this day as the story says, that Shiva played with Pārvati and lost every thing. She went to live on the banks of the Ganges. Shiva's son Kārtik saw that his father was depresse d in spirits on accouut of his loss in gambling. He learnt the art of throwing dice, went to his mother and regained for his father all the wealth he had lost. This was taken to heart by Pārvati. She now became melancholy. Her son Ganesh learnt the art from his mother and defeated his brother Kārtik. Shiva deputed Ganesh to bring Pārvati home. Ganesh was riding his mouse along the banks of the Ganges to reconcile his mother with his father. Saint Nārad gave intimation of this fact to Vishnu. "When Vishnu came to the banks of the Ganges to meet Shiva he assumed the shape of a set of dice. Shiva, and Nārad, and Rāvan began to play the game. Pārvati lost every thing, and was about to curse Vishnu for cheating her, when the others intervened and said it was not a nice thing to do so. She therefore pronounced a blessing instead upon all those who in future played with dice on the first day of Kārtik so that they might he successful in all dealings throughout year."

**Divyáchi Avas, or Divyáchi Amávásya.**—The day of the new moon of the tenth Ashādh on which the worship of lamps is celebrated. For folklore see Lamp-day.

**Dolhára.**—A swing, a litter. A festival held on the full moon day of Phālgun, when figures of Krishna are worshipped in swings.

**Dolhára.**—A swing, cot, or litter, for Gauri the Goddess, worshipped in Chaitra. See Gauri for folkore.

**Durga Shashthi.**—On the 6th day of the bright half of Ashwin (September and October) the goddess Durga expressed her desire to her Lord Shiva that she felt a craving for a babe to suckle. Shiva smiled and remarked "Why? you are the mother of the whole Universe." But she said that it was sad to miss the pleasure of actually nursing a babe and demanded that at least Kārtick his son born in another way and kept aloof from her, should be brought to her. He consented and left Kailas to bring him. Durga was however so intent on having a babe that she made a doll and was looking at it. Vishnu the Protector noticed it and thought it a good opportunity to please her. He therefore entered the doll, and it came to life. When Shiva returned with Kārtick he found that his wife had already one child in her lap. She explained what had happened. They were both overjoyed and invited all the gods to have a look at the lovely babe. Among the guests was Shani or Saturn, notorious for his evil eye. As soon as he threw a glance at the babe, its head dropped off! Alas! everybody was distressed and all the gods were alarmed! Durga began crying, and Shiva could not bear it. At her request, he sent his *ganās* or attendants to find the lost head, but they failed! At last he directed that the head of any creature sleeping with its face towards the North should be chopped off and brought to him forthwith. An unfortunate cow-elephant was found in that inauspicious position. Its head was severed and taken to Kailās. Shiva placed it on the mutilated body of the doll which came to life again! But the hideous disproportionate figure of a man with the head of an elephant, distressed Durga. In order to compensate for the disfigurement, Shiva ordained that he should be appointed the head of the *ganās* or attendants and called Ganapati (*pati-Chief*) or Ganesh "*ish*-chief or head", and that in all *pujas* he should be the first deity to be invoked. He further added that he who invokes Ganesh at the beginning of an undertaking shall have his efforts crowned with success, and bestowed the title of Siddhidātā "Success Giver" on the boy. Ganesh thus became the departmental deity of success. In Bengal it is believed that the doll was made on the sixth day (*Shashthi*) of Ashwin.

[Compare Ganesh Chaturthi or the Ganesh day of Bombay which falls in Bhādrapād, August-September.]

**Ekādashi** or the eleventh day of each of the two halves—is also a fast day. The story runs that there was a giant named Kumbh. He had a son named Mrudumanya who performed severe austerities. The God Shiva was pleased. He asked for freedom from death through any men and women. Shiva granted the boon on condition, that he was subject to death at the hands of a woman not born out of a womb! Believing that to be impossible, the giant became very bold. He conquered Brahma, Vishnu, and Mahesh, (Shiva) the three Gods of the three heavens. They ran from place to place with their wives Sāvitri, Lakshmi and Pārvati and at last entered the hollow of an old *Phillanthus emblica, amlaki* tree. Being closely packed together the three gods and their wives had their joint exhalations so mixed up, that they produced a girl! Thus born without entering a womb, this girl was destined to kill the giant. She fought a battle and destroyed the enemy who was standing near this tree with the hope of meeting one of the three gods to fight again. This mysterious woman is called *Ekādashi*—the eleventh, and therefore the eleventh days are observed as fasts, in commemoration, and have the virtue of destroying all sorts of sins committed, during the interval! On the preceding, or the tenth day of each half of the month, only a limited kind of food comes be taken; on the eleventh no food is allowed, and on the twelfth, a Brahman has to be fed. If a Brahman is not available or is unwilling to share cooked food (with non-Brahmans for instance), uncooked food stuff has to be given to a member of that caste before any one breaks his fast. If two *ekādashi* days are announced in the calendar, as sometimes happens, the first is held sacred to Shiva and the second to Vishnu.

**Ekādashi.**—Āshādh (June, July) is the fourth month of the Hindu Calendar of the Shālivāhan era. It has two very important fasts and feasts, both are *ekādashis* or the 11th days of the first and second half, respectively. On the former day a very large fair is held at Pandharpur the seat of Lord Pāndurang, better known among the lower classes as Vithoba. One folk-lore story recording a miracle may be added here. It is the history of Saint Sakhubāi published in the *Sant Lilāmrita purān* or the "Nectar of the pastime of Saints" compiled by the poet Mahipati Bāwa. It runs that in the town of Karhad situated on the banks of the Krishna there lived a Brahman, his son Digambar, and his daughter-in-law Sakhubāi. This Sakhu was the daughter of a *vārkari* or pious man who had vowed to go on foot to the shrine of Pandharpur for the annual fair. He always sang verses of Tukaram and others in praise of Pāndurang, and so devoted were the parents of the girl that even while at work or while talking to friends they would quote appropriate passages from Tukārām. The girl acquired the same habit. She also became a devoted and religious woman, so much so, that she was taken for a religious maniac. Her mother-in-law ill-treated her. She was assaulted, branded, kicked, abused and ill-fed. Yet so patient and so enduring was the girl, that she never complained of it to her parents while they were alive. Her father left her a large set of ornaments, jewellery of sorts and cash worth about ten thousand rupees, but the poor girl could not even see them. They were locked up in the chest of her cruel and covetous mother-in-law, and she was made to do menial's work. To clean pots, to wash clothes, to sweep the floor, to cowdung the house, and to fetch water from the river, were the duties assigned to her. To add to this drudgery the mother-in-law used often to throw the freshly washed clothes into the street, and compel her to go to the river and wash them again. The girl would, without losing her temper, only sing :

"My Mother is dead, my father is gone.
Lord Vithal! thou art my shelter alone."

One day while she was returning from the river, she saw an old man and his wife going to Pandharpur. She recognised them as the friends and associates of her own parents and accosted them. She expressed her desire to accompany them to the shrine. This visit was misrepresented to the mother-in-law by a girl cousin of her husband; with the result that the mother-in-law caused her to be tied down to a pillar in an underground cellar of her house. In this dark room she only recited the prayers she was taught, never complaining against her persecutors. Those humble prayers reached Lord Vithal! He turned to his wife Rakhumâi and asked her to lend him her jewels and clothes, because he had to dress himself like the wife of the pilgrim to save the girl. He got what he wanted, went to Karhad, and, dressed like an old woman entered the dark room. He broke the ropes with which Sakhu was tied and told her that her father's old friend (the pilgrim) was waiting for her. They both started, but on coming out of the house he told the girl that she was to meet her and *her* husband at an appointed place, and that he was obliged to leave her in charge of a guide named Garud, who would quickly take her by the shortest route. But this Garud happened to be no other than the celestial half-man half-eagle charger of Vishnu. Vithal himself being the manifestation of that God. He was of course transformed into a coolie! He took her on his back and carried her to Pandharpur just in time to meet her father's friends at the out-skirts of the sacred city. Sakhu bathed herself in the river Bhima and was taken to the temple by her divine guide in the midst of a crushing crowd. Sakhu looked at the image—the goal of her life, she stared, she lost consciousness, she placed her head on the foot of the image and expired! Sakhu was dead! Her body was indentified by the old pilgrims, the friends of her parents and by some residents of Karhad, who were present near the shrine. She was cremated. All this took more than a week, and yet she was not missed at home! That is the miracle! Lord Vithal had substituted himself in her place, had promised to be 'good' by abstaining from singing thos 'cursed' psalms! He or rather 'she' as Sakhu was released from the dungeon at short intervals and worked amicably and peacefully to the great chagrin of her mother-in-law, who coveted her legacy and wished her death. Lord Vithal influenced and charmed Sakhu's husband. He began treating her very kindly in spite of his mother's promptings. On one day Lord Vithal transformed himself into the old pilgrim and replaced Sakhu in her place. On this day the pilgrims had also come back to Karhad and they were surprised to find Sakhu alive. They assured her family that they met her in Pandharpur and that she had died and was duly cremated! The father-in-law, the mother-in-law and the husband of Sakhu put her again in the cellar and began ill treating her for being a witch. But lo! Lord Vishnu appeared in full blaze and assured them that it was all his doing. That the old pilgrim woman and the young wife, were no other than himself and that the coolie-guide Garud was his own celestial charger! Apologies and reconciliations followed and Sakhu or Sakhubai became Saint Sakhubai!

**Ekādashi** The 11th day of Kārtik is named (*prabodhini*) *ekādashi.* It is considered specially meritorious to fast on this day because the gods who had gone to sleep on the 10th of Ashād awoke on this day. Baths in the river, visits to temples, gifts to Brahmans, and prayers unto the God Vishnu are all advised. In the *pothi* called Kārtik Mahātmya it is said that in *Krit Yug* there lived a Brahman named Deva Sharma in the city of Mayāpur. He had a daughter named Gunavati who was married to one of her father's pupils whose name was Chandra. One day, while collecting flowers and sacred grass for the usual worship, a demon killed Chandra and thus Gunavati became a widow and fasted. She used to go every morning to the Ganges for her bath and one day Vishnu come down in his *vimān* or celestial car and took her to Heaven. In Krishna or the 8th incarnation of Vishnu, she became his wife as Satyabhāma her father was re-born as Satrājit, and her Brahman husband as Akrur. The 11th day is therefore accepted as being efficacious fast-day for securing happiness in future births.

**Fāg** *see* **Phāg see also** ***holi*** **for folklore.**

**Fālgun,** *see* **Phālgun.**

**Falguni.** *see* **Phalguni.**

**Fugdi** *see* **Phugdi**

**Faski** *see* **Phaski**

**Fig tree (Indian)** *Ficus Indica* **worship of the,** *see* **Varat Sāvitri for folklore.**

**Friday fast.** There was a King in a certain city who had no son. His Queen managed to adopt secretly a new born child stolen from a Brahman family. The poor Brahman mother was told that it was necessary to blindfold her at the interesting moment, because she had no previous experience of child birth and would get frightened. While thus blindfolded, her babe was removed and a curry-stone was placed in front of her to show that she had given birth to an unnatural stump. The King was told that a son was born to him and there were great rejoicings. The pseudo-prince grew into a man. But the poor Brahman mother gradually began to suspect the midwife. She acepted the *Vrat* of the Fridays of Shrāvan, by worshipping Jivantika the Goddess of longevity. At the end of the *puja* she used to throw a pinch of coloured rice into space and say "May Goddess Jivantika protect my lost son, wherever he be." Curiously enough these grains of rice always fell on the head of the prince. In due course he succeeded his father. He could not account for the weekly shower of rice, and the conversation between a calf and a cow disclosed to him that he was born of the Brahman mother. He felt uneasy, and left for Benares. On his way to the sacred city, he happened to put up in a Brahman's house. The landlady was unfortunate enough to always lose her babies on the fifth night after they were born. She had just given birth to a new child. It was the fifth day. The King was travelling incognito. He had to sleep in the verandah in front of the door leading to the *accouchement* room. At midnight a ferocious looking evil spirit came. It was Satvāi the devil who eats the hearts of infants. She had come to kill the child, but seeing a man sleeping in the passage she inquired who he was. She was replied to by the Goddess Jivantika who stood at the door and said that her 'protected' child was there, and that she dare not cross over him. The struggle continued for some time. At last, Satvāi was forced to go back disappointed. The parents were keeping up all night for fear of losing their babe. They over-heard the conversation between the Goddess and the evil spirit, and they asked the guest to stay for one day more because the 6th night after a child's birth was the one during which, they believed, Satvāi would visit it again. He did so. He slept again in front of the door way. The child-killing Satvāi came. Jivantika also came. The first wanted to enter the room to kill the babe, the second prevented her from approaching her protected child—the King. The struggle continued until the early hours of the morn, when the evil spirit was forced to retire and the child was saved. And why? Because the natural mother of the King regularly worshipped Jivantika on Fridays in Shrāvan and threw the rice-blessing to protect him wherever he was. The Goddess Jivantika like a guardian angel was protecting him and the evil-spirit dared not cross him. The King reached Benares and thence went to Gaya. While offering rice balls to his dead *pitris* he was surprised to see two hands stretched out instead of one. He asked the priests of

Gaya how it was that there were two hands instead of one. They advised him to return to his capital and to invite the whole of the town to a banquet. 'You will,' they said, 'then learn the reason of the phenomenon'. He returned; he gave a feast on a Friday of the month of Shrāvan. The Brahman mother was invited. She sent word that she was sorry she could not comply with the request of the king, because she had to fast on that day, and had to observe some ceremonial taboos. She was asked to mention them and said that she would not pass over the washings of rice, she would not wear green bangles, she would not pass beneath a bower of the *Kārle (Momordica dioica)*. After the *puja* she threw the pinch of rice and it fell as usual on the King's head. At the end of certain enquiries and measures the queen dowager confessed that she was not his real mother, and explained that the poor Brahman woman was the one who gave him birth. He was thus restored to his parents. He built a separate palace for them and lived a happy and prosperous life. Such is the power of the Friday-*Vrat* as observed during Shrāvan, in honour of Jivantika the Goddess of longevity.

**Friday Fast.** There was a very poor Brahman who was unable to feed his wife and children. His wife went to her neighbour's house and told her how helpless she was. She advised her to fast on Fridays, to begin the *vrat* in the month of Shrāvan to observe which one should fast all the day. In the evening, a married woman should be invited to the house, she should be offered turmeric, saffron, and other ingredients. She should have her lap laden with cocoanut, rice and a piece of bodice cloth. She should also be given milk and sugar with parched gram. After thus honouring the guest, the devotee should take her meal. This should be repeated on every Friday for one year. At the end of that period, Brahmans and

Brahman women should be fed. The poor woman accepted this advice, and began fasting on Fridays. Her brother was a very rich man, but he was ashamed of his poor relations. One day, he invited one thousand Brahmans to a banquet, but studiously omitted his sister for fear people would laugh at him. The poor sister thought that her brother might have forgotten to invite her, and that there was no harm in going to a brother uninvited. She wore her sacred silk cloth, took her children with her, went to her brother's house, and they seated themselves among the guests. After every body had taken his or her position the brother—as is the custom—came with a potful of *ghi* to pour on the rice of each. He saw his sister in a beggarly dress. She was looking down, out of shame. He called her by her name, and said that all the guests were laughing at him at seeing his sister so wretched without ornaments or rich clothes, and warned her that she should not come again. The poor woman took her food with tears in her eyes, and quietly returned home. On the next day, her children asked her to take them to their uncle's house to enjoy the feast—which was still continuued. She could not say nay, and thought that a brother however rich would have at least affection enough to allow her to take her food. Her poverty, she thought, enforced tolerance. She must bear insults. She therefore went again. When the rich brother came to distribute *ghi* with a blazing silver pot in his hand, he expostulated with and even insulted her by calling her a *beggar* and her children *pigs*. He warned her not to step into his house. She bore the insult with patience for the sake of her starving children. On the third day—the feast was still continued, and the sister went again but she was dragged out, and forced to go away without taking a morsel! She was very sorry and cried. She had to go without food, so she prayed unto the Goddess of Wealth. The Goddess was moved. Brighter days followed. In the course of a year the poor Brahman woman became very rich. On the last Friday of the year of the *vrat*, she held a feast and invited her rich brother to dine. He felt some hesitation but did go after all. He was sumptuously treated on silver plates and in gold cups. He invited her in return. She accepted the invitation. On the day of the feast, she wore as many necklaces, and other ornaments as she could with difficulty carry. She wore a gold and silk *Sāri*. Her brother came to the door to receive his wealthy sister in due form. She was offered a seat on a stool inlaid with silver and was given the first seat next to his own—the place of honour. The brother sat near her, but the sister stood up and removed her shawl to place it on her seat. She then took out all her ornaments and arranged them in a row. Doing this, she began placing morsels of food on the shawl, on the necklaces, bracelets, rings, and armlets! The brother asked her to explain, and she said in retaliation that the dainties were not offered to her, but to her jewels and that she was giving them their share! She said, "You turned me out on the day I could only wear rags, and now that I am rich you are offering me so much hospitality, I cannot accept it. It is the due of the goddess Laxmi. She must get it." The brother repented and apologized. She then took her meal and reconciliation followed. May the goddess Laxmi enrich every one that observes this *vrat* of fasts on Fridays for one year.

**Friday Fasts.** There is a *vrata* called Vara-Laxmi which implies the worship of the goddess of Wealth.

In the Bhavishottar-purān, Shiva tells his wife Pārvati that it grants wealth and happiness. When the full moon falls on a Friday in the month of *Shrāvan* this special worship should be performed. The story runs, that there was a city called Kaundanya encircled by a rampart of gold-bricks. In this city there was a house inhabited by a Brahman woman named Chārumati. She was a pious, and very virtuous woman. She was good looking and had a charming voice. The Goddess Laxmi appeared to her in a dream and told her to prepare a gold image of Vara-Laxmi, to get her house thoroughly washed and decorated, to obtain a brand new set of pots for the worship, and to select a spot to the East or North East of the house for the ceremony. A *Swastik* should be drawn on the floor, one *sher* (two pounds) wheat flour should be placed on the symbol so drawn, and on it should be placed a *kalash* or *lota* filled with rice. All about this *lota* new pieces of cloth should be arranged. The *lota* should then be worshipped with flowers and sacred leaves, gold and cloth. Then on top of it should be placed the gold image of Laxmi and worshipped. The best possible dainties should be offered for food. Of the twenty one balls and patties placed before the image, five should be left there (for the priest) and the rest partaken of by the household. After dinner, there should be singing and dancing.

Shiva assured his wife that she herself, as well as Saraswati, Sāvitri and Indrāni had all observed this *vrata* in order to attain the high positions they now occupy among the gods.

Laxmi thus instructed Chārumati in her dream, accepted her thanks and disappeared. Chārumati related her dream to the members of her house and carefully performed the *puja* on the full moon Friday of Shārvan. She used to sit in front of the image and pray. The result was that all her wishes were fulfilled. She got elephants, horses, carriages, and many other treatures. When her old friends enquired how she became so rich, so be-decked with priceless jewels, she explained to them the *puja*. All her lady friends also became rich and happy on worshipping the goddess of wealth in the same manner, and similar good luck is promised to every one that performs the *puja* on the full-moon Fridays of the months of Shrāvan in future!

**The Ganesh Chaturthi** or the fourth day of Bhādrapad, sacred to Ganesh, is a feast day. As soon as the Haritālika are sent away, Ganesh is brought into the house with music of all notations. He is the elephant-headed big bellied god of knowledge and success.

Once upon a time, Shiva left his home for Shikār. His three hundred *ganās* or attendants are not taken into account. Perhaps they accompanied him as beaters. Any how Pārvati was left alone. Pārvati desired to take a bath but having nobody to keep watch while she bathed was obliged to make a figure out of the scrapings of her body and set it outside her door to guard it. When Shiva returned he was prevented by the clay *chaukidār* from entering the house. He was wild with rage and cut off the head of the fellow who dared prevent him from entering his own house. Pārvati was taken by surprise. She asked her husband how he could' enter the room in spite of her *chaukidār*—her *gana*, her attendant. Shiva explained, Pārvati was angry and refused to allow him to touch her until her child (because her creation) was restored to life. Shiva could not find the head and had to get one of an elephant to replace it. The *gana* came to life again and was awarded the highest prize, the headman's place, that is *pati* or head of the *ganas* or attendants. Promotions followed, and he ultimately became the God of knowledge and success— a Departmental deity holding plural appointments. [For the Bengal Story of the birth of Ganesh. See Durga Shashthi.]

Philologists and ethnographists have tried to trace the the origin of Ganesh to the harvest season, comparing Pārvati to the Earth, and the clay of which the figure was made to the alluvial crust found on the banks of rivers soon after the Bhadoi or Bhādrapad crop. Some derive his origin from the letter 'om' [3s] but a recent examination of the signs of the Zodiac discloses the origin of Ganesh's belly from the big body of the crab or cancer which stands in heaven just near Shiva who, as the male part of the Gemini or Mithun, intervenes between the female part of that sign (Pārvati) and the zodiacal sign of cancer the crab, or big belly

There are many *purānās* and traditions published about Ganesh. In some families Ganesh 'goes back' on the second day; in some he stays from five to seven days and is sent away to the river along with his mother.

**Ganesh.**—On the fourth of Bhādrapad, Ganesh is worshipped in the form of a clay figure, representing a fat human body with an elephant's head, riding on a rat. The terms Ganesh and Ganapati both mean the head or chief[1] of the people, from *gaṅa*, servants, and *isha* or *pati*, master.

From the primæval attributes of this deity, he seems to represent the harvest festival. He is called Mushhak-váhan, rider on a rat, but the word *mushhak* comes from a Sanskrit root, which means a thief. The title therefore implies that he is riding over the thief of the field (field-rat). The elephant's head and snout have possibly their origin in the appearance of a farmer, carrying on his head a load of the corn-sheaf, particularly when the lower or lowest ears swing to and fro. The appearance was readily passed to the symbol possibly owing to the mythological fable of the four *diggajàs*, or elephants, who are supposed to support the heavens in the four directions represented by the points of the compass. In India at any rate the idea of hugeness is conveyed by comparison with an elephant, the biggest animal known. For instance, when a strong young man dies unexpectedly, people say:—'What an elephant of

---

1 The headman, or Patel, always commands the position of a *tikáit* and is offered the *pán* first of all and so is Ganesh in the verse which runs:—

Ghána bharila. Vida thevila.
Adhi namila, Gana Raja.

The *pán* is first placed before Ganesh, I have bowed unto him.
And now I put the grain into the mill to grind,

prowess he was, but within a few hours Death has levelled him to the dust.' Rám is compared in the *Puránas* to the young of the elephant, Diggaja Dasaratha, when he broke the bow of Parasuráma.

The idea therefore of a bumper crop over-riding the pestilence of the rats might well be expressed by a god with an elephant's head, ridihg a rat or *mushhak* (thief), and possessing in addition a 'fair round' belly, the latter evidently symbolical of the barn. Conquest is very often symbolised in this manner. Siva rides the bull (Nandikêsvar) he conquered; Krishna dances on the hood of the snake Káliyá, whom he vanquished; and so Ganésa rides over the rat he destroys as Lord of the Harvest. The origin of the gigantic head of an elephant on one side and the little field mouse on the other can thus be accounted for in his figure.

As to the particular form which the elephant-headed god has taken on in representations: the human body of the figures may have originated from the primitive effigies in vogue, and the well-known titles of Gaṇêsh, Surpakarna, and Ekadanta, one-toothed, gives a clue to the rest. *Surpa* or *supa* is the winnowing basket so essential at harvest time, and the one-tooth may well represent the ploughshare. Then let two winnowing baskets and a ploughshare be added to the fat body as shown in fig. 3, and one fairly gets the form of the elephant's head with which the god Ganésh is usually endowed.

The food offered to Ganesh connects him with the harvest, as it consisis of balls, called *modaks*, made of rice, flour, raw sugar, and the kernel of the cocoanut; all in season at the time of the festival in the month of Bhádrapad. And there is a symbol attached to him which speaks for itself in relation to the harvest. Round the fat belly, representing the full barn, is shown a hooded cobra, the great destroyer of the field-rat.

When the clay figure of Ganesh is taken away, it is customary to turn its face back thrice towards the house, in conformity with the belief that such a step ensures the speedy return of the man or woman leaving the paternal roof on a journey. This custom is always followed by good Hindus. The compiler was compelled to do so, when he left for England in 1886.

The new crop or harvest ceremonies connected with the cult of Ganêsh seem to confirm his primitive origin as above explained. After the clay figure is thrown into a tank or river, a handful of clay or sand is brought in the tray, or on the stool used for carrying it, and ceremoniously thrown into the barn and the grain barrels, and particularly into the room is which provisions are stored. This is an exact counterpart of what the people did on the continent of Europe and elsewhere in primitive days. The Indian Ganêsh may in this matter be compared with the grain goddess of Mexico, the Alo Alo of the Tonga Islands, the Demeter of the Greeks, or the Ceres of the Romans.

As society advanced and philosophical speculation usurped the domain of direct argument, Ganêsh seems to have obtained rapid promotion and came to be styled Siddhidâtâ, the Giver of Success, an ideal in the production of a good crop. He was also styled Vighna-hartâ, the Remover of Distress, which is the peculiar power of a bumper crop. So success in every undertaking began to be attributed to him even in learning and he acquired another name as the Lord of the Goddess of Learning, Sarasvati.

During the performance of the death ceremony of the Old Season, represented by Gaurî, Ganêsh is naturally invoked and asked to return soon, as, the sooner a new harvest-season returns, the happier will it make the simple farmer-worshippers. That is why they say:—"*Ganapti, báppa, moria,*" Father Ganêsh, Lord of the people, we wish you a speedy return. In the Marâthâ Country, children add :—" *Pudhaliyâ varshi laukar yâ !,*" Come early next year. *Moriá* may be the corruption, or rather transformation, of an exclamation of the simple Kunbi (farmer) :—" *Mhora ya,*" Come before all. The Kanaits of Kângrâ say "*more ye*" when they want a friend to return quickly. This expression has been transformed by the learned into the grandiloquent title Morêsvar, or still more grandiloquent Mayùrêsvar, Lord of the Peacocks. *Moryâ* therefore represents the welcome with which Ganêsh is hailed every year at the harvest season, Bhâdrapad, rice-in-ear month, which occurs just when his mother Gaurì (Mother Earth) is *enceinte* and cries out "touch-me-not," through the balsam which is used in the preparations for the ceremonies in her honour then performed.

**Gancsh as the God Siddhi Vināyak.**—Saint Shaunak and his associates in the Naimish forest asked Suta to tell them how people would achieve success in every undertaking. If husbands and wives quarrel what will bring about their reconcilation ? How to induce indifferent strangers to take interest in one's affairs ? In education, trade or agriculture, what will ensure success ? Which God will grant success ?

*Suta said*: When the Kauravās and the Pāndavas stood ready to fight duly arrayed on battle-field, Yudhistir, the senior Pāndava, made a similar request. He said, "Oh Krishna, what God will grant us success on the battle-field ?" Krishna replied that the God Ganesh *alias* Ganarāja will do it. He was then asked to describe the way in which that God should be propitiated and the day auspicious for the *puja.* He was told of the fourth day of the month of Bhádrapad or the fourth day of Mágh. The fourth day of the bright moon is of course the most auspicious, but one can perform the worship on any day he feels inclined. No date can be fixed for devotion. That feeling may rise at any time. White *til*, gingelly seed, should be ground to paste on the curry-stone and applied to the body of the worshipper. He should then bathe and begin the *puja* in the middle of the day (12 noon). Three and a half *tolas* in weight of gold, or half of it, or a quarter of it or as much as one can afford should be used in making an image of Ganesh. If one is too poor to buy gold, he should take silver. If very poor indeed he should take clay for the image. But none should commit the sin of Cupidity in dishonestly avoiding this out-lay. Ganesh should be shaped with only one tooth, with ears like a winnowing basket, *surpa*, mouth like that of an elephant, with four hands, a noose and a battle-axe in the hands. The image should be offered a welcome and duly worshipped in the usual form. It should be specially offered 21 fronds of the *durva* grass (*cynodon dactylon*). Twenty-one sweet balls prepared with flour, *ghi*, sugar, &c. Out of these 21, ten balls should be given to the Brahman priest, ten should be eaten by the family of the worshipper and the remaining one should be offered to the God. The gold image should then be given to the Brahman along with the cloth, etc., with which it is worshipped, saying "Oh Brahman I give you this duly dressed image of Vināyak. May the God be pleased." After thus respectfully asking the Brahman to accept the image the God should be addressed :

"Oh Vināyak, oh Ganesh, all gods pay their respect to thee. Oh thou favourite (child) of Pārvati, Oh destroyer of impediments, I pray to thee. Ganesh gives and Ganesh takes, and therefore Ganesh is the salvation of us both. I offer my obeisance to Ganesh." The Brahman should then be offered a good meal. The worshipper should also take his dinner, but should eat nothing cooked with or fried in oil.

He who worships Siddhi-Vināyak gets what he wants *i.e.*, knowledge, wealth, success in battle-field, son, husband &c. If a widow worships him, she will never be widowed in future births. Ganesh should be worshipped in the first instance before the commencement of the *puja* of every other God or Goddess such as Vishnu, Shiva, Devi, Pārvati, or the Sun. If the God Ganesh is worshipped all the Chandikas and Mother-Goddesses are pleased.

Oh Dhrama, if you perform the *puja* of Ganesh you will be able to conquer your enemies in this battle and will soon be crowned. You will attain success in every undertaking no doubt. At this advice from Krishna, the Pāndavas worshipped Ganesh and were crowned with success. This God grants *siddhi* which means success and that is why he is named Siddhi Vināyak. He who attentively listens to this book when read to him, also gets success.

Krishna proceeds :—

Of Raja Dharma ! The *puja* of Ganesh performed on the 4th moon of the month of Bhādrapad is much appreciated in the Kailas, the abode of Shiva. Whatever you give away to Brahmans on that day is returned to you a hundred fold. Saint Parāshar mentions a curse on the head of those who see the moon on that holy day. It is this: While the sun stands at the constellation Kanya (Virgo) on the 4th moon of Bhádrapad, if any one sees the moon, an "allegation" or "false accusation" falls to his or her lot before the following year ends. If one sees (the moon) accidentally he or she should repeat the charm, *mantram* "*Simmha prasenamavadhit simhe Jāmbavanta hatah.*"

This charm will counteract the curse.

The Skandhpurān describes the origin of this curse. In the forest of Naimish, Suta described it to the Saunakas.

He begins :—

SUTA. Oh Sanat-Kumār, I describe to you the most important *vrat* or *puja* of Ganesh. Listen attentively. It should be performed notwithstanding all obstacles on the 4th moon of Bhádrapad. Be he a man, or be she a woman, he or she who desires to be prosperous should perform this *puja*. The worshipper is immediately dragged out of the slough of despond due to overwhelming misfortunes. All false allegations (scandals) against him vanish and all calamities disappear! In the midst of a thick forest, in any misfortune, on the battle-field or in a political plot wherever one be overtaken by misfortune this is the only *vrat* which grants success. The God Ganesh is very fond of this *puja*, and the three worlds (universe) know it well. There is no *vrat* which can grant relief like this.

To the enquiry as to who first introduced this *vrat* the reply was:—

Krishna was once falsely accused of having stolen the great gem *Syamantak*. The lord of the universe, the Great God, the bravest of the brave, Krishna was in trouble over the allegation. He consulted Saint Nārad and the latter initiated him.

*Question.*—Sanat Kumār says. What? He who is full of virtues, He who is all powerful, He who is the cause of the origin, existence, and destruction of the universe, He who is all pervading, He the Lord of Lords, how could He be accused of theft? Yes, it is an astonishingly wonderful tale. Do describe it.

*Nandikeshwar* replied:—In order to relieve Mother Earth of the crushing weight of sin produced by the Demons, Vishnu and his cobra Shesh appeared on earth as Krishna and Balrām. They became the sons of Vasudev. For fear of the Demon Jarāsandh, Krishna asked Vishvakarma, the celestial architect to build Dwarka in the midst of the ocean. It was built with gold bricks. There were in it 16,108 palaces for so many wives of Krishna. In the centre was the celestial *pārijāt (Necthathes arbar-tristis)* which diffused the perfume of its flowers. It granted all desires. There were 560,000,000 houses for the Yādavs. There were many other people also living in the city. Dwarka contained every mortal thing that could be seen anywhere on the face of the earth. In this city lived a Yādav named

Ugrasen. He had two sons named respectively Satrājit and Prasen. Satrājit performed austerities on the seashore by staring at the sun all the day. He took no food. The sun was pleased and stood before him in human form. Satrājit prayed heartily.

The sun asked him to name the favour, the Yādav asked him to give him the great jewel named Syamantak. He gave it, but warned him thus :—

Take care, this is no ordinary jewel. Every morning it gives out, from its body eight times its own weight of gold, but he alone can wear this gem who is all pure and has never committed sin. If an impure man dare touch it, he would be destroyed forthwith. So saying the sun suddenly disappeared !

Satrājit returned to Dwarka with the gem. The citizens were 'dazzled' at the lustre of the gem. They thought that the Sun himself was approaching them to pay a visit to Krishna. Krishna told them that it was the great gem, and not the sun. Satrājit approached Krishna. Looking at the wonderful gem, Krishna wished he had one like it, he did not take it. But the wish of the powerful Krishna produced the fear that he would one day take it away by force. Satrājit therefore handed it over to his brother Prasen, and warned him to remain pure in thought and deed. One day Prasen went out for *shikār* with Krishna and was wearing the gem. Krishna returned, Prasen disappeared !

Satrājit accused the "sinner" Krishna of having murdered his brother for the sake of the gem! Citizens of Dwarka began 'talking' of the matter in a suspicious way ! Krishna was very sorry at being underservedly accused of so horrible a crime ! He went out in search. He had some attendants with him. They saw the dead body of Prasen lying along with the carcase of his horse and guessed that he was killed by a lion. Krishna followed the footprints of the lion, and saw that the king of the forest was killed in turn by a bear. He followed the footprints of the bear to a cave. He left his guard at the mouth of the cave and entered it alone. It was 800 miles in length! It was dark, but Krishna's own lustre illuminated it as he went along. At the end of the cave, Krishna saw a palace. It contained a cradle in which lay sleeping a babe. That babe was the son of Jāmbuvant the king of bears. The lost gem was hung up over the cradle as a toy! There stood a young and beautiful maiden rocking the cradle? She was the daughter of the bear-king! He was charmed. The girl began singing a lullaby to the following effect :—

"Prasen was killed by the lion, the lion was killed by Jāmbuvant. Do not cry dear child, the gem is now yours."

The girl saw Krishna. She fell in love at first sight and said :—

"Do leave the cave at once, before my father Jámbuvant awakes. Take the gem, but run away?" Krishina smiled but instead of following her advice, blew upon his conch shell—the challenge signal!

Jámbuvant came forth and began the battle. It was a terrible fight!

Krishina's attendants watched at the door of the cave for six days, and thinking that he was killed by the bear, returned to Dwarka.

The obsequies of Krishna were duly performed!

On the other side, Krishna fought the battle for twenty-one days and defeated the king of the bears. He was pleased with Krishna. He then recollected that he was not fighting with an ordinary mortal! His adversary was God himself.

Jámbuvant said :—"Oh God, I am invinicible to all the gods, demons, demi-gods and men, and yet you have defeated me! You must therefore be the God of Gods.

You are Vishnu. I know it. How could you otherwise possess such prowess ? I offer you this gem along with my daughter Jāmbuvanti. Krishna was married to the princess and returned to his capital with his prizes. He informed the citizens of what happened. He then held a general meeting and in that open Durbar he handed over to Satrājit the lost gem. In order to remove the ill-feeling that would arise, Satrājit also offered his daughter Satyabhāma to Krishna.

Poor Satrājit! The possession of the gem was his misfortune! One Shatdhanva and one Akrur coveted it. They were watching for an opportunity to kill him. During Krishna's absence to Hastinapur (Imperial Delhi) Shatadhanva killed Satrājit, and carried away the coveted gem! At this time Satyabhāma was in her father's house. She immediately went to Krishna and told him how her father was murdered!

Krishna was a diplomat! Inwardly he was glad, but out wardly he showed that he was very angry. He proposed to his elder brother Balarām that they should both follow Shatdhanva to kill him in return. Shatdhanva heard of this. He was afraid. He handed over the gem to his associate Akrur. He ran away riding a favourite mare of his, and went to the South, Krishna and Balarām followed him. They travelled 800 miles, and Shatdhanva's mare dropped dead through over exertion. He therefore began running on foot. Krishna thereupon left his chariot and followed him. He overtook and killed him! But alas! there was no gem with him! and when Balarām arrived Krishna said to him :

"Oh Dada! I have in vain killed Shatdhanva. He had no gem with him. Balarām was very angry. He said :

"Oh Krishna you are a sinful man. There is no doubt! For the sake of mean lucre you have killed a member of your own clan. How will people believe you? Krishna swore in a thousand ways to assure Balarām that he really did not get the gem. Balarām was pacified, still there was some suspicion. He expressed his regret at Krishna's killing Shatdhanva for nothing and left the territory to go and live in the Vidarbha country. Krishna returned home.

People said that Krishna was a wicked man. He must have appropriated the gem after killing Shatdhanva. He was also charged with having got rid of his elder brother for the same reason.

The God Krishna, the Lord of the Universe could not bear the charge. He became humbled like an ordinary mortal.

The gem was all along with Akrur, who ran away, when he heard of the death of Shatdhanva. He went to Benares, and there he spent in charities the gold given out daily by the gem. He was very clever, and lived a devoted and pious life, adding many architectural gems to the city of Benares. Wherever the gem—the gift of the sun—was carefully kept by pious men, there would be no famine, disease, flood, or similar misfortunes. Krishna being the incarnation of the all pervading Vishnu of course knew where the gem was, but as he was in a human birth he assumed the role of a man and showed that he was very sorry for the disagreement caused by the gem between himself and his brother and the disgrace of being accused of coveting it. At this moment Saint Nārad came to him. He was welcomed. He asked Krishna why he looked so sad? Krishna told him the history of the gem. Nārad replied, that he knew why he was so accused. It was the effect of the curse of Ganesh for having seen the moon on the fourth day of Bhādrapad. Krishna thereupon asked Nārad why it was unlucky to see the moon on that day and why was it lucky to see the same satellite on the 2nd day of each month? Nārad replied "The moon became arrogant at being born beautiful and insulted Ganesh. He was cursed by that God. Listen how.

When Ganesh came to life, Shiva appointed him the head of his servants *(gana)* and gave him the eight goddesses of success to wife. Brahma praised and worshipped Ganesh.

At this praise the God Ganesh was pleased and asked Brahma to name the favour he sought. Brahma begged that he might be able to perform his duty of "creation" without a hitch. Holding a ball of sweets in his hand Ganesh after thus blessing Brahma, was returning to Swarga. He arrived at the Chandraloka, the region of the Moon, stumbled, and fell. The arrogant Moon, ridiculed him. He laughed at him. The God Ganesh could not stand the insult. With his eyes as red as fire through wrath, he cursed the Moon. He said, Chandra! Thou thinkest thyself very good looking. Take then this curse, that he who from this day forward will look at thee shall suffer from the distress of being falsely accused. The moon went down the water and lived in the lotus which opens at night. When the moon thus disappeared all the Gods, Saints, Demi-Gods and people became alarmed. They went to Brahma for advice. Brahma said that he was unable to remove the ill effects of the curse of the powerful God Ganesh. Neither Shiva nor Vishnu could do it. He therefore advised all the Gods to go to Ganesh himself—the God of Gods. They asked Brahma to show them the way to propitiate Ganesh. He explained the *puja* of Ganesh. The image of Ganesh made of gold should be given to a Brahman, with cash (*Dakshana*) in addition. When one has power to pay large sums to Brahmans, he should on no account be miserly.

Accepting this advice, all the Gods deputed Brihaspati their preceptor to instruct the moon. He instructed the moon as to how the *puja* was to be performed. The moon propitiated Ganesh who appeared. The moon expressed his regret at insulting him and begged his pardon. Ganesh was asked to remove the curse, but he refused, then all the Gods intervened. They prayed for mercy.

Ganesh modified the sentence by deciding that those who see the moon on the fourth day of *Bhādrapad* will be subject to the curse of being falsely accused during the twelve months following that day. Those who see the new moon on the 2nd day of each month will not suffer from such distress. But the moon asked Ganesh to name the remedy for removing the ill effects of seeing him on that one day in the year—the 4th of *Bhādrapad.* Ganesh said :—

" He who will worship me on every 4th day of the dark half of every month, and will worship you and your wife Rohini, he who will give to the Brahmans, my images in gold, he who will listen to this *pothi* (book), he who will feed Brahmans, will always obtain success in every undertaking. In *Bhādrapad,* my gold or clay image should be worshipped. Take a pot without any puncture or hole in it, place it on a heap of rice and upon it place the image. Two cloths (shawls, etc.), should be wrapped round the pot. A heap of sweet balls should be offered. The worshipper should wear a red cloth. If he has no money to buy a gold image, he should buy one of silver. Then he should offer me dress, flowers and cash. He should then light the sacred fire, into this fire he should throw some pieces of sugarcane, and some sweet balls. The whole *puja,* including the image, pots, cloths, balls, fruits, cash, etc., should finally be given to a rahman. He should then ask Ganesh to grant him whatever he wants, such as honour, kingdom, son, grandson, cows, grain, clothes &c.

In the food to be given to Brahmans that day, there should be no pungent or sour things—they should all be sweet. The God Ganesh added that such is my *puja,* and this is the way, to success."

Saint Narad advised Krishna to perform the *puja.* Krishna did so in order to remove the false accusation of having coveted the gem. He was freed. If the moon be not visible when the *puja* is performed, the hearing of this *pothi* is sufficient, (Skandh puran.' Syamantkopakhyan).

**Ganesh as God Satay Vināyak.**—Satya Vināyak means the *true* Vināyak or Ganesh or Elephant headed god of success. The story is given in the Brahmānd Purān.

Suta a saint tells some Rishis :—He says,

During the Satya Yug, golden age, Brahma "once upon a time" sat steeped in meditation when his son Nārad came to him and said,

*Nārad.*—Dear father, you are omnsicient and therefore pray tell me what *puja* should people perform to ensure happiness in the universe. Which is the God that will grant all desires in all ages ?

*Brahma.*—Oh Nārad the God that existed even before the *Vedas,* that is the one from whom the *Vedas* themselves emanated, one who is shaped like "Om" is the God that grants all desires in the Iron age—I mean Satya Vināyak. History speaks of him in the form of conversation between Shiva and Pārvati. While sitting at ease on mount Kailās, Shiva was asked by his wife Pārvati this very question.

*Shiva* said :—Dear Pārvati, there once lived a very learned and pious but poor, Brahman named Sudāma. He was liberal hearted but was unable to support his family. Finding him in a distracted mood, his wife said to him that it would do them all much good, if he (Sudāma) were to go and see Krishna, the rich Prince of Dwārka, who was his class fellow and friend. He was reputed to be very kind to the poor and to the *Brahmans.* Thus advised, the poor Brahman prepared himself to go to Dwārka. There was nothing in the house to offer to Krishna as *nazar,* and so she went from door to door until she could collect on loan two or three handfuls of parched rice. He tied them in a rag and went to see his old friend. Krishna welcomed him most cordially. He offered him the best bath, the best flowers, the best clothes, the very best dinner, and excellent *pān*. After dinner, they were talking together of old school-days. Krishna divined the object of the visit. Out of formality, however, he asked his guest what he had brought for him and extracted the little bundle of parched rice from under the armpit of the poor emaciated Brahman! He took a handful and swallowed it. He, the great incarnation of Vishnu was satisfied and thought how poor, how miserable was his playmate. "Very well." He thought "I will see what the difference between a king and Brahman is! I will remove the mist of poverty that envelops my Brahman friend with the help of God Satya Vināyak." He then turned to Sudāma and said:—"I hope your children are doing well. I hope you are able to support them. What profession do you follow?"

*Sudāma*—(ashamed to raise his head) Oh God! the whole world is happy because you are its Lord. Where then is the necessity for enquiring about the circumstances of your own personal friend? I support my family without begging.

*Krishna.*—Without begging, that is, by the sweat of one's own brow; yes, it is a very difficult, task, but it is the one that has been counted as a duty and is acceptable to God. You had better worship God Satya Vināyak. He will grant you all desires.

*Sudāma.*—Friend! Who is the fittest one to be worshipped.

*Krishna.*—He who is served by Brahma, Vishnu and Mahesh the three chief Gods, whose servants they all are, He who is devoutly worshipped by men and *Yogis*, is Satya Vināyak. Do worship him, my dear friend. You will surely be successful and the *Vrat* you will perform will set an excellent example before all people. People will follow your good example. This is the only *puja* which brings fulfilment of all desires.

*Sudāma.*—Dear Krishna! in what month, and on what day should this *Vrat* be performed, who performed it first, and with what result? Pray, tell me all this for the benefit of the people.

*Krishna*—Oh Brahman, listen. The protector of the poor, God Vināyak, was born on the full moon day of the month of *Vaishākh.* He should therefore be worshipped on that day or on the *Bhádrapad* fourth, and on a Monday, or on a Friday. In fact on any auspicious day, let the votive oblations showing the resolution of the mind to perform the *puja* be offered in the morning. Paste made of gingelly seed and *Avali, Phylanthus emblica,* fruits should be applied to the body to be followed by a bath. The worshipper should again bathe himself in the evening and worship at first the nine planets. Then in the centre of a bower made of plantain trees and decorated with floor drawings in different colours, wreaths of flowers and mirrors, he should place a *kalash* or pot full of water. On the pot should be placed the emblemetic diagram on a copper sheet representing Ganesh. On the four corners of the engraved square piece of copper, he should put symbols of Lakshmi-Nārāyan, Pārvati-Maheshwar, Prithvi-Varāh, and Shakti-Madan. If the copper engraved mystic *yantra* be not at hand, a lotus with eight petals should be drawn with sandalwood paste. In the centre of the lotus so drawn, should be placed God Satya Vināyak, and at the time when the town is full of the dust raised by the cattle returning home (sunset) he should *without* reserve offer all that he can to the god, and worship him. One and a quarter weight or measure of flour, sugar, and solid (boliled to solidity) milk should be fried in *ghi,* sweet balls of the mixture should be offered to the god as food along with other dainties in proportion to the wealth of the worshipper. "Afterwards guavas" pomegranate and other fruits of the season should also be served. The leaves of the *Shami*, *Prosopis spicigera*, *Rui*, *Calatropis gigantea*, and *Durva*, *Cynodon dactilon* should be placed over the image. After the *puja*, all present should attentively listen to this book which shall be read by the priest. Then Brahmans should be worshipped with sandal-wood paste flowers &c. Married women should be given turmeric cosmetic, red powder, and Brahman women should be offered a sumptuous dinner. The worshipper should after this, take a portion of the food in company of his family. The whole company should keep up all the night, discussing *shāstras* or dancing, singing, acting, or in out-door games, chess, &c. &c. Until the next morning the devotee should keep all his thoughts pure. He who performs the *Vrat* in the manner prescribed will achieve success. One desirous of wealth will get that, of grain, cattle, woman, son, long life, health, honour, good knowledge, whatever he wants shall he get. One who has no desire for these, will obtain salvation. When there was nothing, but water all over the universe, Brahma performed this *puja* and Ganesh granted him power to create the universe. Oh! Brahman, Vishnu himself performed this *Vrat* to attain the power of Protection. Dear friend! I myself did the same to acquire the power of protection as well as of incarnation at will. I perform this *Vrat* on every Friday. My priest Saint Garga will come tomorrow to remind me that I have to perform the *puja* on Friday. Krishna then advised Brahman Sudāma to take religious instructious about this *Vrat* from his priest. The latter performed the *puja* and offered a vow that with the money he would get without begging, he would perform the *puja* himself. He kept up all the night singing in praise of the God Ganesh. The next morning he started on his return journey, On the way, he met a rich Bania named Mani who was carrying one hundred gunny bags full of gold coins loaded on buffaloes.

He rested in a village for the night, where he was looted by *dakāits*. He was much distressed at so heavy a loss. He exclaimed that if he recovered his lost treasure, he would give away half of it to the first Brahman he should meet. As soon as this thought crossed his mind, he saw a bag containing one thousand gold *mohurs* and simultaneously saw Brahman Sudāma. He therefore hospitably called him and offered him five hundred coins out of the amount so miraculously recovered. Sudāma spent the amount on the same day in performing the *puja* of Satya Vināyak. He then began meditating on the virtues and powers of the God, and saw the deitiy before him, He the God gave him more wealth than that possessed even by Kuber the Treasurer of the Gods!

Pārvati again enquired of her husband as to how her son Ganesh could give such untold wealth, when the Brahman devotee was neither a beggar nor a merchant.

*Shiva* replied:—"Listen, when Sudāma distributed the money he had got, Bania Mani saw it and he asked him why he squandered away his wealth in this manner when he said he was too poor to support his own family. Sudāma explained to him how he was advised by Krishna to perform the *puja*. When the people of that town saw that Sudāma was so devoted a worshipper, they gave him, bags of coins! When he returned home his hut had undergone such a transformation that he was amazed to see a palace in its place. His wife saw him in that puzzled state and sent her servants to fetch him. They most respectfully bowed unto him, told him that he was their master, and taking him inside the palace, bathed him, dressed him, and put on jewelry on him. Sudāma and his wife saw that even the walls of their palace were studded with precious stones, and that the house was full of all comforts, there were gold plates all over the place, and servants were busy arranging for a royal banquet. His wife then asked him to explain the cause of such a magical transformation of their poor hut. Sudāma explained how the God Satya Vināyak was worshipped and how he granted the boon, and how his school friend Krishna had introduced him to his priest Saint Gargācharya and how the latter initiated him into the mystery of the *Vrat*.

The Bania Mani who was in turn initiated by Sudāma, returned to his house in Kutch Bhuj and explained the *Vrat* to his family and his friends. The next day after his arrival, he himself performed the *puia*. To this *puja* he invited the king, the Brahmans of the city, and his friend and minister named Chitrabāhu. After the worship, the minister made enquiries about the commercial success of his tour. The Bania explained how he was looted, how he recovered only one thousand gold *mohurs* and how he gave away half of that to Sudāma. Wonder of wonders! At this very moment the thieves who had looted the Bania came to the place to offer for sale to Chitrabāhu some jewelry. They were courteously invited to take part in the *puja* and asked to sit near the minister. They handed over some ornaments to Chitrabahu and he in his turn, handed them over to Mani for examination. But Mani immediately recognised his stolen property. Turning then to the minister he said that it was his own lost article and that the *pseudo* merchants were the thieves! "This was the very ring, for instance," he said "which my friend Chitrabāhu was pleased to bestow on me as a mark of favovr." Chitrabāhu identified the ring. He became angry. The thieves were frightened. They then vowed to the God that if the minister would allow them to escape unpunished by merely confiscating the ill-begotten property, they would perform the same *Vrat* which brought them into the clutches of the law. The minister turned towards them and thundered out.

"Look here, you *Badmāsh*! How did you come by this ring? If you speak the truth you will be allowed to go unpunished, but if you do not, you will all suffer the severest punishment possible." Poor souls! They confessed their guilt. "It is Lord Satya Vināyak who has caught us," they said. Bania Mani thus recovered the whole of his property.

Thus experiencing the wonderful effect of the *Vrat* minister Chitrabāhu offered a vow that he would perform the *puja* with the object of getting a good-looking son. He got one. He was in ecstasy and forgot to perform the promised *puja*. He was soon overtaken by calamities after calamities. He came under the displeasure of the king, who took by force all his wealth and turned him out of the city. Poor Chitrabāhu, the Diwan of Kutch, wandered to the banks of the Narbada as a beggar. One day he went to the hermitage of Saint Shuka for alms. He prostrated himself before the Saint, and was in tears. The Saint easily divined the cause of the grief and said, "Diwan Chitrabāhu, do not cry. Worship God Satya Vināyak who stands at the head of those considered worthy of worship. You forget the vow you offered to him. Let me remind you." The minister immediately performed the *puja*. That acted on the mind of the king, and His Majesty repented of doing an innocent man harm. He recalled his minister, and re-installed him.

The thieves gave up their unjust profession and became good citizens. They went to the banks of the river Falgu. There they gathered and worshipped the God Satya Vināyak. While they were thus engaged there came a woman in distress. The Brahman priest who was directing the *puja* was named Bhārgav. He made enquiries about the woman. She said "Oh Chief of Priests! There is a King named Chandrasen who rules over the province of Malava. He is very religious, very liberal, truth-loving, and learned in the Vedas. He has a large army. He is the Emperor of the world and the protector of the poor. He treats his subjects like his own children. I am the queen of that great man! I have no issue! He has therefore married a second wife, Madanāvati. The king has with him two very just and upright ministers. They are as brave as they are just. But this sixteen year-young woman Madanāvati has enchanted the king. He is night and day "looking babies in her eyes." He cannot bear a minute's separation from her. He hates me! He does not respect me! He never listens to me! He looks furious at me! He never accepts anything from me! I have thus become the slave of my co-wife. Moreover, she has given birth to a son. He is named Padmasen. He has grown and is given the sacred thread. He is educated and is married to Padmasena the princess born of the king of the Madra-country. My husband, the king, has come to Gaya on a pilgrimage. His Majesty has finished his ablutions this day. He was tired, and went to sleep. My-co-wife went to him. She saw me there. She kicked me and turned me out! Oh Brahman! I am tired of my life and have come here to kill myself! You know well, good priest, that the woman who is not respected by her husband is despised by all. What then is the use of remaining alive? Better to go to a *jungle* and fast and meditate on God; or drink a cup of poison! or, to drown one's self. These are my thoughts. I have not yet decided what to do. It is a sign of good luck that I see your sacred feet. Oh kind Brahman! Oh Ocean of Sympathy! What are these people doing here? Pray tell me."

The priest explained to her the efficacy and the history of the *Vrat*.

He said, "Oh Queen! all these were once thieves but by the grace of god, Satya Vināyak, they have now turned themselves into honest men. They have acquired riches by good hard work."

She then retracted her footsteps vowing a *puja* to the great God! She performed the *puja* after her return to her capital Karnāvat, with her husband King Chandrasen. He proved himself a successful ruler, because he was just. When his first queen Sunita began worshipping the god, his mind gradually under went a change and she became his beloved wife once more. When she was restored to favour, she sent for her Priest Bhārgav and performed the *Vrat* again and again with royal eclat. She invited the king to witness the ceremony. He asked his second wife to accompany him. She pretended illness and did not go. The king went alone. His old queen begged of him to share the worship with her. He did so. He fed couples (men and women) of married Brahmans and gave them plenty of cash, clothes, ornaments, perfumes besides other things. She fed them with choice dainties of which boiled solid cream formed the chief ingredient and gave them singing parties, theatrical entertainments &c. &c. The result was that old queen Sunita became *enciente.*

Next morning, she went to her co-wife and courteously offered a part of the god's offerings, but she became angry and turned her out of her palace. She had even the impudence to throw away the offering! The result was, an attack of leprosy! The moment king Chandrasen saw her horrid figure he turned her out. He lived happily with the first queen. She gave him a son. The King was delighted. He fed and heaped bounties on priests. The second prince was named Lakshipad. Queen Sunita was now placed in the height of her joy. She always performed the *puja* with devotion. The co-wife became very ill. She repented. She begged the pardon of the senior Maha Rāni, who advised her to perform the same *puja* every month feeding Brahmans and priests as often. His Majesty built a bejewelled temple for the God. Ever since that time, the town of Karnāvat has become a celebrated city well known all over the world. King Chandrasen enjoyed happiness even beyond the reach of the gods of of Heaven! He ultimately handed over his Raj to his son, and abdicated himself only to go to the forest to perform austerities, along with his two queens. He thus prepared himself for the attainment of salvation. He got it.

Such is the fruit, in this mortal as well as in the celestial world of the *puja*!

Pārvati the wife of Shiva thus listened with admiration to the history of the exploits of Ganesh, but she had one doubt. She sought explanation as to how the milk-made and other sweets could be eaten on a fast day? The solution suggested by Shiva was, that on the fast day the worshipper should only drink a small quantity of the washings of the image of the Elephant-headed god, and should eat the dainties on the following day.—*Brahmānd Purān.*

**Gauri.**—On the sixth day of Bhādrapad or thereabouts, a bundle of the wild flowering balsam plants—touch-me-not (Impitiens Sp.)—is ceremoniously collected by maid-servants, brought home, and placed in the verandah on a low stool with the roots towards the main entrance of the house. Under the stool is drawn a magic square with turmeric powder, fig. 1. Care is taken by the maids that, before the plants are removed from the soil, they are worshipped, wrapped in a cloth, and placed in a winnowing bamboo tray, fig. 2, previously decorated with the *svastika*. At sunset the bundle is worshipped and taken to the entrance, when rice and water are waved round it and thrown to the left side to guard against the evil eye. It is then placed on a chair or high stool and again worshipped, along with an unmarried girl, and all married women are served with the red powder, &c., the emblems of conjugal or married life.

The next ceremony consists of carrying the bundle from room to room, while the supposed foot prints of the Gauri. fig. 3, are being impressed on the floor with *gulāl* (red powder) paste. As each room is entered, the girl, who had been previouly, worshipped has to reply to the questions, (1) Gauri, Guari! whither have you come? and (2) what do yo see?

The first room so honoured is generally the central or chief hall. The girl then replies, (1) I have come to the *dîwân-khânâ*, and (2) I see that *Râvsâhîb* So-and-so has been sitting on a high cushion, reclined against another, and dictating orders to his secretaries, and that sepoys and *chôpdârs* are in attendance, and so forth, generally depicting the highest desire as the prosperity of the bread-winner. The girl is then given a mouthful of sweets, and the mistress of the house says, "Come with golden feet and stay for ever."

The middle room is next visited and the questions repeated. This is the dinning-hall, and a suitable "tall" description is given of feasts and banquets. The same request is repeated as she is taken from room to room. The important "lying-in room" is never neglected, and the description of the cradle, the babies, and their pleasure-giving pranks are minutely detailed. The bundle is then replaced on high stool or chair.

On the first night the chief food offered is the milk and sugar *kshîr*, or porridge with wheat-flour rolls resembling small pieces of vermicelli. Before retiring for the night the plants are tied up into a mummy-like figure, with a woman's mask, dressed and decorated with ornaments, and treated as the Goddess Gaurî.

Next morning the goddess so formed is worshipped as usual and is offered a rice-cake, prepared like an omelette, with the aid of cocoanut kernel and raw sugar. Every married woman now takes a hand-spun cotton-thread of her own height, counted sixteen times over, places it before the goddess, and worships it.

If there be a new bride in the house, a daughter-in-law, pan-cakes with pounded gram pulse (*puran*) and raw sugar are specially offered. Twenty-five bamboo winnowing trays are then filled up with bangles, combs, red-powder boxes, turmeric-tubers, rice, a necklace of glass-beads, dates, almonds, betel-leaves, betel-nuts, a cocoanut, some fresh fruits and a bodice-piece. They are distributed by the new bride, who is carried in a palanquin with tom-tom accompanied by female friends.

On the second night, all the girls in the house sing songs and dance, keeping up late, visiting the houses of girl friends for dancing and singing in front of the Gaurî. At midnight she is supposed to have to go away, that is, her 'spirit' departs, when an *ârtî*, consisting of incense and camphor, is offered.

The third day again sees her figure worshipped. The food offered consists of crescent-shaped pan-cakes, containing cocoanut kernel mixed with sugar. The 'one's-own-measure-skein' of thread of the previous day, which had been placed before the figure, is then lifted up, folded into a smaller skein and to it sixteen knots are tied. It is then worshipped, dyed with turmeric and tied by each woman round her own neck. This curious necklace is retained until the eighth day of the second half of Âshvin, the next harvest time, and removed before the sun sets on that day. The knots are untied, the skein worshipped, sixteen *ghî*-lights are burnt before it, sixteen *til* seeds (the crop is *then* ready), sixteen grains of rice, and flowers of cucumber are offered to it. The food prepared in honour of this necklace, called *Mahâlakshmî*, after the goddess of plenty and wealth, consists of the porridge. The thread is ultimately thrown into a river.

In regard to the chief goddess Gaurî, the Goddess of Harvest, one great peculiarity remains to be mentioned. She is supposed to have been followed secretly by her husband Siva. who remains under the outer fold of her *sârî* (garment), and is represented by a *lôtâ*, covered by a cocoanut and filled with rice carefully measured.

When the lay figure of Gaurî is thrown in a river or tank on the third day of the ceremoney, a handful of pebbles or sand is brought home from that place, worshipped and thrown all over the house and over the trees (1) to bring good luck to tbe house and (2) to protect the trees from vermin. Before the image is taken away for disposal, in a fold of the *sârî* it wears, are placed rice, turmeric-tubers, and betel-nuts. The woman who carries the figure is warned not to look behind her, as is the case when carrying dead bodies. The rice in the *lôtâ* representing Siva is finally carefully measured, to see if the quantity has increased or decreased, in order to prognosticate the results of the next harvest. In some families *aghâda* (*Achyranthes aspera*) plants are used instead of the balsam or touch-me-not.

The fable to account for the ceremony is given below verbatim as taken down :—There was a big town, in which lived a poor Brahman, with a large family. The month of Bhādrapad, came and he saw the Gaurî figures in all the houses of the town, and heard the music in their honour. His children saw them too. They asked him to bring the Gaurî to them. He could not. He was too poor. He had no money even to buy the little rice-flour and sugar required for the offering.

"He went to a tank to drown himself, but was accosted by an old married woman. She dissuaded him from the resolution, and accompanied him home. His wife made enquiries. He told her that she was his grand-mother, whereupon the wife went in search of some grain for food for her. To her surprise, she found her barn quite full. Porridge was prepared and all partook of it.

"Next morning, the old woman asked the Brâhman to tell his wife to bathe her. and added, 'Do not deny and do not demur.' He did so, and left the house on his daily begging-tour. He received plenty of alms that day.

"The old woman asked for rice and milk *kshîr (kônjî* or gruel), but there was no milk. So she advised him to make a number of pegs and strings for tying up cows and she buffaloes, and advised him to call by name at sun-set as many cattle as he could accomodate in his farmyard. They came and were milked, and so the *kshîr* was prepared and partaken of by the whole family.

"The honoured guest then asked leave to depart. The poor Brāhman expressed his fears at losing what he had got, through her favour. He was blessed and assured. The Brahman took her to the tank, where she gave him some sand and asked him to throw it over every mortal possession of his to secure 'plenty.' She advised him to repeat the ceremony in honour of Gauri every year on a suitable day in the month of Bhâdrapad." (August—September.)

This story, however, presupposes the existence of the annual worship. and is therefore merely a record of its introduction into a new family.

The rationale of the ceremony suggests, the alluvial soil of the river-side or tank as the original seat of the crops, (2) the old woman as the old season going out, (3) the young girl as the new season budding up, ready to burst out, as the symbol touch-me-not specially suggests, (4) the lay figure as possibly the dead body of the old season, the rice and the millets being just in flower at that time of the year, and (5) the food offered as the expected Bhâdvi, new rice-crops. The distribution of the trays, fruits, &c., represents the usual materials in use. But, (1) the loss of the spirit in the lay figure at midnight, the last day of the particular season of 'field work," (2) the drowning of the lay figure into the bowels of Mother Earth, (3) the sprinkling of sand, and (4) the skeins with sixteen knots are symbolical, as the simultaneous death and resurrection of the season celebrated all over the world by primitive races is found here stereotyped into a Hinduised form. The sixteen knots and the sixteen folds of the skein turned into a necklace, suggest the number of weeks a rice-crop takes to grow.

**Gudhipādma**—The Mahābhārat gives the story. Among descendants of Pururavā, there was a king named Vasu. He left his capital for a *Shikār* expedition but instead of returning home became a recluse and performed a long penance. Indra, the King of Gods was pleased and gave him a *Vimān* (celestial car), some arms, and wreath of flowers with the virtues of *aegis*, that made him invincible. He returned to his capital on the *first* day of Chaitra, and therefore all the citizens decorated the placc to welcome him.

**Gudhipadwa**—*Chaitra (March-April.)*

**New Year's Day.**—(1) Varsha Pratipadā or Gudhipādvā is the name given to the new year day of the Shālivāhan era which is in vogue in the Marātha country. Shālivāhan was the son of a potter. He headed a successful popular movement and became the chief of a powerful monarchy in Mahārāshtra. He ruled at Mungī-Paithan. The ruler whom he overthrew was Vikramāditya the last of the Gupta rulers of Mālwa. Shālivāhan's era is reckoned from A.D. 78 the supposed year of his coronation. It marks the beginning of the solar year. On this day Hindus raise their standard on a long pole. It is made up of silk-and-gold clothes. Then a flower wreath is added and the whole topped by a silver or brass *lota* to give it the appearance of a lotus bud shaped *Kalash*. This standard is worshipped in the usual way, and a family feast is observed. It is customary to eat a few tender leaves of the *Melia azadirachta* or *neem*-tree on his day, as it is supposed to prevent disease during the year. Every one is addressed in a gentle tone and blessings are poured on the younger members when they bow to the elders. No abusive language or harsh words are used to any one.

**Hanumān Jayanti**—

**Hanuman's birthday**—On the full moon day of Chaitra (March-April), is celebrated the birth day of Hanumān the monkey general of Ramā. It is supposed that he was born of the wife of *Bander* (monkey) Kesari, as the result of the rice-ball she got one morning by accident. Rāma's father Dasharath had just performed a special sacrifice for securing a son and heir. The god of fire gave him three balls to be eaten by his three queens. The second queen carelessly left it on the terrace or threw it away. A kite took it in its talons and flew away, but it dropped its prize where Kesari's wife Anjana was living. She ate it and conception followed. It is also said that Hanumān was an incarnation of Shiva, who was born to help Rāma in destroying demons.

**Haritālika** is a feast followed by a *puja* (worship). Literally it means the history of an Abducted Friend.

Pārvati, the daughter of Mount Himāchala or Himalaya, was about to be married. She was one day told that she would be married to Shiva, the Destroyer of the Hindu Trinity, but on one occasion Saint Nārad came to see her father and during that visit described the wealth and importance of Vishnu. When Pārvati heard of this change of mind of her father, she was very sorry, because she was all alone thinking of Shiva and no one else. She therefore opened her heart to her maid of honour and cried. She expressed her desire to marry Shiva, and said that she would on no account change her mind. Her maid therefore suggested that they should run away from her father's palace, go to the forest and there perform austerities for the attainment of this object.

She was under this inducement abducted and taken away. At her sudden disappearance, her father suspected that she was carried away by some gods or demons or demi-gods. He began the search himself. He was so overtaken by grief at the loss of his beauteous child that he fainted. He was immediately surrounded by the people. They asked him why was he so sadly overtaken by grief. Why so powerful a prince, as firm in the battlefield as a rock, should shiver like a tall tree in the midst of a hurricane. He thereupon explained to the assembled public that the loss of his daughter preyed upon his mind and that he could not bear the idea of the princess being taken away by force. All the people tried to trace her but without success. The old king at last entered a forest infested with furious beasts of prey and venomous reptiles. His daughter Pārvati had established herself in a cave on the banks of a stream and was performing austerities along with her maid. She made an emblematic figure of Shiva in sand and began worshipping it. It was the third day of the month of Bhādrapad and the moon was in the constellation known as Hasta (a hand). She kept up all the night singing songs in praise of Shiva. The result was that the Mountain of Kailās, the abode of Shiva, shook to his foundation as if by an earthquake. Shiva knew what it meant and forthwith hurried himself to the cave where Pārvati and her maid were engaged in the *puja.* He appeared before the former and asked her to name the blessing she desired as the fruit of her devotions. The recluse princess said that she was pining for him, it was to get him as her husband that she was performing the *vrat.* She explained that her father at first intended that she should be given to him (Shiva), but that he had changed his mind, because he (Shiva) was poor and Vishnu was very rich, but that as she once began thinking of him she would on no account change her mind. Shiva granted the boon and disappeared. The next morning Pārvati performed the closing ceremony of the *vrat* and consigned the figure to the stream. At this juncture her father Himāchala arrived on the spot and discovered his daughter fast asleep along with her maid on the bank of the stream. He lifted up his lost child, and asked her why she had left the luxuries of the palace to come to such a dreadful place full of ferocious beasts of prey. Pārvati replied "Dear father, you forget; that you once offered my hand to the God Shiva and then changed your mind, dazzled by the jewels and wealth of Vishnu. But I would on no account change my mind. I have mentally married Shiva and will ever remain faithful to him, like a religiously chaste woman." This confession emanating from the honest and chaste thoughts of the daughter convinced the father of her sincerity and he promised to comply with her request. He then took his "abducted" pet to his palace and ceremoniously performed her marriage with the god of her choice. It is thus a case of a Pahādi woman—abducted by her maid or maids—to enable her to secure the husband of her choice.

Based on this experience, Shiva ordained that his wife should be worshipped under the name Haritālika by those girls who long for husbands of their own choice. The *modus operandi* consists of the intended devotee fasting all day on the third of the month of Shrāvan when the moon ascends the mansion Hasta. This, it may be remembered, is the memorable day on which Pārvati succeeded in securing him. During this day all women (of course Hindu) should eat nothing but plantains. They should drink no water. A bower formed of plantain trees should be fully decorated with various sorts of flowers and flags. It should be sprinkled with sandal-wood paste. Musicians should be kept in attendance. An emblem of Shiva made of sand and earth should be prepared. An image of Pārvati *alias* Haritālika should be placed near the emblem with that of her maid of honour both in praying *mudra* or attitude. Both the images and the emblem should be worshipped together in the usual way. Dainties of all sorts and fruits of the season should be offered as food and distributed among Brahmans and others. The following prayer should at last be recited :"I offer salutations to Him who is calm, Him who has five heads, unto Him who holds a trident, to Him who has in attendance Nandi, the sacred Bull, Bhringi, the attendant, and Mahānkāl, the God of death. I offer salutations to Her the beloved wife of Shiva, the essence of the Universe, the Mother of the Universe, the source of all happiness, the Omnipresent, the giver of all blessings, she whose presence is felt in the mortal span of life, she who is the Protectress of the people. I offer my salutations to the one who rides a lion. Oh Goddess, protect me, Oh Goddess, grant me my desires, Oh Mother, grant me a Rāj (Kingdom), a happy life with my husband living, and wealth."

After the *puja* and the prayer, every woman should attentively hear the story or history of the abduction. Brahmans should be fed to satisfaction, they should be offered good and substantial presents, such as clothes, gold, and cows. The fruition, the result, the blessing promised consists of release from all sorts of sin, and a principality for seven births one after another, with the blessing of a long lived husband.

But listen! Here are the curses levelled against those women who dare take any food (except plantains) on the third of Bhādrapad, the day on which the moon graces the constellation Hasta. If she takes food, mind, she shall become a widow for seven successive lives. She shall be a penniless wretch, she shall suffer the pangs of witnessing the death of her son, she shall prove to her husband a veritable Xanthippe. She who does not fast on that memorable day shall go to Hell.

On the second day of the *puja*—further adds the text—an emblem of Shiva made of gold, silver, copper or at least sand, according to means, should be devoutly offered to a Brahman with a pot full of rice and other estables, and along with clothes and cash.

In conclusion it is ordained, that she who will perform the *vrat* will get as good a husband as Shiva himself, will enjoy all blessings on earth, and on release from this mortal frame will be blessed with a palatial residence in Kailās, the abode of Shiva, where, with her husband, she will enjoy endless blessings. So says the *Bhavishottar purān*.

**Holi**—The *Holi* is a saturnalia connected with the spring equinox and the wheat harvest of the Western part of India. It is observed in its indecorous and boisterous form by the lower classes. Tradition ascribes it to the death of a giantess, at the hands of Krishna, who on her death-bed asked for the favour of a festival in her name but the time fixed for the festival and the ceremony observed, point to the "death of the season." The preparation of the bonfire, and the sound produced by beating the mouth with the back of the hand, form part of the cremation ceremony observed all over India. On the full-moon day of the month of *Phālgun* a hole is dug in front of every house, and a castor-oil tree is transplanted into it. Grass, cowdung-cakes, and other fuel, are heaped round the tree. *Holi* or *Holika*, who is at the time called a goddess is worshipped, and the sound above described is made, with the accompaniment of a certain word. The people throw red powder at each other, and play outdoor games all night. Next morning, which is called *dhulvad* (from *dhul*, dust), people of the lower orders throw dust at one another, and all sorts of improper expressions are vociferated in the streets. No woman in Western India leaves her house during this festival, and if one is seen by accident she is liable to be accosted in very unpleasant language. Among the Marāthas proper the *Vir*, or people who died on the battle-field, are "danced" by their descendants, who go round the fire with a drawn sword until they get into a trance, or believe themselves possessed by the spirits of the hero. After the sports are over, everyone bathes with water boiled on the *Holi* fire. In some places goats are sacrificed. Among high class Hindus cakes (*puran-poli*) made of wheat flour, and stuffed with pounded gram and raw sugar, are thrown into the fire, with a cocoanut. It is the prerogative of the Rāja to light the palace bonfire first; until that is done no one will commence the festivities, as fire has to be taken from the palace bonfire to the *Holis* kept ready at other places.

*Not of Bengal Origin.*—Writers of the *Purānās* have prescribed many variants. In Bengal *dolas*, or swings are made for Krishna, and no bonfire is prepared. This in itself is sufficient to show that it is originally a harvest festival of the wheat producing tracts and not of rice-producing Bengal. The *naivedya* or food, consisting of wheat, gram, and sugar, confirms this belief, and the indecent saturnalia finally settles the origin. A similar festival is observed among the *Santals* and *Mundas*, when the *sāl* tree flowers. Corresponding harvest festivals of ancient Europe leaves no doubt as to the real origin. It is interesting, however, to compare the *purānic* variants given below :—

Jaimini says that fire should be worshipped in front of a bower in which is a *dol*, or swing, for Gopal (the cowherd king, from *gau* a cow). He tells us that Rājarshi, or the warrior-saint Indradyumna, was the first to perform this ceremony, in the jungle of *Brindavaṇ* (*Brindaban* in the Bengali pronounciation).

The *Pātālkhand purān* mentions the *dol*, but not the fire. It prescribes the use of red, yellow, and many-coloured powders.

The *Utkalkhand purān* also advocates the *dol* worship.

The *Garud purān* does the same, but adds the use of the coloured powders.

The *Hari Bhakti Vilās pothi* (in Bengal, *puthi*) mentions *Chaitra* as the month in which the swing ceremony should be performed.

Some families among the the *Prabhus* of Bombay do not worship the *Holi* fire, nor the *dol* either, but they do prepare the *purān-poli* wheat-gram-sugar cakes in the morning, and send them to the *grām-Holi* (from *grām*, town), the chief bonfire of the town, with cooked rice and cocoanut, to be thrown into it. For the next day's bath they obtain water boiled on the *holi* fire.

Prescriptive rights of igniting the chief bonfire of the town, of heating the bath-water on that fire, and of dancing the *Vir*, or heroes, round it are still respected by all Hindus. In the Rajput and Marātha Native States the palace *Holi* is guarded by sentinels for four days, and people who do not possess this right are prevented from encroaching.

## Interesting Theories.

In the Madras Presidency, except at Tanjore (a Marātha State), the bonfire is not prepared, and many Madrasis assert that no improper epithets are uttered. It is further added that low class women freely mix with men in celebrating this festival. The songs sung contain the lamentations of Rati, the goddess of love, at the death of her husband Kāmadev under the fire which emanated from Shiva's third eye. It therefore follows that the resort to improper language and expressions represents the disgust of Shiva with the female sex, and extends over the Scytho-Dravidian tract occupied by men who did not bring their wives with them when they immigrated; that the wail in the Dravidian tract represents sorrow of the females at the loss of their fair-complexioned emigrant husbands; and that in the Gangetic tracts the lower classes regard the day as a saturnalia while the upper classes accept it as dedicated to their polygamous God Krishna.

In some parts of the Madras Presidency a mock fight takes place between men and women. A woman takes a bundle of sheafs and ascends a tree, and the men try to capture the bundle, the women preventing them from doing so. At Indore, the *Baniyas* erect a colossal figure made of straw and clay, of Nāthurām, about 40 feet high. Owing to an objectionable feature, this was prohibited, but the Durbar received a numerously signed petition and sanctioned the resumption of the practice on certain conditions.

On the fifth day after the chief fire ceremonials, presumably representing the cremation of the season, a grand Durbar takes place in native States, in which coloured powders and fluids are thrown at the *sardārs* and officials. It is called *Rangpanchami*, and is also observed by people in their houses to mark the conclusion of the festivities. It may represent the resurrection of the season,—four days after the cremation. As a result of environment on even the non-Hindu Parsis, the following proverb has been quoted from a Guzerati book :—"To the *Holi* of the Hindus the simple Pārsi-woman offers a cocoanut."

## DERIVATION OF THE WORD.

The word *Holi* has its derivation in the Sanskrit word *Sol*, meaning "bitter of sour;" *solika* means "coldness." Another name for *Holi* is *Phalguni*, curiously resembling the *Phagasin* of the Greeks. The *Pallica* of the Egyptians resembles the *Holika* of the Sanskrit writers. *Phul* means flower, and there is a *Floralia* and *Phalarica*, to be compared with the *phallus* of Osiris, the *thyrsus* of Bacchus, and the *lingam* of Shiva. Then we have the God Horus in Egypt as the avenger of his father, and the vivifier of the two lands (of Egypt). In one place he is represented as "weighing the hearts of the deceased in the presence of the God Osiris, while Thoth writes down the result." There is also the ceremony of "opening the shrine of Horus and offering incense to a king's deified father and mother." (Burge's History of Egypt, Vol. 3, pp. 19, 202; Vol. 4, pp. 144; Vol. 7, pp. 33, 238, &c.)

These quotations speak for themselves in tracing the real origin of the festival, and the fact that the Western part of India is more affected than the Eastern and Southern portions, that the indecent phase is confined to the servants, slaves, and depressed castes formerly under the sovereignty or rule of the Rajputs or Marāthas, together with the "dancing" of the *Virs*, lead to the discovery of some important ethnological data. The meaning and derivation of *Phalguni, i.e.*, "fructifier"; the connection of the festival with the vernal equinox, its relation to the wheat, gram, and sugar harvests; the nature of the offering, of the *puran-poli;* and the resurrection ceremony of the *rangpanchami*, possibly point out its origin from harvest festivities imported from Egypt or Greece. The digging of the hole, and "dancing" of the heroes may have some connection with ancestral worship. The meaning of the words *Holi* and *Holika* ("sourness" and "coldness"), the mock fight between men and women, and the disgusting epithets hurled all round, particularly at the sight of women, may lead to a connection between the festival and the temporary disagreement between foreign men and local women, due to difference in colour and and to the approaching separation of the nomad men. The wailing may signify its result on the womankind. The *Holi* therefore appears to be a conglomerate of festivities, with its origin in the astronomical equinox and the agricultural harvests, its evolution in the nomadic habits of the first immigrants, the ancestral worship of heroes, the leisurely adoption of a tribal festival by a Mongoloid race too anxious to retain men hailing from the Western parts of India, like Brindaban and Dwarka (the seats of Krishna), and finally in the embellishments of the *Purānas*.

**Itu Worship.**

Itu is the name of a Bengal goddess who confers all sorts of favours on those who worship her. She is represented by an earthen jar filled with water and topped over by plantains. The Sankrānt of Agrahāyan is sacred to her.

There lived a greedy Brahman who felt a craving for some sort of pan cakes, and asked his wife to prepare them, but the poor woman had no materials to make them with. Full of resource, he went begging and collected sufficient stuff for a full meal. Late at night his obedient wife sat frying the cakes, but her husband was so suspicious that he was secretly watching her all the time and tying knots to a string to record the actual number of cakes prepared. After the operation was over he went to sleep. His two daughters named Jumno and Umno awoke early and out of motherly love they were each fed with a single cake. They were warned not to ask for more. As the Sun rose, the Brahman got up and demanded the cakes. He found that there were two short, and knowing that his two daughters consumed them, took them to a forest and cruelly deserted them. The heartless greedy priest returned home, the poor mother dared not complain! The girls wandered until they came across a place where some fairies were engaged in worshipping the goddess Itu. They learned the process, followed it, received blessings, came back to their father and made him rich. A king who passed their house, sent for some water, and it was supplied by the girls in a pitcher. He was angry at the small quantity, but found that it contained an inexhaustible store, so he took a fancy to the girls, married one himself, and gave the other in marriage to his minister. His wife Umno did not perform the *puja* and came to grief. She was ordered to be beheaded. The executioner saved her life, and handed her over to her sister Jumno. She lived incognito. The father of the girls neglected the *puja*, kicked the sacred pitcher and suffered the consequences. He became a beggar. He then went to the prosperous daughter but the gifts she gave were looted by the emissaries of the goddess Itu. His wife then went to her daughter, stayed there until the *sankrānt* day in Agrahāyan, worshipped the goddess, and became rich. The other daughter did the same. The king repented, and in his foolish way asked the minister to restore his wife on pain of death. The prime minister came home dejected, and told his wife what an impossible order he had received. She disclosed the secret of the queen's incognito and restored her to the king on condition that he planted an avenue of plantain trees and pitched tents covered with cowries. This was done and all became happy and went to heaven in the end after full enjoyment of life.

**Janmāshtami.**

In the second half of Shrāvan there are two fasts and feasts. The first is the birth-day of Krishna called *Gokul-āshtami* or Janmāshtami. Krishna of course is the accepted eighth incarnation of Vishnu. His maternal uncle Kansa was told by the Divine Echo that his sister Devaki, whose marriage he was celebrating, would give birth to a son who would kill him. On further enquiry from astrologers, he learnt that the eighth boy born unto her would be that one. Even during the nuptials, King Kansa wanted to kill his sister to remove all anxiety. He was advised not to kill an innocent woman, but to destroy his future enemy as soon as he was born. At this stage he was further advised, that there is no knowing which would be the exact eighth, as counted from one end the figure eighth stands last, but counted from the other end the first becomes the eighth. Similarly the second or any other may become the eighth. He therefore put his sister and her husband Vasudev into prison. They were closely watched, each child as it was born, being killed by the king. The seventh and the eighth were saved. This eighth child of Devaki and Vasudev became the hero of the Mahābhārat. He killed his uncle and helped the Pāndavās in their struggles with their cousins. It is the celebration of his birth that gives its name to the *Janmāshtami* day from *Janma*, birth *ashtami* the eighth. In some families this ceremony begins on the first day of the dark half of Shrāvan and lasts for nine days just as the Durgāpuja does in Bengal. But the difference is this. Only a few families celebrate the former all over India, while the Durgā-puja has attained the position of a provincial or territorial festival in Bengal. The general holiday aspect of the Goddess-worshipper is not met with, with regard to the birth-day of Krishna. Another essential difference consists in the total absence of any animal-sacrifice from Krishna's birth-celebrations. The writer knows of a family feeding as many learned Brahman priests as could be collected together in a city for the first three days, their number ranging from 100 to 150. During the next three days all Brahmans whether priests or no-priests, are similarly fed, numbering as many as 400 to 500; and during the last three days beggars of all sorts are fed by thousands. *Kathās* or *Kirtans* consisting of meetings in which recitations from the Mahābhārat intermixed with interpretations, traditions, and funny stories are held during the eight nights. On the eighth night, the birth ceremony is celebrated and on the nineth day a row of unglazed ceramic pots containing sour milk is hung from a pole supported by two uprights and broken. Devoted old and young people dance below them in supposed imitation of the pranks of Krishna during his stay among the cowherds. Thus ends the ceremony.

**Jitāshtami.**

Jit means life and *ashtami* the eight day of a month. The eighth day of the latter half of the month of Ashwin is observed in Bengal as a fast by women in the hope of ensuring long life for their babies. The story runs that a certain king had no child. He sacrificed many animals and secured a number of charms from ascetics but all to no purpose. One day the queen dreamt that if she performed the *Jitāshtami Vrat* by planting a plantain tree and a *bael (Ægle marmelos)* tree in the midst of a miniature tank and worshipped them in the prescribed form, she would get a son, who would be married to a princess. The queen performed the *puja* and observed the fast every month on the eighth day of the dark half. But her daughter-in-law ridiculed the idea and called it gross superstition! The result was that her children died young. At last, the old queen persuaded her to adopt the *Vrat* and to observe the fast. She did so with excellent results!

**Kālashtami.**

The eighth day of the second half of the month of Kārtika is observed as a fast in Benares and the night is spent in prayers, etc. The story is, that once upon a time there rose a dispute among the gods as to who was the chief. Brahma claimed the honour, but there appeared out of Vishnu's body the personification of the Vedas to claim that exalted position on behalf of Shankar. Brahma would not accept that, and began speaking ill of Shiva. At this moment there appeared the vision of Indra. Every body bowed except Brahma. He said that he was the Creator and he made Shiva and named him Rudra (from *Rodan* —cry) because he cried. He asked Shiva to bow down his head to him. Shiva was angry. He created Kāl-Bhairav and asked him to chop off one of the five heads of Brahma. It was immediately done! Shiva then asked the Kāl to go and live at Benares. Ever since that time Kāl-Bhairav has been the presiding deity of that sacred city, and the Hindu inhabitants of the place keep up the day in his honour.—[*Kashi khand Purān.*]

**Kapila Shasthi.**

On the first of October 1912, there fell a *Yog* or conjunction of stars and planets which comes only once in about sixty years and is called Kapila Shasthi.

The definition given as in the Dharma Sindhu, Purān-Samuchchaya, Nirnayāmrita, Hemādri-Skandapurān and Vratrāj, says that the following conjunction is necessary to form this Yog or opportune time:

(1) The month of Bhādrapad.

(2) Its second or dark half.

(3) Tuesday.

(4) The Sun to be at the *Hasta* constellation.

Hasta is the thirteenth asterism of the Lunar mansions according to Ratnamāla. It is shaped like a hand. According to Shripati, the number of stars constituing this group is five. Its apparent longitude according to Surya-siddhānta is 170, and its latitude 11 South. According to Colebrooke, Burgess and Bentley its principal star is 7, 8, Corvi.

(5) Vyatipāt. When the sun and moon are in the opposite *āyana* and have the same declination the sum of their longitudes being 180°; that astronomical Yog or conjuction is called Vyatipat. [Sir M. Monier-William's Dictionary.]

(6) Rohini constellation.

Rohini is the fourth asterism consisting of five stars according to Shripati. According to Surya-siddhānta its longitude is 49°-50° and its latitude 5°-0 South. According to Colebrooke its principal star is *a, Tauri*, and according to Burgess and Bentley it is Aldebaran. Its shape is supposed to resemble a wheeled carriage.

(7) The sixth day of the dark half.

All these must co-exist *during the day*, because, says the text: *It is a Yog sacred to the Sun.* If it falls at night, it is considered abortive.

The previous Kapilā-Shasthi fell on the 28th of September 1858, that is about 54 years ago according to Christian era. This difference may be due to the different system of caclulations of the calendars, as is noticed in the fact that according to the Shaka era this year is 46th in number, while according to the Samvat era it is 57th in the series.

The tradition is, that once upon a time Saint Nārad the celestial celibate saw, while bathing in the sacred Ganges, a pair of fishes in conjugal happiness. His passions were excited and produced in him the desire to lead a married life. The happiness of a family and the pleasure of children playing about, and a thousand and one things which make life enjoyable tempted even this citadel of celibacy, this ever youthful ascetic. He made up his mind to give up his *Brahmacharya* and lead the life of a householder. But, he thought, who would give him a wife, and besides, he had no money to expend on the costly ceremony. What should he do? He thought, he had found out a solution. The best course was to go to Krishna, the King of Dwarka, and the husband of sixteen thousand one hundred and eight wives! The lord of Dwarka could easily spare one, and would not miss her! And he was so fabulously rich that he could easily pay all the expenses! This unholy thought affected the sanctity of the great saint to a certain extent. God however felt himself bound to satisfy every desire of his devotees and Nārad stood at the top of them all! All-pervading Vishnu therefore organized a counterplot. Vishnu as Krishna was full of humour. He took no offence even at so insulting a proposal. Noticing that Nārad laid much stress on the large number of his wives and hinted at the impossibility of one man meeting them every day, he asked the saint to go round his houses and to pick up that woman with whom he was not living. Poor Nārad! He was not in his senses. He took the bait, and actually went round the whole city, but in every house he visited in quest of a "vacancy," he found Krishna present, either playing with his children or enjoying the company of his wife in a thousand and one ways. Always happy, always jolly, always in the enjoyment of the highest blessings possible for a married man! That sight still more excited the passions of Nārad. He was still thinking how to get a wife when his time for prayer came. As he always bathed and repeated his prayers very punctually he involuntarily went to the Ganges to bathe. Nārad was thinking of going again to Krishna for a wife when he took another dip, and on coming up to the surface of the water was astonished to see that he was turned into a woman! She (now of-course *she*) got out of the stream and was going to change her wet cloth, when, lo! a big tall, stout, manly, good-looking *sanyāsi* accosted her. He caught her (Nāradi as she must hence be called) by the hand, took her to a cottage and marriage-by-capture followed. She gave birth to sixty sons one after another—one every year! Worried, exhausted, fatigued, bored to death by these numerous sons, she at the end of the sixtieth year involuntarily prayed to Lord Vishnu to relieve her of this worldly misery! Repentance did not come too late, for, the long eternal (free from death) life of Nārad! The *sanyāsi* disappeared and there appeared in his place the Glorious Lord of the Universe, God Vishnu, with four hands holding *shankha, chakra, gada* and *padma!* and said "What are your wishes Oh penitant woman, they shall be granted!" Nāradi looked aghast, looked at the lord again, wiped her eyes and said "You know it my lord. Fool that I was, I thought married life was a bed of roses, full of happiness and pleasures. Save me my lord!"

"Rise dear Nārad, rise!" was the response. He was transformed into a fully equipped young ascetic in every detail! The God Vishnu embraced him as a friend and asked him to name any other desire, but by this time the sixty sons had gathered round their mother clamouring for food! Nārad appealed to Vishnu to silence them, Vishnu gave them the Rāj of the world to be enjoyed by turns for one year at a time. This is how each Hindu year has a separate name for a cycle of sixty years. At the end of this cycle falls the *Kapila Shasthi,* the sacred day on which Nāradi, was re-transformed into Saint Nārad!

Here is the list of the sixty sons of Nāradi after whom the lunar years in the cycle are still being called. The name of the year 1912 A.D. according to the Shaka era is No. 46, Paridhāvi, while according to the Samvat era it is No. 57 Rudhirodgāri. The former year is 1838, the latter 1968-69 while the A.D. is 1912.

Prabhav, Vibhav, Shukla, Pramoda, Prajāpati, Angira, Shrimukha, Bhava, Yuva, Dhata, Ishwar, Bahudhānya, Pramāthi, Vikrama, Vrisha, Chitrabhānu, Subhānu, Tāran, Prārtiva, Vyaya, Sarvajit, Sarvadhāri, Virodhi, Vikriti, Khara, Nandana, Vijaya, Jaya, Manmath, Durmukha, Hemalambi, Vilambi, Vikāri, Sharvari, Plava, Shubhakrit, Shobhana, Krodhi, Vishvavāsu, Parābhava, Plavanga, Kilaka, Saumya, Sadhārana, Virodhikrita, Paridhāvi, Pramādi, Ananda, Rākshasa, Nala, Pingala, Kalayukta, Sitdhārthi, Raudra, Durmati, Dundubhi, Rudhirodgāri, Raktākhi, Krodhana, and Kshaya.

## DISSERTATIONS.

In this *yog* or conjunction, there are simultaneously present the Sun, the sixth day of the Moon, the symbol hand or *Hasta* and Rohini constellations the Vyatipāt or Sun and Moon in juxtaposition at 180° and a Tuesday. Let us bear this in mind and note the curious resemblance of ideas as recorded by Sir George Cox in his Manual of Mythology.

"Zeus" says Sir George, "is found in the Hindu Mythology as Dyaus the god of the bright sky or heaven. Dyaus-piter may be compared with Zeus-Pater and Jupiter which means father Zeus. By the Anglo-Saxons he was called Tiu (a word traced in Tuesday"—the day on which the Kapila-Shasthi must fall).

Tiu also means, the pure blue sky, the abode of light. On the other hand Vishnu, who became the father of the sixty sons by Nāndi, is blue. "In the West the Earth had been spoken of as the bride of the sky. As Zeus is derived from the same root with the Greek Theos, and the Latin Deus or the Sanskrit Deva, which all mean God, and as Krishna or Vishnu is supposed to be all-pervading (from *Vish* to pervade) and blue in colour, he is in this story made to represent Zeus-Pater. The Tuesday of course points to Tiu or Zeus. The presence of the moon in juxtaposition is necessary in this conjunction. In the Hindu popular belief the Moon is a male but according to Western ideas it is a female. It therefore perhaps supplied the ideas of male Nārad transformed into female Nāradi. Thus the story possibly mixes up the two ideas, turns the Moon into a woman and makes the sixty lunar years, the sons born of Zeus the blue or sky-coloured Vishnu. The Sun and Moon brought face to face at 180 degree are the emblems of eternity and may be the witnesses of the marriage as is conveyed in the adage *Yāvat chandra-divākarau*, that is as long as the Sun and the Moon do exist. It is a blessing.

It is thus seen that the Kapila Shasthi tradition has a striking resemblance to the story of Zeus and his sons. They do not exactly agree, but "these stories" says Sir George Cox, "differ so much, that it is often impossible to make them agree together, and we can only say, in many cases that each country or city followed its own version."

This is therefore a case in point in which Zeus the father and Earth the mother are supposed to produce sixty children, from a marriage, which takes place this day when the asterism Hasta or hand is in evidence to symbolize the ceremony of a bride giving her hand in marriage to her husband, in the presence of two eternal witnesses the Sun and the Moon, on a Tuesday—the day sacred to him.

W. Brennand in his Hindu Astronomy tells us at pages 22 and 23, that this is Brihaspati's Cycle. "This cycle of 60 years was brought into India by some of the immigrant tribes, and was afterwards known as the Cycle of Brihaspati, *i.e.* of Jupiter. It is a combination of five years, from the Astronomy of the Vedas, and siderial period of the Planet Jupiter, which was at first reckoned to be 12 years, but was afterwards found by the Hindus to be 11.86,0.962 years, admitting an error of about $8\frac{1}{4}$ months in 60 years, which would require periodic correction."

**Khas Shasthi.** *Khas,* or Khus is a grass known also as Bena in Bengal *(Andropogon muricatus)* and Shasthi in this case means the 6th day of the bright half of Paushya (December-January). It is a fast followed by a *Puja* of the goddess presiding over the day and also named *Shasthi.* The story current in Bengal where this *Vrat* is observed, runs, that a certain Brahman's daughter-in-law was a naughty girl. She did not work well and stealthily ate things prepared or reserved for the family gods. Her children therefore died young. With the object of improving her conduct under the influence of the goddess Shasthi, her mother-in-law decided upon making her observe the fast. She therefore gave her a large number of clothes to wash and sent her away to the river for that purpose. The woman took nearly the whole day to finish her job, and as she could not take any food, she had to fast. During her absence from home, her mother-in-law worked hard and cooked a nice set of dainties and made every preparation for the worship of the goddess as symbolized by the *Pātai* or *Bena* plant. She dug up a small ditch to represent a tank, planted the sacred grass on its bank, and arranged the materials for the *Puja* in front of it. The family priest and the musicians were also kept in readiness. When the woman heard the music, and saw on her return, that so much trouble was taken for her by her kind mother-in-law she repented, and devoutly worshipped the goddess. The result was, that her children henceforth lived long, and her sin was expiated. She and her neighbours therefore adopted the *Puja.*

**Kojāgari Puja.** It falls on the full moon day of Ashwin. (September-October). In Bengal, the story runs that there was a king who made it a rule to encourage industrial pursuits in his capital by purchasing all unsold articles brought to the weekly market. It attracted many clever artisans. He once bought a statuette which was not sold. It happened to represent the goddess of Poverty ! On the very night of the purchase, he heard a plaintive voice from the room in which he used to worship his family gods. It was midnight. He entered the room and saw a beautgous woman crying. He asked her who she was. She said that she was was the goddess of prosperity and was crying because she could not stay where the goddess of poverty lived. Saying so she departed but before leaving the house, she granted a boon to the king. She said " As I have always been respected and well treated by you, I grant you the power of understanding the language of all birds, beasts and insects." Do follow the following commandments :—

(1) Good behaviour is the essence of manhood.
(2) Restraint is the highest virtue of a woman.
(3) Clarified butter is the essence of good food.
(4) Watchfulness is the essence of night.

Following these precepts, the king never slept at night. He once saw a woman leaving his house and asked who she was. She said that she was the Goddess of fortune and that she could not stay where the goddess of poverty (Alakshmi) lived. On another night, he met another lady leaving his palace. She said that she was the goddess of success and that she could not stay because the king had brought the image of Alaxmi. Finally he saw a man and a woman walking out of the house. On enquiry he learnt that the lady was the family goddess and the man was Dharma the god of virtue. The king allowed the goddess to pass ; but he stopped the man and said " Sir I bought the image in order to keep your rule. I made a certain promise to traders and by your own rule, I was obliged to keep it." You must therefore support me now that

I am in distrees. Dharma stayed. Gradually the king became poorer and poorer. Every day at his dinner ants used to gather around his dish. One day the king ordered the Queen not to put clarified butter to his rice. The next day it was not given. The ants that were moving about were speaking among themselves and said that the king was gradually becoming poor—so poor as not to be able to allow clarified butter with his rice. The king understood this, and laughed. The queen noticed it and asked the king the cause, which the king said he could not disclose. But the queen was obstinate. At last the king agreed to tell her the fact. He asked her to accompany him to the Ganges. He would then, he said, disclose to her the conversation of the ants and die on the banks of the sacred stream. On reaching the place he asked her whether she wanted him or the secret. The queen risked even that and preferred the latter. At this moment the attention of the king was drawn to a pair of goats grazing in the vicinity. A sheaf of grass was floating down the mid-stream. The she-goat asked the male to bring it for her to eat. He sharply said "I am not a fool like that king to risk my life to please a wife." The king took the hint and tried to bring his queen to her senses. As she did not give up her stubborn resolution, he deserted her, and she roamed over a forest. In the evening she heard the blowing of the conch-shell and the ringing of bells. She went in the direction of the sound and reached a place where some young ladies were worshipping the image of Laxmi. It was the night of the Kojāgari day. She was advised to perform the *puja* and she did so. The result was that the iron image of Alaxmi in her husband's house melted away and the king regained all his wealth and glory. Finding this miraculous change in his affairs, he asked Dharma to explain the cause. The God of virtue told him that the change was due to his queen's merit in performing Kojāgari Puja. The king therefore went in search of his wife, and found her still in deep meditation seated in front of the idol. He brought her back with great pomp and became happy. The Kojāgari *puja* has henceforward been carefully observed.

**Kokila Vrat.** It is an observance which·begins on the 15th or full-moon day of the intercalary month when it occurs in Āshādh (June-July). It recurs about every twenty years.

*Kokil* literally means the Indian cuckoo, or *Koel, Eudynamys Orientalis* it is much respected by Hindus. Cuckoo is held sacred to Sati or Gauri, the wife of Shiva, because it is supposed to represent that goddess in connection with a curse. The story runs that Dakshya, the son of Prajāpati or Brahma, had no son. He wanted one. At the advice of Saint Kapila he undertook to perform a sacrifice for the fulfilment of his desire. To this grand assemblage he did not invite his daughter Sati and her husband Shiva. When Sati heard of the great sacrifice, she was surprised at not being invited, and attributed the omission to her father's forgetfulness. She thought, it was no dishonour to go to one's parents uninvited and begged her husband's permission to do so. After some hesitation, Shiva allowed her to go. She went to the place. On entering her parental home Sati, after paying her respects to her father, began arguing with him for disrespecting her lord by omitting to invite him. Dakshya found fault with Shiva's mode of living among ghosts and other uncanny spirits, and reminded her of her marriage against his wish, and asked her to leave him. Sati was very angry, as she was a devoted wife and a great admirer of Shiva. Words ran high, father and daughter got excited over the dispute. Sati could not bear her husband being insulted in that way, and jumped into the sacrificial fire! Nārad, the celestial news-carrier informed Shiva of what had happened. Infuriated Shiva dashed his long hair against the mountain.

The moment he did so, the hero Virabhadra and the terrible goddess Kāli issued forth! Shiva told them to destroy Daksha's sacrificial fire. They started with their armies, including eight Durgas and sixty-four Mātrikas. Daksha took help of all his allies, the gods assembled for the sacrifice. They mobilised at Kankhal situated in the North-West. They were all defeated. At last Vishnu the great Protector of the Univsrse, stood between the opposing armies. Terrible Virabhadra with his destructive arms bowed his head down as soon as he saw Vishnu, but told him that he had to 'obey orders.' He then disarmed the great god by swallowing his luminous weapon *Sudarshan*. Vishnu then went home. Victorious Virbhadra and Kāli began the wholesale spoliation of the ceremonial altar by extinguishing the sacrificial fire. Virbhadra dragged Daksha out of the ladies' apartment, twisted out his neck with his mighty nails, and threw the head into the fire!

Brahma the father of Daksha was overtaken by grief. He begged Shiva to forgive his offending son and to restore him to life. Shiva ordered his Field-Marshal Virabhadra to produce the body of the unfortunate Daksha. As the head was already destroyed by fire a sacrificial goat's head was chopped off and placed over his trunk. Daksha the penitant father-in-law of Shiva, came to life, prostrated himself before Shiva, and begged forgiveness. Yes, he was forgiven, and in order to compensate him for the loss of his human head, it was ordained that at the end of the worship of Shiva, every devotee must make a sound resembling that of a goat or his *puja* will not be accepted. This is the origin of the practice in vogue in all the Shaivite worships. Sati had however committed the sin of polluting the sacrificial fire by burning herself in it and had to atone for it! She was turned into a cuckoo. At the earnest solicitations of her grand-father Brahma, Shiva decided that after passing her days as a bird for a thousand celestial years, she would resume her former shape and would be accepted as his wife.

In commemoration of this event, it is further decided that women who observe this *vrat* will never lose their husbands by death.

On the full-moon day of the intercalary month Āshād (June-July), therefore women bathe themselves in the nearest river, sea, or tank, worship the gods in the temples situated in the vicinity, and returning home worship also the gold image of a cuckoo studded with eyes made of rubies and provided with legs made of silver, if they can afford to pay for it. If not, a figure made of pounded sissamun, *Til,* is substituted. They also worship the bird, if they can get a specimen. Then they fast until the evening. This process is repeated for a month. One condition attached to this observance of one-meal-a-day consists in taking no food at all if the cry of the cuckoo is not heard during its course.

*Desertations.*—This ceremonial is evidently based on astronomical phenomena. The solution of this interesting myth becomes easy on examining the first six signs of the Zodiac (see plate). Let us compare. The first one in the East is *Aries,* the ram-headed Daksha, the second is *Taurus* the bull, or Shiva's Nandi, the third is *Jemini,* the Mithun, or Shiva and Pārvati, the fourth is *Cancer,* the big bellied crab or the snouted, or elephant-headed Ganesh, the fifth is *Leo* the lion the charger of Sati, and the sixth *Virgo* or Sati herself. After thus imagining the family of Shiva, let us place the altitude of Virgo at the N.W. corner of the Indian horizon, above the city of Kanakhal, the place where the sacrifice is mythologically located. Added to this the *aurora borealis,* of the Western sky with its flaming red colour or the Himalayan scenery in the month of Ashādh may be compared with the fire of the sacrificial altar. To complete the figure we have only to add the well-known belief that the celestial bodies sink into the

Western ocean for rest and come out by the Eastern gate! It is their home. In this case the home of Daksha. Here then we have a complete picture. What remains to be accounted for is the connection of the twenty years' cycle, and the cuckoo-shaped constellation.

*The cycle.* Brennand tells us in his "Hindu Astronomy" (page 29) that "The Chaldeans had in use several cycles. They had also a period called the Saros, consisting of 223 complete lunations in 19 years, after the expiry of which period, the new and full-moons fall on the same days of the year." This is possibly the cycle represented by the *Kokila Vrat*, because the author further proves that "the astronomies of existing Eastern nations had a common origin." The Chaldean *Saros* is therefore the Indian *Kokila Vrat* cycle, and the moon represents Virabhadra rising from the matted hair of Shiva simultaneously at sunset with Kāli (night *i.e.* darkness) to destroy the glorious effect of the *aurora borealis*, to produce a visible prototype of the fall of Virgo as described below.

One constellation is called *Corvus*, literally a crow, but a crow resembles a cuckoo in shape and colour. Dr. J. T. White tells us in his Latin Dictionary that Corvus is akin to the Sanskrit root *kruc*, to cry. It is therefore necessary to hear the cry of the cuckoo before taking the evening meal! A crow is an unclean bird and therefore Hindus have substituted cuckoo for it. This constellation *Corvus* (crow, cuckoo) is in the altitude of Virgo just below it. Again it is said that Vishnu stood between Virabhadra and Daksha. But Vishnu is a manifestation of the Sun. His bright arm *Sudarshan* or the last rays of the Sun, were, it is said, swallowed by Virabhadra or the Moon with his reflected dull light and by Kāli, possibly a personification of darkness is this myth. Vishnu then went home, that signifies sunset. That so many things in this story should so closely fit in with the theory that this myth originated from a celestial phenomenon of the fall of Virgo as typified by similar oracular spectacle of the well-known *aurora borealis* at the time Virgo is in the West and the Corvus is in the same altitude in the lower hemisphere cannot be said to be a mere coincidences.

But there is another astronomical fact to be considered in connection with the mention in this folklore of the probable period of one hundred Deva's years after which Sati will be restored to her former position. A year of Deva's Brennand tells us, is equal to 360 of the Saura years. One hundred of Deva's years therefore would represent 36,000 (thirty-six thousand) of the Saura years (p. 177).

Taking these data, we find that the fall of Sati into the sacrificial fire records the fall of Virgo recorded by William Peck, F. R. A. S., in his work called "The Constellations and how to find them." He says "more than 2,000 years ago the middle of this constellation was on one of the Equinoctial Points (*i.e.*, the points where the Equinoctial cuts the Ecliptic), from which it has been called 'the first point of Aries:' but owing to the precession of the Equinoxes, or the motion of the axis of the earth round a perpendicular to the Eclipt the Equinoctial Points have moved to the right on the Ecliptic about 30 degrees, which gives the whole heavens an apparent motion round the pole of the Ecliptic in about 25,900 years. Thus Aries 2,000 years ago occupied the same position with regard to the Equinoctial as Pisces now does, but since then it has *apparently* moved to the left a whole sign; so that the *constellation* of Aries is now in the *sign* of Taurus, Taurus in Gemini, etc."

Here is the astronomical solution of the fall of Sati or Virgo. I give it in Peck's words:

"It is probably more than 4,000 years ago since the oldest star groups were first named, and by a people—as it is thought by some astronomers—who lived in a country at no great distance from Mount Ararat. At that time,—when the present names of the constellations were first invented—the heavens did not present the same appearance as they do at the present day; for we know that the earth, besides rotating on its axis and revolving round the sun, reels like a mighty gyroscope, but with so slow a motion that it takes nearly 25,900 years to make one complete revolution of its axis round an imaginary line perpendicular to the plane in which the earth moves."

These 25,900 years of 365.550 days each have to be reconciled with the 36,000 Saura years and we get the possible time at which Virgo or Sati will complete her cycle. For our purpose it is sufficient to say that Aries will then be the first visible sign on the horizon at the equinoctial point and Virgo the sixth or the last, that is just where she was before she jumped into the sacrificial fire!

This method of composing folklore from celestial phenomena was possibly introduced by the ancients to aid memory before the art of writing was invented. It is certainly the best method, and is even now followed in certain places. In course of time these stories became versified into mythological lyrics called the Puranās.

**Kshetra Vrat.**

Kshetra means a field, Kshetra-Devi is the fairy of the field. She is worshipped in Bengal on Saturdays in the month of Agrahāyan (October). The story runs that a boy named Bishu lost his father when he was only five years of age. He and his mother had to live with his maternal uncle as they had no one to support them. But the wife of the uncle was a cruel woman. She persecuted them, and inspite of caste restrictions, made Bishu work as a shepherd and his mother as a menial. Brahmans as they were, they felt the humiliation and propitiated Kshetra-Devi. When Bishu came to age his termàgant aunt turned him into a ploughman. He was so degraded in his position as a Brahman, that people nicknamed him Lāngla Bishu or ploughman Bishu. The food he received in exchange for wages was bad. His mother was half starved. She was forced to go begging, after finishing the drudgery of her daily duties and collect some food for her son. She used to take it to the field. But Bishu never took a morsel without first offering a portion to the goddess of the field. One day the mother was seen by the aunt feeding her son, and accused her of stealing food from her house. She had great influence over her husband. He therefore turned them out. They had no food. They went to the field to sleep in the open air without bed or covering. They were crying. At that moment the goddess or fairy appeared to them and gave them some grains. She advised them to sow them in another field lying fallow, and to go and sleep in an empty hut there. She also asked them to sell a very small portion to a Benia to get some food in exchange. They did so. After taking a repast they sowed the seed and went to bed. On rising, they were astonished to find the field full of a fine crop quite ready to harvest. The news reached the owner of the field. He went there, and saw these forlorn people and asked them to explain the phenomenon. They did so. He took them to his house, patronized them, and offered his own daughter to Bishu in marriage. They thus became rich. Bishu employed men and artisans to build a house for himself. In the mean time the aunt and the uncle lost every thing. They became poor and had to seek work. They came to the very village in which Bishu's house was being erected, and worked as coolies. They were recognized. Reconciliation followed. They returned laden with gold and became happy. They repented, and began worshipping the Kshetra-Devi in turn.

**Kushmānd 9th.**

The 9th of Kārtik is named after 'Kushmānd' the fruit of the *Cucurbita pepo,* as the story will explain :—

On this day the calabash—like large fruit of the *Cucurbita pepo* should be hollowed out, then filled up with gold, silver and jewels and finally given to a Brahman. The reward promised is residence in Heaven in proportion to the number of seeds removed to make room for the gems, and others. In the Kārtik Mahātmya *Pothi* (book) it is said that in the tract situated between the Ganges and the Godāvari, there was a city. In this city there lived a rich Brahman called Rāma Sharmā. He had two sons named Krishna and Dhananjaya respectively. After the demise of their father, they divided the property among themselves. Both lived the life of the profligate son known to Western scholars, and became very poor. They then left the city and lived in a forest the life of *dakāits*, and *shikāris.* On one occasion they charged a lion and were both killed. Their souls were taken to Yama the Pluto of India. Chandragupta the recorder of good and bad deeds was consulted, and he advised the transfer of one to Heaven and the other to Hell. Dhananjaya enquired on his way to Heaven why his brother was sent to Hell when they both had lived similar lives. The heavenly guide explained that while they both were studying the Vedās together, they were asked by their teachers to bathe in a river every morning during the month of Kārtik but he (Dhananjaya) bathed for three days while his brother Krishna never did so. One bath destroyed all his (Dhananjaya's) sins, the second secured for him a seat in Heaven, and the third would prove of use there. The brother solicited advice as to the way to obtain his brother's release from hell, and to attain a seat in heaven. The angel told him that on the 9th of Kārtik (October-November) a calabash fruit should be filled with gold, silver and gems and given to a Brahman. He did so in heaven, aud got a seat for his beloved brother.

**Lalita Panchami.** The fifth day of the moon's increase in the month of Ashwin (September-October), is sacred to

Lalita a form of Pārvati the wife of Shiva. The story runs, that in a certain town there lived two twin brothers, the orphans of Brahman parents. Their relatives mis-appropriated their father's property and turned them out. They wandered alone until they reached another town at mid-day. They were very hungry, poor souls! They were standing in the street when, as luck would have it, a Brahman came out to feed crows with the offerings he had just made to his ancestors. He saw them. That was a moment at which every good Hindu offers food to the hungry. He asked the boys who they were, and when he learned that they were of his own caste, he took them into his house, fed them, and asked them to tell him their little history. He ultimately kept them in his house as pupils and taught them the *Vedas*. They saw their patron performing the *Puja* of the goddess Lalita and begged of him to explain to them the object of performing it. He said, that it was the *Vrat* of Upāng Lalita Panchmi. Its performance grants education, wealth, and happiness. In fact it grants all the wishes of a devotee. They therefore began performing the *Puja*. They were very succeseful in their educational career and became rich. They got themselves married and ultimately returned to their own town. After a lapse of time, they lived separately. The elder brother punctually performed the *Puja*, the younger carelessly neglected it and became poor. He therefore returned to his elder brother with his wife and lived with him. One day, the wife of the elder brother, insulted the younger. He was angry. He repented his neglect of the *Puja*, and left the house to propitiate the goddess. His brother tried his best to trace his where abouts, but could not. The wanderer roamed over the country until he reached the city of Upāng. The king of the place was also named Upāng and the city goddess was called Upānd-Lalita. He went to the temple. He prostrated himself before the image of the goddess, begged forgiveness and worshipped her. He slept in an adjoining shed alloted to pilgrims. The goddess appeared to him in his dream, and advised him to see the king, to ask His Majesty to give him the lid of the box used for keeping turmeric and other powders for her worship, and to worship it devoutly. He did so, took it home, and resumed the worship. He again became rich and happy. He got a daughter. She was named Lalita after the goddess. One day, while she was bathing with her friends on the banks of the river that flowed near the city, she saw a dead body floating down the stream. Out of childish curiosity she threw some water on it, out of the lid she had in her hand. But lo! The man came to life! He looked so beautiful, so young and so attractive that she fell in love and asked him to marry her. But the poor young man got confused and said that as he was a penniless stranger, how could he induce her rich father to offer him such a gem! She suggested that she would invite him to a dinner and when he was seated there, he should refuse to eat a morsel unless she was offered to him. The first rule of Hindu hospitality would prevent her father from refusing to accede. He did so. He succeeded. He was married to the girl and received a big dower. On her way to her husband's house, Lalita took away that lid,—that charm which her father had received from the King of Upāng. This loss resulted in poverty to her parents. The mother asked the daughter to return the lid, but she refused to do so. The dame was angry, and became vindictive. One day she met her son-in-law on her way to the river, killed him, and carried away the charm. But the daughter had continued her devotion to the goddess and therefore her husband came to life again. He returned home hale and hearty, and told his wife what had happened. She was overjoyed at his escape. The mother-in-law heard of the good luck of her daughter and son-in-law. She went to their house, and expressed her regret at the stupid blunder she committed in a fit of anger. But the sin she had committed resulted in reducing her to abject poverty. Her husband could not account for these ups and downs and went to his elder brother for advice. His brother explained to him the cause. It was simply his gross neglect of the *Vrat.* He advised him to be more punctual and devotional. The young brother promised to follow this advice, returned home, and resumed the *Puja.* His poverty disappeared. He became rich and all his wishes were satisfied. May the reader be equally happy and prosperous!

**The Lamp-Day.** Distinct from the Divāli, which is a well-known period of annual festivities, is another day called the *Dipāmāvāsya* or the last day of Ashād (June-July) devoted to the worship of the family lamps or *dips.* There is a folk-lore story attached. The adage that Lamps bring Wealth has for its text

*Dipam Laxmikaraṃ.*

In the city of Govindpati in the Tamil country, so runs the tale, there was a banker called Pashupati Sheti. He had two children, one son and one daughter respectively named Vinita and Gauri. These two promised each other, that when they had become adults, they would contract marriages between their children if found suitable for a matrimonial match. Gauri, the sister, was married to the son of a very rich man. There were three daughters born to her. The youngest was named Saguna, the good-natured. Vinita, the brother, had three sons born unto him. But fate intervened, and these children could not be married. Pashupati Sheti got involved in financial transactions and after his demise, his creditors sold all his property. Vinita thus became very poor, while his sister remained immensely rich. But he was a very sensible man, he bore his misfortune with manliness and with courage. He curtailed his expenses, brought them down to the level of the present day circumstances and lived like an ordinary *rayat.*

Rich Gauri, his elated sister, did not feel inclined to keep her promise. She thought it below her dignity to marry her daughters to the sons of a poor man though her only brother. She therefore selected two millionaire families for her first two daughters and got them married to their scions. The youngest was still unmarried. Vinita was very sorry for the change in his sister's temperament. He always thought that his once affectionate sister would not forget him in his adversity, but he never spoke to anybody about his disappointment. The mutual promises of the brother and sister were, however, no secret, and many people came to console the brother and to express regret at the breach of promise of the sister. They threw the whole blame on her. This public reproach reached the ears of Saguna, the youngest daughter. She was very sorry to see her mother transgressing the limit of the unwritten code of society. She was always pleased to find her poor uncle a typical member of the genteel society—honest, sober, modest, obliging, and good-natured. Vinita's sons were also very good boys and were equally popular. She was very sorry to see that her parents selected the sons of rich people for her two sisters. It is an unpardonable breach of etiquette in a young girl to mention her own selection of a husband. Saguna however gathered courage enough to meekly place before her mother her decision as to her own choice of her husband. She said: "Mother, is it really so that you promised to marry your daughters to uncle Vinita's sons? and that you have broken that promise in getting my elder sisters married to outsiders? May I respectfully take the liberty of reminding you of that promise in my humble case? I feel humiliated when girls tease me about your broken solemn promise. I have made up my mind to marry our uncle's youngest son or to remain unmarried all the days of my life." Gauri, the mother, was astonished at this little speech. She got excited and expostulated. "Wretched girl!" said she, "are you going to marry a beggar? No, we sha'n't marry you to that boy, and if you dare insist, beware, once you are given away to that fellow, we shall never see your face again! We shall be dead to you and you to us!"

Sagūna was very sorry to see her mother so angry, but she did not change her resolute decision. She had to be married to her cousin, in spite of the objections of her parents to a matrimonial alliance with poor people. Vinita never spoke to his sister on this subject. He had resolved to postpone his sons' marriages until all his sister's daughters were married. When he heard of Saguna's determination to marry his youngest son he was greatly delighted. He therefore selected brides for his first two sons, as no younger brother could, according to custom, be married before the elder ones were matched. The marriages over, Sagūna remained happy and contented with her lot, so much so that the girls of her age began emulating her. Daughter of a millionaire, free from false pride and mean vanity, she was seen working with cow-dung cakes, fetching water from the river like an ordinary poor man's wife, and mixing freely with girls of the poorer classes. She proved a very obedient daughter-in-law and served her father-in-law, mother-in-law, and brothers-in-law most heartily and meekly. Vinita and his sons used to go to the jungle every morning to collect fresh figs (*Ficus Indica*) leaves for stitching into plates and cups, and the women of the household had to shape them, with reed pins. They were sold at one anna per hundred. So modest was their income that they had to do all their work without the help of a single servant. But Saguna commanded so much respect from her own people, that although she was the youngest, all the family income was handed over to her and she regulated the expenses of the day in proportion to the sale proceeds. After the male members were fed, the poor women had to distribute the remnants among themselves and to be satisfied with what was left unused, or to pass the day without any food. But they were all contented and happy. Sagūna was considered the Devi or goddess of the household and all loved and respected her. Her cruel parents never thought of her. They did not even care to enquire if she was dead or alive.

Time passed. Time waits for nobody. One day, the King of the realm placed a lucky nine-gem ring in a niche while bathing. A kite lifted it up and carried it away. It was a valuable jewel and a talisman. While flying over Vinita's house, the kite dropped the ring in front of Sagūna who was smearing her court-yard with cow-dung. At the sound of the fall, Sagūna turned her head to see what it was. It was a valuable jewel. She carried it into the house and placed it in trust in front of the family Gods where a lamp was burning. The lamp is the emblem of honesty. The lamp is the giver of fortune. "*Dipam Laxmikaram!*"

A *batāki* was beaten in the after-noon announcing the loss of the Mahārāja's nine-gem talisman ring and offering a big reward to any one restoring it to His Majesty. Sagūna heard the town-crier's call and on the return home of the males, she placed the ring before them. She then respectfully suggested that they should all go to the Mahārāja to tell him of the find and to say that as she found the jewel she should be allowed personally to return it and to mention her own wishes as regards the promised reward. They agreed to follow her advice, went to the palace, and delivered the message. The King granted her an audience. While placing the ring before the King, she described how she got it. The King was so pleased with her modesty and courteous behaviour that he asked her to name her reward.

"Mahārājā-dhirāj," said Saguna, "this humble subject of your Majesty has but one desire. On a Friday it should be ruled that there be no light in the capital, not even in the palace, and that your Majesty's humble subject alone be allowed to illuminate her poor cottage." The King smiled, and said "Granted, to-morrow is Friday and your wishes shall be fulfilled."

The girl bowed and left the court. Next morning she handed over to her father-in-law the only necklace she had left to her, out of her jewellery, and asked him to sell it. She fasted. In the afternoon, she told her brothers-in-law that she had arranged to buy buntings and lamps of sorts and to illuminate the whole of their house. She earnestly requested them to help her in keeping a close watch at both the doors, without taking a wink. She then told them that a richly dressed group of women would try to enter the house. Before allowing them to enter, they should be made to promise that they would never leave the house again. They should be made to take an oath to that effect, and then respectfully escorted. If on the other hand a woman in rags begged permission to go out by the back-door, she should also be compelled to swear that she would never return to this house.

The brothers-in-law thought this a fit of madness, but they knew that Saguna was a sagacious girl and promised to carry out her wishes scrupulously.

The whole household was anxious to see what was in store for them. The whole of the city was enveloped in darkness. Saguna's was the only house where bright lights were burning. The eight-fold group of Laxmi or the goddess of wealth searched in vain for a resting place until they came to Saguna's house. They tried to enter but were stopped by the honest guard. He compelled them all—eight in number—to take the oath of never leaving the premises, and then allowed them to enter. Their presence in the house was a signal for a ragged old woman to leave hurriedly the abode she had occupied for years. She was ugly and repulsive. She begged permission to fly away, but was made to take the oath of never returning. While crossing the threshhold, she muttered "I am the goddess of poverty, the elder sister of those eight goddesses who have just entered by the front door. I dare not stay where they are. May God bless you all. I do solemnly affirm that I shall never come to this house again." She then ran away in hot haste.

With the next morn, there came a complete metamorphosis of the house—graneries innumerable, treasures of gold mohurs, milk-jugs overflowing and the eight beauties working heart and soul to fill up every receptacle with luxuries of sorts. Saguna's wisdom became the most interesting subject of conversation all over the city. Every one called her the *Avātar* or incarnation of the Goddess Laxmi.

The King paid a visit of deference to the family and showered honours on the old father and his three sons. Saguna's parents repented their haughtiness in neglecting her and went to her house to beg her pardon. All became happy.

This is the reason why Friday is kept sacred to the Goddess of wealth. Friday evening-twilight is considered the time of the arrival of Laxmi at one's house. At that time it is considered lucky to concentrate all attention on the Goddess, to discard all wild talk, and the absence of a lamp at that hour on Friday is not tolerated. Every Hindu house has always a lamp at least near the *Tulsi* plant opposite the front door on all Friday evenings. Laxmi is worshipped, and parched gram and sugar-candy are distributed by the chief married lady of the house. One day in the year all the lamps in the house are artistically arranged within an auspicious drawing on the floor and devoutly worshipped by the married ladies of the household. Sweets are prepared as *naivedya* or offerings to the God of Light, and served at the meal. All this because, "*Dipam Laxmi karam*"—*Lamp brings wealth.*

**Lamp-Day** (in Bengal). There was a king in a certain city. His young daughter-in-law one day stealthily ate some sweets and falsely accused rats of the offence. All the rat tribe of the palace held a protest meeting and resolved that the girl be punished for that wickedness. They therefore conspired in placing her bodice in the bed of a guest. When this was discovered, the girl was disgraced and turned out. But she had been very carefully observing the *vrat* of the lamp day. She used to polish and clean all the brass, silver and gold lamps very carefully and to worship them, keeping them burning all the night. The rats were jubilant over the revenge but the lamps were very sorry. On the following lamp-day, it so happened that the king was resting under a tree after a good day's hunting expedition. Curious to behold, he saw that the lamps of all the houses in his capital held a meeting on the branches of the tree. Each of them was relating his experiences as to the dainties prepared in its owner's house, or the interesting incidents which brightened the prospects of the family. While this was going on, the chief lamp of the Royal Palace sat dejected and seemed to be very sorry. It related its loss of the premier position it held in such meetings, as it was always the brightest and the most luminous. When asked to explain the cause, it stated that the good and virtuous daughter-in-law of the king who cleaned and worshiped it had been turned out on a false charge trumped up by the wicked rats of the palace. The loss of its position was due to the absence of the valuable services she rendered. The king could overhear this conversation. His Majesty repented of the hasty step taken in expelling his daughter-in-law, went home, made fresh enquiries, could get no direct proof of the crime of which she was accused, sent a palanquin for her, expressed his regret at the injustice done to her, re-instated her, and made her the chief controller of the palace.

**Laxmi.** Laxmi, the Hindu goddess of prosperity, is called also Sri, Padma, Hira, Indra, Jaladhija (ocean-born), Chanchala or Lola (the fickle, as goddess of fortune), Loka-māta, mother of the people, and other names. There are several legends as to her origin. The Taittiriya Sanhita describes Laxmi and Sri as two wives of Aditya. The Satapatha Brahmana describes Sri as issuing forth from Prajāpati. The Rāmāyan legend makes her spring forth from the ocean, like Aphrodite, in full beauty, with a lotus in her hand, when it was churned by the Asurās and the gods hence called Kshirābdhitanaya, daughter of the sea of milk. According to the Purānas, she was the daughter of Bhrigu and Khyāta, and she was the wife of Vishnu in all his incarnations. These legends are all comparatively modern, for though in the Rig Veda the word Laxmi occurs, it is not a goddess personifying good fortune, but one of a kindred significance.

As the consort of Vishnu, she is painted yellow, sitting on the lotus or water-lily and holding in her hand sometimes the *Kamala* or lotus, at others the shell, or the club of Vishnu. At her birth, she was so beautiful that all the gods became enamoured of her, but Vishnu at length obtained her. She is the Hindu Ceres, or goddess of abundance; Sri, goddess of prosperity. She is called Padma or Kamala, from the lotus or nymphæa being sacred to her; also Varāhi (as the energy of Vishnu in the Varāha *avatar*); Ādi Māya, the first mother Nārāyani, etc. She is also described as the daughter of a man-Bhrigu; but in consequence of the curse of Durvāsa upon India, she abandoned the three worlds and concealed herself in the sea of milk, so that the earth no longer enjoyed the blessings of abundance and prosperity.

"Queen of the gods, she leapt to land,
A lotus in her perfect hand;
And fondly, of the lotus sprung,
To lotus-bearing Vishnu clung,

Her, gods above and men below,
As beauty's queen and fortune, know."

When as Ramā, the sea-born goddess of beauty, she sprang as one of the fourteen gems from the ocean, she assumed the character of the Venus Aphrodite of the Greeks, who, as Hesiod and Homer sing, arose from the sea, ascended to Olympus, and captivated all the gods.

The followers of Vishnu esteem Laxmi as the mother of the world, and then call her Adi Māya.

The name of this goddess is given to the last stalks of grain which the Hindus, as the Scotch, carry home from the field and preserve until the next harvest; and from all who desire that prosperity attend their efforts, she receives adoration.

In the Belgaum district, until the early part of the 19th century Maha Laxmi was regarded as the goddess on whom the productiveness of the land depended.

The Maratha cultivators are still attentive to her worship, and when the *rabi* crops are well above the ground, they proceed to their fields, where they place five stones around a tree, on which they set spots of vermilion and some wheaten flour; they worship these as the five Pāndavs. In the evening they take a few stalks of *sorghum*, with a lamp surrounded by a cloth, to their homes, which they regard as their Laxmi. It is an interesting sight to see the wives of the cultivators each returning to her home with her lit-up basket of sorghum. The ceremonial is performed on the 28th day of the moon, *Amās*, which in 1867 coincided with the Christmas day. The Hindus have other things which they adopt as their Laxmi or luck-token.

In Rajputana, in one festival, Laxmi is depicted by the type of riches. She is evidently the beneficent Anna Purna in another garb. The agricultural community place a corn-measure, filled with grain and adorn her effigies, they are those of Padma, the water nymph, with a lotus in one hand and the *pāsh* (or fillet for the head) in the other. She should not be confounded with Rambha, chief of the Apsaras, the Venus of the Hindus. Though both were created from the froth (*sara*) of the waters (*ap*), they are as distinct as the representations of riches and beauty can be. Laxmi is the wife of Vishnu, and is represented at the feet of his marine couch, when he is floating on the chaotic waters.

Laxmi has no temples, but, being the goddess of abundance and good fortune, she is assiduously courted, and is not likely to fall into neglect. She is worshipped on the new moon of Aswin (September-October), by bankers and merchants especially. A ceremony in her honour is performed by a bride and bridegroom when the bride has been brought to her husband's house.

Gaja-Laxmi, in the Ellora caves is represented with a lotus in her hand, and four attendant elephants, who are pouring water over her.

She is called Lakkhi in Bengal where it is believed that Indra the King of Gods, was once cursed by Saint Durvāsa with the result that he was reduced to poverty. The gods shared the misfortune. They went to Vishnu and propitiated his wife Laxmi. They became rich again.

She is worshipped in Bengal in two ways. (1) A clay figure is prepared, painted yellow, and suitably dressed. She holds a lotus flower in each hand and sits on the same floral throne. (2) In the second form she is represented by symbols. A basket is filled up with paddy, half a cocoanut is placed over it. To its right is placed a *kowri* shell. *(Cypress moneta)* filled with water. A shoe-flower (*Hibiscus rosa sinsensis*) is added. To the left of the cocoanut is placed a model of a granary made of plantain sheaths, and the whole thing is covered with red cloth. This covered symbol is then placed on a low stool decorated with coloured drawings of which the footprints of the goddess form an important part. Owls are drawn on the floor on either side of the seat.

The articles necessary for the *puja* are, a seat made of *Kusha* grass [*Eragrotis Cynosuroides*] a shell, a pair of copper vessels, flowers, rice, *durva* grass *(cynodon dactylon)* yellow myrobolan, sesamum seed, betel leaf, lotus, sandal-wood paste, *ghi*, milk, parched paddy, rice, sugar, sugarcane, *kowri* shells fruits, eatables specially prepared, betel nuts, and cocoanuts. The conch *Turbinella pyrum* or other shells required for her worship possibly refer to her birth and her connection as goddess of wealth to the *kowries* (the *Cypress moneta)* the primitive coin of India. The *kowri* is itself Laxmi—the wealth of the ancients. The lotus is a flower sacred to Vishnu, his son Brahma in born out of a lotus, and therefore there is nothing special is his spouse using it as a throne, or holding it in her hands. The paddy and the basket for storing it are peculiar to Bengal and along with the barn owl connect her with the harvest season. The footprints shown as if she is entering the house are significant, but above all there are three symbols which indicate the inter-mixture of the Shaivite worship of the female organ of generation. They are the (1) triangle, (2) the double triangle, and the *shankh-lata* or the creeper with conch-shells worked up into it. The opening of the conch-shell has the resemblance of the *yoni*. Bengal worships Kāli the consort of Shiva and every ceremony is connected with her. This is possibly a modern innovation due to the increasing influence of the Shāktas. The barn owl, is given a seat near the Goddess of Wealth and is actually worshipped along with her.

That Laxmi should be painted yellow is natural as she represents gold; that she should have a corn measure indicates the time of storing corn, and the paddy basket is the actual wealth adored as Laxmi. Laxmi is worshipped on the *Divāli* day all over India, but in the West there is no image, a trayful of the silver or gold coin of the day, suffices. Laxmi is never invoked by herself in the Western Presidency. She is always worshipped along with her husband Nārāyan, who is accepted as the giver of wealth as in the following translation of a couplet :

"If the husband of Kamla begins to give you with his thousands of hands (innumerable) how much can you take with the only two you possess ?"

There are temples dedicated to Laxmi-Nārāyan, and none dedicated to Laxmi alone, except as Maha Laxmi or the great Goddess of wealth, where she is enthroned and attended by two white elephants who are shewn pouring water over her head or holding lotus flowers. She is shewn squatting, and not with her right leg resting on another lotus used as a foot stool. In Bombay, white elephants take the place of the owls of Bengal.

The Bengal Laxmi is worshipped generally by the dame or priest of a house on a Thursday of the bright half of the months of *Pausha* (January) *Chaitra* (March) and *Bhādra* (August) of every year, and specially on the full-moon day of the month of *Aswin* (September) on the new-moon-day of Kārtik (October). It is believed that she should not be worshipped on any other days. Her worship should be solemnized in the evening not in the afternoon, nor at night. [ *Skandh Purān* ].

It may be noted that in the Bombay Presidency the worship of Laxmi with liquid lamp takes place on a Friday at twilight, while in Bengal it takes place on a Thursday.

An up-to-date Bengal tradition of Laxmi runs :—Once upon a time Laxmi sent her son Kubera to her daughter Bhushna to instruct her in her own history. Kubera asked her to listen to the story of Laxmi, but she replied that she could not do so, as by mistake she had chewed betel leaf that morning. Another day Kubera went and asked Bhushna to listen to the story, but on that day she said that she had herself cooked rice for her children and as she was hungry she had partaken of it on that morning. A third time did Kubera go again to Bhushna for the same purpose. Bhushna on that day was so angry that she threw her bracelet at Kubera and wounded him on his forehead. Kubera was never assaulted by any body before. He thought, if his wound were seen by his mother she would surely curse Bhushna and put her into great trouble. So he, instead of going to his mother wandered about here and there during the whole day and went home in the evening. Laxmi called him and made him to sit upon her lap. While examining his body with motherly affection she saw the wound and asked him how he got it. Kubera in order to protect his sister said—" Mother, while running in the street, I suddenly fell down and got wounded." Hearing this Laxmi was very angry with the Goddess Earth, she called her to her presence and said—" Oh Earth, as you have injured my son Kubera, I will withdraw your fertility." The Earth was afraid and replied—"Oh Mother, what power have I to injure your son? I never did it." Laxmi suspected Bhushna, and asked Kubera if she did it, but Kubera denied by saying that the wound was caused by a fall from a tree. Laxmi called the tree and said—" Oh tree, as you have injured my son I will cut you to pieces." The tree was frightened and replied—" Mother, what power have I to injure your son? I never did it." Laxmi then understood that the wound was surely caused by her daughter Bhushna and not by any body else, in as much as no one dare injure her son.

Thereupon Lakshmi cursed her daughter Bhushna in the following words :—" Bhushna, whereas you, through arrogance of your wealth, have injured my hitherto uninjured son Kubera, you shall lose all your beauties and shall be an eyesore to your husband—the King." Bhushna's charms disappeared, her ornaments made of gold and precious stones were transformed into iron. Her husband's horses and elephants were burnt to death, and he was, so displeased with her, that he ordered his hangman to kill her and to bring to him her blood. The hangman took her into a forest and said—" Queen-mother, I have been brought up by you, so it will be an ungrateful act to kill you. Moreover, Kings are fickle-minded men and act according to the advice of their ministers without looking into the good or bad side of a thing. I know not if our King will ask me one day to bring back his Queen. So you may go to your father's house. I will get the blood of some dogs and cats and take it to the King." After saying this the hangman went away.

Night came, and she took shelter under a banian tree. After some hours there came a huge boa constrictor to devour Bhushna but it was burnt to ashes by her breath. There lived a pair of birds on that banian tree. Their young one asked the mother-bird—"Mother, when will my eyes be opened?" The mother said "When the lady who is now under this tree will anoint your eyelids with the blood of her little finger, then your eyelids will be opened. But this lady is in great distress; you should in return for her service to you, help her by carrying her to Laxmi." Bhushna heard this and climbing the tree anointed the eyelids of the bird with the blood of her little-finger, the eye-lids were opened instantly. The grateful bird carried Bhushna on its back to the Laxmi Forest.

There was a large lake in the Laxmi Forest. Nārāyan the father of Bhushna and husband of Laxmi used to bathe in this water. So the maid servants of Nārāyan came there to fetch water. Bhushna asked them—"Who will bathe with the water you are taking?" Bhushna dropped her ring into a jar, and the maids did not know this. When Nārāyan was bathing he found the ring in the water and reproached the maids, saying. "Well, wherever you find anything, you like to pour it on my head. Here is a ring. I know not if it is with a good or bad intent that you have dropped it on my head. Tell me where you got this." They said—"Lord! we are but servants; we do not know the virtue of the ring. While we were fetching water from the lake in the Laxmi forest we saw a very ugly woman. She talked about you and Laxmi. She might have thrown it into the jar without our knowledge." Hearing this, Nārāyan went to the lake and found that the ugly looking lady was none other but his daughter Bhushna. She began to weep when she saw her father and told him everything that had befallen her. Nārāyan instructed her to cry loudly uttering the names of her father and mother, when the bell calling him to come to his breakfast rang. He turned back and bathed. While going to his breakfast he heard the cry and asked Laxmi "who was crying." Laxmi knew that her daughter was crying, but suppressing that she said—"Somebody in distress." Nārāyan said—"No doubt; but I think it is my beloved daughter Bhushna who is in distress. I hear our names called out." Hearing this Laxhmi said—"When a man grows old he loses his common sense and such is the case with you, otherwise you could not apprehend the distress of Bhushna. She is a queen; how should she be in distress? Old fool! mind your own business, and let not the cry disturb you."

Nārāyan said that he could not eat unless he ascertained who was crying. He went to the spot and brought Bhushna home, and asked Laxmi to forgive her. Laxmi was obliged to favour Bhushna and to remove all her calamities.

Bhushna was called back by her husband, the King, and with him lived a happy life. While Bhushna was going to her husband's place she was instructed by her mother not to again forget to worship Laxmi in proper time and to listen to her *purān*. From that time Bhushna never forgot her duty to listen the sacred *purān* of Laxmi. Her husband, when he became aware of the power of Laxmi, prepared a golden image of her and kept in his house.

The text ends with the following para.:

Here the 'story' of Laxmi has gone home, after conferring boons upon the housewife. Do worship Laxmi in *Pausha, Chaitra* and *Bradra*—the three harvest seasons, and never let Laxmi go out of your house.

Quite human is this tradition. The origin, manifesttation and worship are given in the Prakriti Khandam of the Brahma-Vaivasta purān, Vishnu puran and Tantrāsāra.

**Laxmi Puja in the month of Chaitra in Bengal.**

One day the God Nārāyan (Vishnu) was coming down to the earth, Laxmi requested him to take her with him. He did so on condition that she would strictly carry out his instructions. He got down from his chariot in one place and asked Laxmi to wait there for him, forbidding her to look towards the south. But her curiosity was raised, and as soon as her husband went out of sight she did look in that direction. She saw there a field of sesamum.

She picked up a few flowers, and decorated her hair, neck and ears with them. On his return the God Nārāyan was annoyed to see his own wife disobeying his orders, and explained to her the Law of the Land. He said that the Law of the day punished the crime of stealing Sesamum flowers by enforced labour for 12 years in the house of the cultivator. Like Daniel, he insisted on her undergoing that punishment. There was no appeal. He disguised himself as an old Brahman went to the owner of the field with his wife transformed into a Brahman woman, and handed her over to him.

Laxmi found that the poor man had no food in his house, that his sons had gone out begging and that the whole family was practically starving. She pitied them and asked one of the daughters-in-law to take a bath, worship her goddess, and then go to her kitchen where she would find every thing ready for her to cook. She also asked one girl after another to open her box after the worship. They obeyed and were all astonished to find them full of clothes and ornaments! The whole household felt indebted to the new comer and served her, instead of exacting service from her for the offence of stealing flowers. But there was one exception. The second daughter-in-law! She was a peevish and very quarrelsome girl and she always annoyed Laxmi. In her turn, Laxmi never accepted anything offered by her or through her. If she brought her food, it was buried under a pomegranate tree. Time runs fast, twelve years passed away. The prisoner Laxmi was free! It was a Baruni day, a festival, held on the 13th of the waning moon of *Chaitra* (March-April). The old mother-in-law of the girls asked Laxmi to accompany her to the Ganges for a bath as she was going with all her family. Laxmi excused herself and remained indoors, but handed over five *kowri* (*Cypress moneta*) shells as her offerings to the goddess of the sacred stream. After the ceremonial bath and worship of Laxmi the eldest daughter-in-law threw the five shells she had received from her guest. Curious to behold; out of the water issued four hands to catch them! This miracle confirmed the suspicion that the prisoner was a goddess in disguise. On return home, they found the old Brahman (God Nārāyan) waiting for them to claim his wife at the expiration of her penal servitude. On release, she disclosed herself and said—" Dig up the things I have from time to time buried under that tree, and you will find sufficient wealth to make you rich. In the treasure there, you will find a separate box containing a necklace. It is intended for the second daughter-in-law.

Do not forget to perform my *Puja* in *Bhādrapad, Kārtik, Paushya*, and *Chaitra*. If you do that, you will never be in want again. Her instructions were carefully followed. The box was handed over to the second daughter-in-law. As soon as she opened it a cobra issued forth and mortally bit her! All the others received valuable jewels and were happy.

**Laxmi Puja in Bengal.** The story runs that a Brahman widow with an only son was so poor that she had to work as a spinner to eke out a living. On a banian tree (*Ficus indica*) in front of her house, there lived a pair of owls employed in the palace of Laxmi the Goddess of Wealth. They had two young ones. During the absence of the parent birds on duty, the Brahman boy used to feed them with whatever he could spare out of his scanty meals. They felt grateful and spoke to their parents of the kindness of the boy and added that something should be done in return. The parents took the boy to the palace of the Goddess Laxmi and presented him to their mistress. While on their way to the palace, the boy was tutored not to accept any gift in gold or jewels, but to beg of the goddess to give him a sheaf of Gingly plant (*Sesamum orientale*). When therefore the goddess offered a substantial reward to the boy, he respectfully declined the offer and asked for a sheaf of the Sesamum called *Til Dhubri*. He got it. He was advised to worship it as the symbol of the goddess every day, and to offer special *puja* to the goddess herself in the months of Bhādrapad (August-September), Kārtik (October-November), Paushya (December-January) and Chaitra (March-April). He was taken back to his home, he followed the instruction and became rich. This created jealousy, the news reached the king, he also became jealous and forcibly took away the sacred sesamum sheaf. The Brahman boy and his mother again became poor, the birds again pitied them, and again begged the goddess—their mistress to help them; she mysteriously transferred the sesamum sheaf to their house, and the worship was resumed. They however became wiser and secreted the sheaf in a safe place. The king again heard of the opulence of the Brahman boy, was afraid that his wealth would enable him to collect a sufficient army to depose him, and out of policy, offered his own daughter to him in marriage. They were married, lived a happy life, and left behind a numerous and prosperous family of princes and princessess. When they died, celestial chariots were sent to convey their souls to *Vaikuntha*, Vishnu's and therefore Laxmi's heaven.

**Laxmi Puja (In Paushya).** In the month of Paushya Laxmi is worshipped in Bengal. The story runs that there lived a poor widow with one daughter and seven sons. She went to her brother's wife for help and was asksd to do menial's work, in exchange for the bran and broken grain that was allowed to be removed. One day she asked for a few leaves of the pumpkin. That little favour was denied and she was stopped from visiting the house again. It was a Thursday, the poor widow was much distressed. She felt so miserable that she wanted to poison herself and her children! With this intention she picked up a dead snake, she put it on the fire to cook and began the worship of the goddess for the last time, as she thought. The goddess was pleased. On her return she wondered why yellow froth floated over the liquid. Her son collected a small quantity. It quickly dried and produced a powder. He took it to a goldsmith who found it to be gold-dust and bought it. The pot was boiled whenever the old widow wanted money, the froth was collected and sold and with the proceeds the family lived in happiness. When her brother's wife saw that she was well-to-do, that her daughter was married to a rich Zemindār, and her sons were married to brides from very opulent families, she invited them all to dinner. The daughters-in-law of the widow had heard of the evil treatment their old mother-in-law had received. When therefore the plates were placed before them, instead of eating food themselves they began placing handfuls on their clothes and ornaments! The hostess was asked to "give some boiled pumpkin leaves," she understood the taunt, knew what it meant and expressed her regret. Reconciliation followed. Then she enquired how the widow acquired wealth and was advised to perform the *Vrat*. She did so, and became equally rich and happy.

**Laxmi Puja**, the story as current in Bengal runs:—

There lived a king who had five daughters. One day, he asked the queen and the princesses to whose good luck they owed their happiness. All of them said that it depended on the king's fortune. But his youngest daughter said, "Every one depends on his or her own fate." The king was much annoyed and threatened to give her in marriage to the first man he would meet the following morning. An old Brahman overhead it and left his son at the palace gate. The king gave his daughter in marriage to the Brahman's son, gave him a small sum as dowry and told his daughter to go away to depend on her own luck. The daughter quietly saluted the king, and followed her husband and father-in-law. They reached a cottage in another king's dominion. There the princess was received by the mother-in-law. She lived there contented, did all domestic work, and used to eat even the the leavings of the family. One day the princess told her husband to bring home whatever he found on the road. The husband brought a dead cobra and gave it to his wife, She advised him to keep it aside. The son of the king was taken ill. All medical aid proved useless. At last, a medical practitioner said "I can cure the prince if I get at once the head of a dead cobra." But it was not to be so quickly found any where. At last the minister proclaimed by a beat of the drum that whoever could produce the head of a dead cobra would get whatever he wanted. It was produced by the princess through her father-in-law, and so the prince was cured. After a few days, the king sent for the Brahman. The daughter-in-law instructed her father-in-law not to accept any thing offered by the king but to say "I wish your Majesty would kindly issue a proclamation prohibiting the burning of any light in the palace or in any other house on the dark night of the *Amāvāsya* of Kārtik." So there was no light in any house on that particular night. The Brahman's daughter-in-law cleaned her house, kept ready a platform, placed a vessel, rice, flower, sandal and wreaths. She fasted the whole day, burned many lights and awaited the arrival of the goddess Laxmi.

The goddess Laxmi riding a barn owl went all over the kingdom. But there was no light. She could only find it in the Brahman's cottage. She alighted there. The princess bowed unto her, took her to the platform, seated her there and supplicated and begged her to accept the offerings: Ths goddess was pleased and said: "Your poverty is at an end. I leave my anklet. Perform my *puja* in this way in the months of *Bhadra, Kartick, Paush* and *Chaitra*. Never be ill-tempered, never complain of want, live a chaste life," she then disappeared. The family became very rich. They began feeding and giving alms to the poor. They constructed a pond, and invited all the Brahman *pandits* and learned men to a feast. The princess remained seated behind a window whence she could see every visitor. Many people assembled, among them, to her great astonishment, she saw her father whom she at once recognised. He was reduced to poverty for neglecting the worship of the goddess Laxmi. The daughter offered him a silver stool and gold plate at the dinner. The king while eating began weeping. His daughter asked the reason. The guest said that he was once a king. He had a daughter resembling her. He married her to a poor Brahman. He did not know whether she was still alive. The princess was also in tears and said that she herself was his deserted daughter. The father and the daughter were then reconciled. The daughter advised her father to perform Laxmi *Puja*. The king returned to his house. The princess was taken to her mother. The king began to perform the Laymi *Puja* and thereby regained his former throne. He reigned for some time and died leaving the daughter and son-in-law as his heirs to the throne. They in turn reigned for some time, and died full of years leaving sons and daughters and instructing them to perform the Laxmi *Puja*.

(*See* Divāli for the Bombay Folklore. Compare also Lamp day folkfore of which this is a variant).

**Laxmi (Maha).**

*Mahālaxmi Puja.* On the eighth day of the first half of Ashwin the Vaishnavās worship Mahālaxmi as distinguished from the *Shaiva puja* and animal sacrifices of the latter sect. In the story ascribed to this ceremony it is said that there was once a king with two wives, the elder called Rāni Pātamādhav and the younger Rāni Chimādevi. He had an enemy called Nandanbaneshwar, who could, like a magician, dive or rise to the sky or disappear, and therefore the King could not kill him. When much annoyed, the King caused to be declared that all the male residents of his city should go in pursuit and destroy him. One poor old woman had a son. He asked his mother to give him some food, but she had only a few crumbs. She advised him to walk faster than other people, to go to a secluded placc to eat his bread, and to avoid being seen with that poor stuff as it would disclose his poverty. He did so. Night overtook him. When the King and the other citizens returned he was left behind. When he was alone in the jungle, at midnight there appeared some fairies and some Nāg-Kanyās or daughters of the Nāg people (snake). They worshipped Mahālaxmi by taking certain thread or charms from their necks. They blew a peculiar musical instrument. It was made by tying a leaf over the mouth of a water pot and passing a thread through it. He asked what was the use of doing all this. They explained that the goddess grants all desire. At twilight the Goddess returned to "Kolhāpur (sic) but before she left the worshippers asked for blessings, which were granted, The old woman's son had also perfomed the *puja*, and so he too begged for a blessing. The goddess said that the great enemy of the King whom he dreaded so much, would die, that the King would be pleased with him, that he would give him half of the territory over which he ruled and half the contents of the royal treasury, that he would build for him a new palace, and that his Majesty would give him a new name, namely Navalvāt. As soon as the sun rose, the elder queen saw that the demon was lying dead in front of the palace! She informed the King of it. His Majesty inquired who killed the demon. Every body denied all knowledge, but it was discovered that the old woman's son had not yet returned home. People therefore guessed that he must have killed the enemy. The King sent for the man. He was just returning. He was frightened. He asked the King why he was sent for. The King showed him the corpse of his enemy and asked him whether he had destroyed him. He explained what happened. He was given half the kingdom and the treasure and a palace as promised by the goddess. The elder queen asked him to show her how the fairies worshipped Mahālaxmi. He did so. She followed his instructions. But on one day the King happened to see the thread. He asked her to explain why she wore a wretched cotton thread when she could afford gold and jewels. She explained, but he felt no reverence, and threw it away. A maid servant found it while sweeping the hall. She gave it to the old woman's son. He handed it over to the younger queen. On the following eighth day of Ashwin (September-October) she worshipped the goddess. Mahālaxmi came to the place to see how she was worshipped. She had assumed the form of an old woman. She at first went to the room of the elder queen. She asked her if there was any ceremony in her house. The queen said there was none. The goddess asked for a potful of water, it was denied; she asked for rice and sour milk or *dahi*. She was denied that favour. The goddess then cursed the queen. She ordained that the elder queen be turned into half woman half frog, to wade in the dirty water from the bath of the second queen. The elder queen was so conceited that she laughed at the apparent old hag! The goddess turned to the quarters of the junior queen. She saw that her *puja* was in full swing there. She revealed herself to her worshipper. When she said that she herself was the Mahālaxmi, the queen asked her how she was to know it. At this, the old woman became a girl, then she assumed the form of an old woman! The queen offered her an honoured place, bathed her, worshipped her, fed her. She sent an intimation to Navalvāt. He came, they both blew the water-pot-musical-instrument. The King sent messengers to enquire what the noise was for. On hearing of the *puja*, His Majesty went himself to see it. He was pleased at the devotion of his deserted queen, and took part in the ceremony. As the cock crew the Goddess Mahālaxmi left the palace, but before doing so, she blessed the devotees and repeated her curse against the arrogant senior Rāni, but the junior begged that she might not be so severely punished. At her request, the goddess reduced the sentence to one of punishment for twelve years. The king sent word to the senior queen that he was returning home with his junior consort and that she should come forward to receive her. She was still so arrogant, and grew so jealous, that in order to manufacture ill-omens, she threw away her gold-and-silk dress, wore rags, let loose her hair, applied a broad hand of red powder to her forehead, held over her head a broken pot containing red-hot coals, and issued out shouting and shrieking like a devil incarnate! The king was angry. He ordered that she be beheaded. The younger queen and king lived happily. The servants, did not however kill the senior Rāni as they had eaten her salt. She was left in a forest. She went to the Potters' Row of a village. The chief potter of that place was shaping a new pot for the new queen, but he could not do so. He enquired if there was an unlucky new arrival in his street. The disgraced queen was discovered, She was turned out. She went to the Glass Blower's Row. The chief artisan was making new bangles for the new queen. They were spoilt. He made enquiries, he found the unlucky woman. He turued her out; she then went to the Goldsmith's Row, the same untoward thing happened wherever she went. She went to the jungle. There she met some Saints (*Rishis*). She served them unobserved as they had shut their eyes in deep meditation. Whenever they left their hut for a bath in the river, she used to sweep and clean the place and hid herself in the jungle before they returned. At last the *Rishis* called forth "who so ever" served them thus. She appeared, she was blessed. They found out from their sacred books that the woman was under a curse of the great Goddess. They made her perform the *puja* by taking a thread with 16 component parts, applying turmeric-paste to it, and offering it with 10 fronds of the *dub (Cynodon dactylon)* grass, and 16 grains of rice to the *tulsi (Ocymum sanctum)* plant after due worship. Then they told her the tradition, and asked her to blow the water-pot-instrument. They finally asked her to tie the thread to her hand, and requested her to perform the next *puja* on the fourth and the third on the 14th day, in Ashwin (September-October). The elder queen followed all these instructions. The goddess was pleased. She asked her to keep water, sandal wood paste, fruits, betel, *Khus* (*Andropogoni muricatus*) fans, etc., ready for the reception of the King, and ordained that he would come to the spot very thirsty. The King should feel that every comfort was offered to him. He would be pleased. The king came, he saw the shaded spot, he ate the fruit, drank the water, and while being fanned enquired who it was that kept all these things ready for him? The queen was produced. The king visited the *Rishis*. They blessed him. He turned back to go home and sent word to the junior queen that she should come forward to receive him and the old queen. She did so in right royal fashion. The king reminded the old queen of her folly when she was similarly told to welcome the other queen. She remained silent, and hung her head down as she had repented. The king and his two queens entered the city amid rejoicings and lived a happy and prosperous life. This *pujā* is very common in Gujarat and the women of that province are seen "blowing the water pot" and dancing round it, singing religious songs all the while. These songs are called *garbhās*.

**Lotan Shasthi.** In Bengal, a Brahman had a son, a daughter-in-law and a daughter. The daughter had three sons and the daughter-in-law, seven. She was thus well-off and happy with her big family. On the *Shasthi* or sixth day of the bright half of *Shrāvan* (July-August). She was arranging for the *Puja*. She was in the habit of offering the goddess six bulls called *Lotans* which she possessed. But on that occasion she found that three of them, were missing from her box. On enquiry the daughter-in-law burst into tears and swore by placing her hand on the heads of her sons, that if she had stolen them may God kill them all. When the daughter was asked, she simply denied all knowledge. The old mother kept quiet and prepared cream-*lotans* and offered them to goddess *Shasthi*. The daughter-in-law was so depressed that she did not take any food that night and retired. When her husband heard of the theft, he was also annoyed and retired without meals. The next morning the seven sons of the daughter-in-law were found dead. She cried helplessly. The daughter told her brother that because his wife falsely swore on her sons they were killed by the goddess. She accused her of the theft of the bulls and abused her. The daughter-in-law entered the room where her sons lay dead, and closed the door. The whole day passed away. Her husband asked her to open the door for removing the bodies of his sons for cremation; but she refused to do so. The goddess

Shasthi had compassion on her. She appeared before her as an old Brahman woman. She explained that it was a serious sin to swear by placing one's hand on the head of one's son. But the bereaved mother said that she did not steal the bulls and had therefore no hesitation in swearing, she had no reason to be afraid. Mother Shasthi said, "Take my advice, and never swear by placing a hand on the head of your son." She then sprinkled water on the bodies with the sprig of a bamboo. The boys came to life again and the goddess disappeared! The happy mother opened the door and came out of the room with her sons. But the three sons of her sister-in-law were dead. It was then the turn of the daughter to cry. At this time there was heard a voice from heaven, it said, "Your daughter stole the sweets and falsely accused the other innocent lady of the theft. Ask her to beg her for forgiveness. She did so. The daughter-in-law then sprinkled water from the bamboo leaves on the dead bodies. The boys came to life again. The daughter-in-law was loved by every one for her good conduct. From that time the worship became popular. Those who perform this *Puja*, have the longevity of their children, assured by the goddess.

**Makar Sankrāt.** This is the day of the transit of the sun at the tropic of capricorn—which falls on the 12th or 13th of January every year, and comes somewhere in the month of Mārgashirsha or Paushya. If in the latter, it indicates happiness and joy, to mankind. If in the bright half of a month it indicates misfortune to thieves, wicked men, and hunters. Similar predictions are vouchsafed when the transit takes place on a particular day of the week, or on particular conjunctions of the stars. Sankrānt or the transit is personified as a female. The animal on which she is shown to ride, the cloth she is supposed to wear, the jewels with which she is made to adorn herself, are all ascertained by some calculation, and made to signify good or evil forebodings during the year to follow. Brahma

Gupta is accepted as an authority on the subject. On this day, Hindus apply to their bodies gingelly seed pounded on the curry stone and bathe; they offer the seed mixed with or coated with sugar to fire, to the manes of their ancestors, to Brahmans, to the members of their families, friends, relations, and acquaintances. It is believed that this six-fold use of the *til* (*sesamum orientale*) destroys all sins. This day is said to be the beginning of the day of the Gods, and that of the night of the demons. The sun begins to turn towards the north.

Among the taboos prescribed are using harsh language, cutting grass, plucking leaves, milking cows, sheep, goat or any other animals. One should take no food, and should not enjoy conjugal happiness! Among the gifts preferentially selected for being offered to Brahmans are, new pots, food for cows, food for priests, sacrifical pots, raw sugar, sesamum seeds, wool, ghi, gold, cows, clothes, horse, etc. The blessings promised are perhaps proportionate!

Giving a cow to a Brahman, ensures salvation to Indra's Heaven, a bull would ensure a seat in Shiva's Kailās, a horse secures prosperity in this world, clothes lead one to a throne, and gold to a leadership. An elephant given to a Brahman on this day, is sufficient to secure the position of an Emperor or king of kings, a piece of land would entitle the donor to a Raj, and the gift of education secures the place of Hari the god of gods!

In practice, men worship the sun and women offer to Brahmans and other married women of their caste, materials required for the toilet such as red powder-boxes, bangles, mirrors, combs and bodice cloths. Betel-nuts, cocoanuts, fruits of sorts, and any thing which a married woman can enjoy are freely distributed. Women take earthen, copper, brass, or silver pots (or lotas) according circumstances and fill them up with certain articles of the toilet and fruit and distribute them. On the next morning they leave their beds before the sun rises, dress themselves, comb their hair and offer betel leaves and spices to their mothers, sisters, daughters and other ladies (excepting widows), chew bits of f esh sugar-cane to clean their teeth, and partake of the *pān*, etc. In the afternoon of the Sankrāt day men visit their friends and relations with their children and distribute the til-seed with sug r saying—"*til ghya gul ghya āni god bola*, viz. accept this til and sugar and speak sweetly to us. They then embrace their equals or salute elders and seniors. This distribution and "wishing" goes on for some days—like the New Year's greetings of the Christian population.

**Manasa.** Is the name of a deity in Bengal, presiding over cobras rattle snakes, or Nāgās.

The story runs that a certain Bania had seven married sons. His wife constantly received presents from all the daughters-in-law except the last. This youngest girl was therefore not liked by the mother-in-law and the girl felt herself slighted. She was depressed. The other girls tried to buoy up her spirits. One evening, they were all discussing the different dainties they liked, but the youngest was silent. She did not speak. At last, when repeatedly requested to do so, she said that of all the items in the menus they described, she preferred rice soaked in water for one night, mixed with *dāl* (the pulse of *Cajanus Indicus*), and cooked into *Khichadi.* As she was *enceinte* and as the object of the other girls was to find out her likings according to the custom of the caste, they all showed that they entirely agreed with her. They then went to the nearest tank to fetch water and to wash their clothes. The youngest thought she saw some fish in the dark and caught them in her pot. She kept them covered for the night. The next morning she was surprised to find that instead of the fish, her pot was full of snakes! These reptiles had just entered the tank to escape from a forest fire and had found the water pot of the girl a safe retreat! The heroine of our story, fed these *nāgas* with milk and plantain meal. The cobras felt much indebted to her as they were very hungry and wanted to repay the obligation. They went to Goddess Manasā and explained to her how the youngest danghter-in law of the Bania saved them from starvation and how affectionately she nursed them. They recommended that the girl be removed to Fairyland as she was ill-treated by her mother-in-law. The goddess or the fairy Manasā, did not like the idea, because, if irritated, the vindictive reptiles would eat her up; and because as a mortal she was likely to commit some blunder, one day. At last, at the earnest importunities of the Nāgas the goddess Manasa went to the house of the Bania transformed as an old woman, and representing herself as the maternal aunt of the girl took her away with the consent of the family. She asked the girl to shut her eyes and not to open them until directed to do so. The girl obeyed, and when she opened them, she found herself in a celestial palace full of all sorts of luxuries and comforts. She was shewn the *nāgas* she had befriended, was asked to consider them as her brothers, and to boil milk for them every morning. She was dressed well and given plenty of ornaments to wear. Like a princess under her father's roof, she enjoyed all sorts of pleasures. But there was one condition attached. She was told never to look to the South. One day she was tempted to do so, and found to her astonishment that the goddess was actually dancing!—a custom unusual among respectable ladies. Attracted by the curious sight she, like Alfred the Great, forgot all about the milk! It was boiling all the while. When the eight *Nāgās* turned up for their breakfast they were hurridly supplied with hot milk. It scalded them! They got irritated and wanted to swallow her alive! But the goddess Manasa appeared and appeased them. She reminded them of her objection to keep a mortal in their palace, as it is always liable to err. The Nāga is a vindictive species. The goddess therefore returned her to her mother-in-law's house, but told her to praise them to her people. She did so, when she was received back blazoned with gold and precious stones. She was asked how she could get such costly ornaments and readily replied that her brothers the Nāgās gave them to her. The cobras had secretly followed her. They overheard the praise bestowed on them and brought more jewellery for the other daughters-in-law. All became rich and happy. Manasa revealed herself, gave more presents, and said that she was not the aunt of the once neglected girl, but a goddess, that she lived in the cactus tree (*Euphorbium pentandra*). She advised the family to bring home that tree on the Dasanand and Nāgpanchami days and to worship it. She prohibited cooking on a given day, in Bhādrapad (August-September). The food to be offered to her should consist of rice soaked in water overnight and cooked into *Khichadi*. Such a worship will, she ordained, protect the devotees from snake-bite.

The goddess disappeared and the youngest daughter-in-law related her adventures with the Nāgas. Thenceforward she became a favourite of the family.

This worship was then adopted by the neighbours with the hope of attaining similar good luck.

*N.B.*—It is customary to feed a pregnant girl with the food for which she may feel a craving in the seventh month of the delicate state, under the belief that such a feast supplies the materials the fœtus requires for its development. It derives its name from Sanskrit, *Sadha* meaning desire in Bengal.

**Monday.** Somavati is the name of the Monday on which a dark night or *amāvāsya* falls. It is observed as a fast. The story begins thus :—

While Bhishma the old grand-uncle of the Pāndavas was laid up on his death bed, he was interrogated by Dharma, the eldest of the Pāndavas. He said "O sir, the principal chiefs of the Kaurava force have been destroyed by my brother Bhima, and others by Arjuna. Through the wickedness of Duryodhan our family has been reduced in number. Excepting old people and young children there remain no kings on earth. In the great family of Bharat we five brothers alone survive and therefore the Empire of which I have just become the ruler does not give me any pleasure. While alive, one has to bear nothing but blame, and even after death, there is no salvation in store. I feel depressed at seeing the wholesale massacre of the family to which I have the honour to belong. Ashvatthāma has through his enchanted weapons (*astra*) killed even the fœtus, Princess Uttara bears. I am therefore doubly grieved at the prospective extinction of the race. O Grand Uncle! What can I do? What will grant me long-lived sons?" . . .

Bhishma replied "Listen O king! I shall describe that *Vrat* which will grant long-lived progeny. O Dharma! on a dark night falling on a Monday, one should go to an *ashvatha* tree *(Ficus religiosa)* and there worship Janārdan (Vishnu). He should offer to God 108 jewels, or coins, or fruits and go round the tree as many times (108). This *Vrat* is much appreciated by Vishnu. Let Uttarā, your brother's daughter-in-law, perform this *Puja* and her fœtus will regain life. That child, when born, will be virtuous and reputed?"

Dharma said, "Pray describe in detail, this the king of all *Vratas*. Pray tell me who introduced it first, and how it became known on Earth."

Bhishma replied, "There is a celebrated city called Kānti. All the Brahmans, Kshatriyas, Vaishyas and Shudras of that city are pious. It contains beautiful palaces, and well-dressed men, and women. It is a lovely place. It also contains many good-looking and intelligent dancing girls. It is as rich as Alakā the capital of Kuber, the Treasurer of Gods, and as beautiful as Amarāvati the capital of Indra. It is as brilliant as Mahāpuri the capital of Agni, the God of Fire. It is full of gems. Over this city there once ruled king Ratnasen. There lived in it during his reign a Brahman named Devaswāmi. He had a virtuous wife named Dhanavati. She was as rich as Goddess Laxmi. She gave birth to seven well-behaved sons and one beautiful daughter named Gunavati. The sons were married. The girl was waiting to be married. At this juncture there came to his house, a Brahman guest. He was a bright young man. He came to the door and poured out blessings. The seven daughters-in-law of Devaswāmi, after paying their obeisance to him offered him alms. He conferred on each the blessing of life-long matrimonial felicity (*Saubhāgya*). Dhanavati then addressed the Brahman and said, 'O Sacred Brahman! pray listen to me. When my daughters-in-law bowed unto you, you conferred on them such blessings as would grant happiness, sons, and long marital life, but when my daughter bowed down her head you merely said "Be pious," Pray enlighten me as to why you differentiated thus. The Brahman Saint replied, 'Listen O Dhanavati! you are a devoted and pious lady. You have gained good reputation. I have conferred on your daughter the most appropriate blessing because, while performing the *Saptapadi* in her marriage, she is fated to become a widow. Let her live a saintly life.' Dhanavati became alarmed at this pronouncement, she repeatedly bowed unto him and begged, 'Oh Brahman! if you know how to counteract the impending calamity, pray describe it to me. O Ocean of Mercy! What can I do if there be no remedy?' The Brahman replied, 'If you can induce Somā to come to your house, her presence would evade the destiny of widowhood that hangs over your daughter's head.'

Dhanavati said: 'Who is this Somā, of what caste is she? Where does she live? Pray tell me at once, there is no time to lose.' The Brahman said: 'Somā is a Dhobi woman by caste. She lives in Ceylon. If she comes to your abode, there is hope.'

Saying so the Brahman disappeared. Dhanavati then addressed her sons and said that their dear little sister was in danger. He who had respect for his father and mother should start at once for Ceylon to bring Somā. Her sons said that she had always been thinking of her daughter alone, and only of her welfare. She always loved her more than her sons, and that was why she was forcing them to go to a country difficult to travel to, a country situated in the midst of an ocean! It was impossible to go there. They were unable to do so. When their father Devaswāmi heard this, he said that in spite of the fact that he was the father of seven sons he had to count himself a man without male issue! He would himself go to Ceylon, and bring Somā who could save his daughter from the impending danger.

At these angry words, his youngest son Shivaswāmi rose and said most reverently: 'O father, do not be so angry. As long as I am alive, who else has the courage to undertake the voyage?

He then bowed to his father and started forthwith with his sister. He reached the sea. He was thinking of swimming across the great ocean, but a large tree attracted his attention. In its hollow the young ones of a vulture were perching. The brother and sister rested under that umbrageous tree for the day. They saw the vulture returning to its young with some food. It offered it to them but they would not take it. It asked them the reason, and they said that it was inhospitable to do so while two travellers were starving under the tree. The vulture turned towards the pilgrims and asked them to name their desire. One of them, the brother, replied that they wanted to cross the ocean to prevent his sister from becoming a widow. The vulture promised to take them to the island the next morning and did so. They went to Somā's house and swept and mud-washed the frontage (of her house) every morning for a year. Seeing this Somā inquired of her sons and daughters-in-law as to which of them was so dutiful. They denied all knowledge. Somā therefore carefully watched the place one early morning and discovered that a Brahman girl was sweeping, and her dutiful brother mud-washing the open space in front of her house. She asked them who they were, and when they told her that they were the children of a Brahman, she expressed her horror at seeing those sacred people doing such menial work for her—a low caste woman. She cried 'O Brahman! The daughter of the impure washer-man's caste that I am, what makes you do a thing that will hurl me down to hell?' Shivaswāmi replied: 'This, madam, is my unmarried sister. She is destined so become a widow while performing the *Saptapadi* or fire worship in her own marriage. But I am assured that the evil can be evaded through your kindness, and therefore we have volunteered to serve you as menials.' Somā told them to desist. She said: 'I will obey you O sacred Brahman! and accompany you to your house,' She then addressed her daughters-in-law and told them to preserve the body of any one that might die in her Raj, during her absence. No one should, on any account, be cremated. She took the Brahman pilgrims across the ocean, through the sky and reached Kāntipur in the twinkling of an eye.

Dhanavati the Brahman woman was delighted. She worshipped the Dhobi woman. Shivaswāmi the dutiful son left for Ujjain in search of a suitable husband for his sister, selected Rudra and brought him down. Somā the washer-woman made all preparations for the marriage. During the festivities the bridegroom died as soon as he commenced the *Saptapadi*. All the relations began lamenting the loss! Somā alone was calm. She stood erect and, in the midst of the wailing, held the sacrificial cup in her hand, and gave away to the girl her own credit for having worshipped the *Vrat Raj* or King of *Vratas!* Wonder of wonders! The dead man was brought to life! Somā the washer-woman returned home. She learnt that the giving away of the merit of her worship of the *Vrat-Raj* caused the deaths of all her sons, her husband, and even her son-in-law. Fortunately for her a '*dark Monday*" Somavati, befell while she was returning home. That Somavati the life-giving *Puja*! On that day she met an old woman carrying a load of cotton. She was groaning under the weight she had to carry. Somā asked her what the contents of the baggage were. Its nature was explained to her, and she was asked to help the woman to put it down. Somā could not comply with the request as the touch of cotton was proscribed on a Dark Monday. Somā, next, met a woman carrying a load of radishes. In this case also she could not touch the vegetable. Somā then went to an *ashvath (Ficus religiosa)* tree that stood on the bank of a river. She bathed herself and worshipped the tree. She then took some sand in her hand, and went round the tree 108 times. As soon as she performed the 108 peregrinations her lost husband, her sons, and her son-in-law came to life again! The city and her house teemed with wealth. When Somā reached home, she was glad to see her own son-in-law come to life again. Her daughter-in-law enquired how all the male members came to life again. Somā replied that when she parted with the accumulated credit of the worship all of them died, but came to life as soon as she refused to touch either cotton or radishes on the first Dark Monday after the event, and performed the *Vrata*. *Ashvath (Ficus religiosa)* is the abode of Vishnu the Protector. If he be worshipped on that day there shall be no widowhood in the family. Every woman will be blessed with happy married life. She then made her daughters-in-law follow her footsteps as regards the *Vrata*. She lived a long and happy life, and in the end reached Vaikunth, the Heaven of Vishnu.' 'I have,' said Bhishma, 'thus described this *Vrata* for your benefit.'

Dharma asked Bhishma to describe it more fully and was told that on the Dark Monday the worshipper should rise very early and bathe herself in the river or in the sea, should wear a silk dress, should observe silence, should go to the religious fig tree, should worship the tree in the usual way, should meditate on the power of the All-prevading, visible as invisible Creator, Protector, and Destroyer, the Origin, Centre, and End for the universe.

The following is the *mantra* of the *puja*:—

"At thy root lives Brahma, in the stem lives Vishnu, and at the top lives Shiva, I bow unto thee O *Ashvath.*"

"Flowers and fruits of sorts should be offered to the sacred tree. The next prayer is: 'O *Askvath*, thou the *abode of Agni* the God of fire and the asylum of Vishnu I bow unto thee.'"

"Then the 108 perambulations should be performed. The offerings should consist of pearls, gold, diamonds, and other jewels, copper and brass, and pots full of food stuffs, All the white coins and other offerings placed before the tree should then be handed over to the Brahman preceptor. In order to to please Somā a married Brahman woman should be worshipped under the tree. Brahmans should be fed well. Finally, the devotee should take her meal observing silence all the while."

"Oh King! Ask Draupadi, Subhadrā and Uttarā to observe this *Vrata.* It will result in the fœtus of Uttara regaining life."

But, out of consideration for the poor, Dharma enquired, how people without means could perform such a costly Puja?

Bhishma said "By offering fruits, flowers, food, clothes and whatever one can afford."

"O King!" entreated Bhishma, "do perform the *Vrata* as quickly as possible!"

The Dhobi is undoubtedly classed with Chamārs, Nats, (Doms), Baruds, Kaivartas, Meds, and Bhils. That a woman of this caste even if pious, was worshipped by a high-class Brahman woman, shows the elevation of the depressed classes under certain conditions.

*On the sanctity of the tree.*

The origin of the sanctity* attributed to the *Ashvath* tree seems to have been recorded in this *Pothi.* It shows that in primitive days, when there were no lucifer matches or flints invented, fire was made by friction of dried wood. Pimpal or Pipal was then used for that purpose along with *Shami*, *(Prosopis specigera)* and *Udumbar* (*Ficus glomerata*). The Namdubri† Brahmans of the Malabar Coast still make fire with pieces of the wood of the Pipal and Jackfruit trees. The maternal grand-father [Dadoba Devāji Mulki] of the writer of this note died in London in 1861, and as his body could not be brought to India for cremation, an effigy made of flour had to be cremated in the course of the obsequies. The fire made at *that time* had to be produced by friction of the dry branches of the *Pipal* and the *Shami* trees. This use possibly accounts for the origin of the sanctity of this tree.

*On Sanitary motives.*

The *Ashvath* produces fire, fire is a purifier, it is indispensable in a Dhobi's house. The Dhobi or washerman washed away all disease-germs from dirty linen, and therefore the presence (or services) of a Dhobi woman in a Brahman family secured cleanliness and ensured longivity. When there was no coinage, when services had to be exchanged, the Brahman was perhaps obliged to render some kind of service in exchange for the work done by the washerman. It may be, therefore, that this story records *that* early exchange of labour or mutual cooperation.

* For sanctity see Cyclopædia of India. By E. Balfour, vol. II, p. 138, second edition.

† Journal of the Royal Society of Arts, vol. 57, p. 422, April 1909.

*On the name of the Vrata.*

Soma means the Moon, Monday is sacred to that luminary, and a dark night sacred to it must have been considered inauspicious like the day of an eclipse. The fast and the prohibition against touching cotton or radishes—both white, may have been designed to intensify the feeling of the loss of the white moon. Somā again, is said to be the name of the Dhobi woman, and it is natural that the dark night on which she fasted was called after her because she was black and untouchable! The mention of Ceylon—which is near Madras, and the names Devas*swami* and Shivas*swami* signify that the story was written in that Presidency where *Swami* is a usual affix,—not in use in other Provinces.

**Monday Fable.** There was a city and, as usual, a king. The King had four queens. The eldest was asked to look after the dairy, the second was left in charge of the kitchen, the third in charge of the nursery, and the fourth was in attendance. After some years, they got tired of their duties and began quarreling among themselves. The first one complained that there was no reason why she should be made to work with the cows and buffaloes, the second one said she could no longer work in the kitchen, and the third got tired of looking after the princes and princesses. When this family squabble reached the ears of the king, he was very sorry. He met Saint Vasishtha, who enquired the cause of his depressed look. The king related the complication of the family dissensions. The Saint sent for the queens and asked each to explain why she was discontented. On hearing the complaints, he said to the first queen that in her former birth she was a cow. She saw a *lingam* and standing over it she dropped milk over that emblem on Mondays. She therefore became a queen, but the *vrat* she had begun was not completed before she died, and therefore Shiva has ordained that she should work in the dairy. He advised her to accept her husband—the king—as the incarnation of Shiva and to feed him with good, pure, unadulterated, home-drawn milk. If she obeyed him she would attain *Kailās* after her death. The eldest queen was thus reconciled. She bowed to the Saint and promised to obey him. The Saint then returned to the second queen and asked her why she was dissatisfied. She said she was unable to understand why she should work as a cook when she was a queen. The Saint told her that in her former birth she was the wife of a poor Brahman and used to beg from door to door for dry (uncooked) food. She, however, observed the Monday fasts, cooked the food-stuff she could collect from five families and offered the preparations to the God Shiva. He made her a queen. But she must continue feeding all the members of her family to complete the *vrat* before she could attain a place in Kailās. She was reconciled, and she also resumed work. The Saint then asked the third queen to explain the grounds of her complaint. She said, she was disgusted and was tired of looking after dirty babies and naughty boys and girls. The Saint explained, that in her former birth she was a female monkey. On every Monday she used to collect a number of good fruits, but did not partake of any. She fasted herself and offered the fruits to the God Shiva. Shiva therefore made her a queen and gave her a lot of children. If she were to take care of them, nurse them, and educate them, the God Shiva would be pleased. She also was reconciled at this phase of her *Karma*. The Saint then asked the fourth queen what made her discontented. She said that the duty of personal attendance on a king was very irksome and onerous and that she could not bear the strain. He told her that in her former birth she was a kite. She saw a *lingam* exposed to the direct rays of the Indian midday sun, and spread her wings over it. The God Shiva was pleased and had given her beds, sofas, chairs, and similar comforts of life. She should therefore continue giving conjugal happiness to her lord to please the God Shiva. She also was reconciled. Let every one (says the story) remain satisfied with one's own lot in the same manner.

**Monday.** 1. There was once a King. He had four daughters-in-law. Three of them were his favourites while the fourth was not. He treated her like a maid-servant, gave her only coarse cloth and food, and asked her to attend to the cow. The month of *Shrāvan* [July-August] came. On the first Monday of the month she went to the jungle. There she met some fairies. They were worshipping the god Shiva with handfuls of grain. She asked them what they were doing. They said that the *puja* was called *Shivā-muth* (literally handfuls to Shiva). She asked them what the fruition of the *puja* was. They said that it pleases Shiva. He grants all desires but specially, the love of the husband and the affection of relations. A woman who performs this worship becomes the favourite of her husband, father-in-law, mother-in-law, brothers-in-law, sisters-in-law, and every one else in the household. She gets children and all worldly happiness, The fairies then asked her who she was. She said that she was the daughter-in-law of the King. They then showed her how to perform the *puja*. "Take a handful, they said, of rice, a betel nut, a pice, sandal wood paste, flowers, and the leaves of the *bel* (*Ægle marrelos*). Hold the rice in your hands and say:

" Oh Shiva, Shiva, Oh Mahādeva, pray accept my handful of grain, and make me the favovrite of my mother-in-law, father-in-law, my husband, my brothers-in-law, and my sisters-in-law." Saying so, put the rice in front of the *lingam*. Go home, take no food, take no leavings of others. If you cannot fast, take only a little milk. Bathe at sunset, offer *bel* (*Ægle marmelos*) leaves to Shiva and take your food in silence. Utter no word." On the first Monday, they gave her the requisite materials. On the second Monday, she was advised to offer *til* (sesamum seed), on the third Monday *mug* (*Phaseolus mungo*) on the fourth linseed, and on the fifth barley. She did so. But on the fifth Monday her father-in-law asked her where her god was, and expressed his desire to see him. She said that the temple was in the midst of a thick jungle full of thorns, brambles, and bushes, impenetrable. Yet the King and the whole of the family followed her. She was accustomed to walk through the rugged paths, but her relations found it very irksome. They reached the spot, with sore feet, but to their amazement they saw a temple made of gold and studded with jewels. They watched the girl worshipping the symbol devoutly and heard her simple prayer. They were moved to tears. They felt great affection for the devoted girl. the King left his turban on a peg in the temple and went to the adjoining tank to bathe. On his return he found that the golden temple had disappeared. One careful search he saw behind a bush a small rustic temple instead. He entered it and discovered his own turban on a peg inside it! The daughter-in-law explained that the God Shiva had mysteriously created the golden temple in order to receive him and his family. They were reconciled. The King ordered a palanquin for the girl and took her to his palacc with great eclat. She became the general favourite of the family and lived a happy life.

**Monday.** There was a once city. In it there lived a poor married woman. During the month of *Shrāvan* [July-August] she used to leave her bed early, bathe herself and perform the *puja*. One measure of rice—a 'palmful' and the other—a 'dorsumful' were taken to the temple of Shiva. She devoutly worshipped the image and prayed:

"Oh God, Oh Mahādeva accept this *phaski*, or palmful of grain and grant me riches."

The remnants were put on the back of the image of Shiva's bull. She did this on all the Mondays of the month. She became very rich day by day. She was satisfied. At the end of the *vrat* she sent a silk bodice to the Goddess

Annapurna of Benares, and a rupee to God Vishveshwar of that sacred city. Shiva sent a message that what she got was only the fruit of her worship of the sacred bull, and that he had yet to grant her a greater blesing as the fruit of her devotion to himself. She then got wealth and happiness beyond description.

**Mondays in Shrāvan** [July-August]. There was once a city, in which there lived a Brahman priest. His pupil who was also a Brahman used to bathe every morning in the adjoining river and devoutly worship the god Shiva. On his return home, he once heard a voice saying "May I come?" It came through a cluster of bamboos. He looked to see who spoke, but no one appeared there! The miracle repeated itself every day. He lost flesh, he was much reduced, he looked worn out. His *guru* asked him what was the matter with him. What ailed him? He confessed that he was afraid of the voice he heard every day "May I come?" His preceptor advised him to take courage, to abstain from looking behind when he heard the echo again, and to respond to it by saying merely "yes." The *guru* promised him that he would see that no harm came to him. The pupil did so. When he reached his preceptor's house, the latter saw that he was followed by an unmarried girl. He got them married. (Her caste is not mentioned in the original tradition). On the following first Monday in the month of *Shrāvan* [July-August], he told his wife not to wait for her morning meal as he was going to Shiva's temple to perform his Monday-*puja*, and as he had to observe a fast. But as soon as she put the first morsel in her mouth her husband knocked at the door. She hastily pushed aside her plate under a cot and attended to her duties. The same coincidence came to pass on all the three subsequent Mondays of the month. When on the fourth, they both went to bed they both saw a glow of light under their cot. On looking at it they discovered that there were four plates full of bright gems! The husband asked his wife how she came to possess such treasure. She was confused, and said that her father sent them. He asked her where her father's house was, and desired her to take him to that place. She consented, but as she had no such house she prayed to the God Shiva to grant a "parental home" for a short time, and under the faith that her prayer would be granted she took her husband to the cluster of bamboos out of which she had mysteriously come herself. There, they found a royal residence, full of people who addressed the husband as "son-in-law" and "brother-in-law" and his wife as their daughter their sister and so forth. In fact the whole affair looked as if the girl had a real father, mother, brothers and sisters with servants of all denominations employed to minister to their comfort. They both (the husband and wife) were feasted, fed, and given new dresses. They started back, but coming forward a few paces the wife found that she had left her necklace on a peg. They both turned back to take it but there was no palace! There were only the bamboos and the necklace lying among them. The husband was astonished. He anxiously asked his wife to explain the phenomenon. She confessed that she had no parents, that the plates full of jewels they saw under their bed contained her own dinners pushed aside so as to enable her to minister to his wants that when she was asked where they came from, she was so terrified that she named her "father" or rather God the father of us all. When he asked her to take him to her parental home, she prayed to the God Shiva to supply the want and Lord Shiva mysteriously did so. May He be as propitious to all those that worship Him on Mondays in Shāravna!

**Mondays in Shrāvan** [July-August].

*A spoonful of milk.* In a city of which no name is mentioned, there lived a king who was a great devotee of Shiva. He thought of filling up the temple with milk so as to drown the emblem of. Shiva in that liquid. He directed that all the people of his capital should carry all the milk they could collect to the temple and pour it over the image. The result was that the children of the city were starved, the young calves were starved, and no drop of milk was available for any body. Every one was dissatisfied and every one was sorry. The whole available quantity was poured into the vault, but it was not found sufficient. At last there came an old woman who had duly fed with milk, the calves, and the children in her house. She worshipped the image and offered only a spoonful of milk, praying that when the whole of the city could not supply enough to fill the vault, it was impossible for her to do so with her slender means. She had therefore done her duty to the dumb young ones of the cows and to the little children in her house. She devoutly hoped that God Shiva would be satisfied with her "drop in the Ocean," her spoonful of milk. Curiously enough, as soon as she poured that little stuff out, the vault overflowed with milk. The same thing happened on all the four Mondays. The king had set a guard to take that woman to him, as soon as she came again. But no one could find her though they watched every old woman On the second and third Mondays the temple vault overflowed soon after she left the place. So, she could not be caught. On the last or fourth Monday the king himself sat to watch for the woman. She came, she offered a spoonful of milk and as soon as she turned her back, the vault overflowed with milk. The king caught her by the arm. She was frightened. His Majesty assured her that she would come to no harm, and asked her to explain the mystery. She said that it was a sin to deprive dumb calves and young children of their only food and to produce discontent among grown up people by forcibly taking away their daily dole of milk. The best course, she said, was to feed every body, to satisfy every body's hunger, and then to offer only a small quantity to God. The king felt grateful for the advice, and made the woman rich.

## THE SIXTEEN MONDAYS FASTS.

**Monday.** There was a city with a sacred temple of the God Shiva, who on one occasion came there in person and was playing draughts with his wife Goddess Pārvati. There arose some dispute as to who was the winner, and the case was referred to the worshipper. This poor mortal said that Shiva was the winner. At this, Pārvati got angry and cursed him, saying that he would become a leper. Poor soul! He suffered for some time, but one day some fairies came to the temple and seeing him distressed, asked him how he came by such a horrid state of health when he was the *pujāri* or worshpper of the God Shiva himself. He explained how he was cursed by the Goddess—Shiva's own wife. They then assured him of speedy cure, if he were to obsevce the *vrat* of the sixteen Mondays fasts. On further enquiry, they explained that the devotee should take no food during the day, should bathe at sun-set, and worship the God Shiva. He should then take half a *seer* of flour, should mix it with *ghi* and raw sugar, cook and partake of it. He should on no account take any salt on this day. This should be repeated for sixteen Mondays. On the seventeenth Monday, he should take five *seers* of flour and prepare balls with *ghi* and sugar. After worshipping Shiva at the temple, he should offer him the balls. These balls should be divided into three equal parts. One should be left for the image, one should be offered to a Brahman or a cow, and the third should be taken home for self and *family*. The fairies then disappeared. The *pujāri* faithfully followed their advice and was cured. When Shiva and Pārvati next visited the temple, the latter was surprised to see the man she had cursed so mysteriously cured.

On enquiry, she learnt the secret, and made up her mind to observe the same *vrat* herself in order to bring back home her own son Kumār or Kārtikeya who had gone away in a fit of temper never to return. She did so. He did come back and asked his mother how his tenacious mind could be so influenced as to yearn for home. She explained the *vrat*, he observed it, and regained his lost friend; the friend observed it, and gained a kingdom; the wife of the friend did the same and got a son; the Prince did the same and got another kingdom. But the wife of the last king committed a blunder. Instead of sending to the temple the five *seers* of the balls she, as a queen, pompously sent five trays of rupees. The God Shiva was offended, appeared before the king in a dream, and advised him to turn her out! But the kingdom belonged to her father, and the minister would not agree to such a rash step. He was however persuaded to yield in the name of the God, whose commandment could not be disobeyed. The poor queen was banished. Wherever she went calamities followed. The food she looked at was spoilt, the river she looked at dried, the tank she stared at got its water full of vermin. She at last went to a jungle and began serving an ascetic. But her evil eye spoilt his little things. He, by virtue of meditation, discovered the cause, and advised her to observe the sixteen Monday fasts. She did so. The God Shiva was pleased, her husband came to *shikār* to the very spot, met her, and through the mediation of the ascetic she was reconciled to her lord.

MANGAL CHANDI (Bāramāsi). [*Bengal Folklore*].

Dhanpati the rich merchant of Ujjain had no issue from his first wife Lahāna. He married a second one named Khullanā. These two co-wives lived together on good terms and prayed to the goddess Mangal Chandi for a son. During the pregnancy of the younger, the merchant sailed for Ceylon to trade. Khullanā gave birth to a good looking son, there was no news from the merchant: but there were rumours that the ship was lost. Years passed away. Srimanta the beautiful child was educated in a school. One day, he came home sobbing and asked his mothers who his natural mother was, and what his father's name was. He was insulted that day, by his fellow students because he could not answer these questions. Lahāna the senior, explained to him, that he was the son of Khullanā, that she was his stepmother and that his father had gone to Ceylon fourteen years ago, with fourteen ships. He never returned. It was said that he had been imprisoned there, by Shālivāhān the king of that island. He saw both of his mothers in tears! He was moved, and said that he would go to Ceylon to get information about his father. His mothers were alarmed, but his resolution could not be shaken. They entrusted him to a trustworthy Captain. They worshipped the goddess Mangal Chandi and instructed their son to pray devotedly to her, if he were ever in trouble. The Captain manned seven boats. They sailed away. Shrimanta was sailing for Ceylon. He forgot the name of the goddess he had to revere. His boats were in danger. One of them sank. He then recollected the name of Mangal Chandi and prayed for help. She was pleased, and the men on board were saved. Then there appeared a cyclone. Srimanta prayed to the goddess Mangal Chandi to save him and his boats.

The mothers grew anxious, but they were assured by the goddess in their dreams that there would be no trouble. While on the high seas, Shrimanta one day saw a goddess floating on a lotus on the surface of the ocean. She had an elephant in her lap. She was swallowing the trunk of the brute and throwing it out again! Shrimanta was terrified. He prayed for help. He reached Ceylon and went direct to the Darbār of Shālivāhān. He was well received. The king enquired what things he saw during his long voyage. He said "I saw a gigantic woman seated on a lotus and swallowing an elephant and throwing it out again." The king got annoyed at such an impossible story and directed the arrest of the boy. At his humble request the king asked him whether he could show him the woman. Shrimanta agreed. They sailed with the staff of the king but Shrimanta could not find her again. The king was very angry, and ordered that he be beheaded, and his head brought to him for inspection. Four executioners tied Shrimanta's hands and took him to the place of execution. When the executioners were ready to strike, Shrimanta begged to be allowed to pray. He invoked the help of mother Mangal Chandi. She appeared before him in the form of an old woman, and placed him in her lap. When the executioners went to kill him, their swords fell broken. They were frightened and ran up to the king. The king went himself to see what was the matter. The terrible howl of the old woman frightened him and his men. Her attendant spirits began giving the king and his men a sound beating. The king prayed to the old lady. She was pleased, and said "You were unable to see on the high sea the goddess "Kamala-Kāmini." You cannot see her because you are a inner. You are responsible for the wrongful confinement of innocent people like Shrimanta's father, and for depriving them of their mcney. "Repent and offer your daughter Sushila in marriage to this boy Shrimanta, and give him a dowry four times the value of the property you have deprived his father of." The king agreed, and begged her to shew him the goddess Kamala-Kāmini. The old lady directed him to go to the pier, and disappeared. The king took the boy Shrimanta with him to the pier. But he could not see the goddess. He then took the boy in his lap, and the goddess became visible. He was delighted to see her. He returned home and released the men he had imprisoned along with the father of Shrimanta. His Majesty himself apologized to Dhanpati. The father and the son were happy. The son was married. The king returned the property of the merchant and gave his daughter some precious gems as her dowry. The merchant returned home with his son and daughter-in-law. In the meantime Lahanā and Khullanā worshipped the goddess every Tuesday, and prayed to her to give them back their son. They had no hope of seeing their husband again. He however returned home with his son and daughter-in-law. They were all glad, and performed the *Puja.* They lived long and happily.

**Mangalā-Gaur.** The Brahman and Prabhu married girls of Bombay perform on every Tuesday in the month of *Shrāvan* for the first five years after marrige a *puja* of Goddess Manglā-Gaur, the Deity presiding over *the Mangala* or good luck. But Tuesday is called Mangal-vār and it is therefore selected for the worship. Sixteen kinds of grains and seeds, and sixteen kinds of flowers are collected and the long-life-giving goddess is worshipped. Girls make it a great holiday, dance, sing, and make themselves merry. The story is given below.

There was a Bania and his wife living in a house. Every morning an ascetic in saffron coloured clothes passed their door, cried *ahallak,* but did not stay to accept the food for which ascetics generally beg. The lady told her husband of this curious phase in the behaviour of the *fakir* and was advised to stand concealed behind the door with a plate of food and to throw it quickly into his *jholi* or begging towel. Next day she carefully followed her husband's instructions, but on throwing the food into the *jholi,* she saw that the saintly person was exasperated beyond measure. He even went so far as to say "Oh you wicked one! you the wife of a sonless man, you the curse of your race, you are a disgrace to your family"—and so forth. He became abusive and so vexed that it was feared he would curse the lady. Her husband dressed as a farmer followed the irate old man to the river, where he forthwith went to wash his towel. While performing the tedious operation of removing the rice that was found sticking to the cloth, he gave full vent to his feelings and showered abuses on the poor woman. Her husband was near, he offered his services, got into conversation with him, and asked him why he threw away the rich, princely dish that was offered to him so devotedly by the Bania lady. "Oh! but she is a *niputrik*, a woman without a son" said the old man, grinding his teetn. It is against the *shāstras* to accept food from people who have no sons born unto them. What can the Bania do to get a son, was the earnest question, and the saint advised that the Bania should go to a certain temple on a certain hill and perform austerities in front of the goddess there. They parted. The Bania returned home and left for the temple. In course of time he performed the austerities and the goddess appeared before him as usual. She asked him to name the blessing he would desire, he mentioned—*a son*,—she said that there was no son nor even a daughter in his *karma* or *takhdir*, but that as he performed the austerities so faithfully, she would grant one boon. He should select it from the offer she was just going to make. It ran: "If you get a son he will be short lived and die at the end of the sixteenth year, but if you accept a daughter, she will live long but will become a child widow. Choose," added the goddess. There was no hesitation and no time was required for consideration as the poor Bania had expressly come to the temple for a son, his dear wife being abused for having none to represent the line. He asked for a son. Then said the goddess, "Go to the orchard behind my temple, and you will find there a big image of Ganesh on a plinth, put your foot on his big belly, do not fear, he will not curse you,—and then you will reach the lowest bough of a mango tree loaded with luscious fruits. Pick only one, take it home and give it to your wife to eat. He bowed, the goddess disappeared, he went to the tree, he found the Ganesh, he bowed unto the Lord of Success and begged to be excused for the liberty he was asked to take, ascended the plinth, placed his foot on the navel of the god, picked one fruit and threw it down. But so tempting was the fragrance of the ripe fruit, that he was led to pick more and more. At last he felt he had picked a sufficient number and looked down to see how many they were. But, alas! there was only one. What on earth could have become of the others? He looked appealingly at Ganesh, but the god merely smiled. He came down, he bowed again unto the God of Knowledge and asked him how it was that all the mangoes except one disappeared. He was told, that the great goddess had granted him only one fruit meaning a child, and that there was no use his becoming coveteous. He must remain satisfied. He picked up the mango, brought it home, gave it to his wife. She in due course, gave birth to a son—as beautiful as Cupid and as lustrous as the Sun. He was the joy, the life and soul of the Bania's abode. No end of charities followed. The son grew into a fine-looking young man. But the fated sixteenth year came and the parents became very anxious about him. At last the maternal uncle of the boy suggested that he should be taken to Benares, the queen of sacred cities, where his fated death might be averted, or at least his dead body consigned to the sacred stream of the Ganges to ensure entrance to Heaven. Such a step would moreover avert the pain of seeing him in the pangs of the last struggle for life. The parents consented, the uncle and the boy started, they reached Benares and halted at a rest-house surrounded by a beautiful flower garden. One morning after their arrival, they saw a group of little maidens collecting flowers and leaves of certain trees. One of them more beautiful than all the others, was seen picking a flower from a branch held down by another with the object of reaching the same prize. The latter lost her temper, became abusive, and said, "Oh! you *rānd* (widow), what business have to you take that flower? Don't you see that I pulled down the branch?" "Rām, Rām" (began the rejoinder) "Oh! you wicked girl. How dare you use that disgusting epithet towards one who has the honour to belong to a race of women, in whose family there never lived a widow? None of my noble ancestresses was so sinful as to survive her husband and to live as a widow, nor shall I—God be with me! You forget that this is a day sacred to the all-powerful goddess Mangalā-Gaur, I have picked up this flower for my mother who has to worship that goddess, and I feel sure she will grant long life to my husband, whoever he shall be!" This little speech cowed the other girl. She begged to be excused, and they both went away. But the uncle, the elder of the two pilgrims in the rest-house, was so struck with the sincerity and divine lustre in that little face, that he followed her unobserved to her father's house, with the object of securing her for his nephew. He hoped, thereby, to ensure longevity through the faith of the girl. But he was disappointed to find that she was already engaged to a citizen's son and that her marriage would be performed forthwith. The brother-in-law was not to be ousted thus. He had money enough to offer. Somehow or other—(how it is not mentioned)—he succeeded in substituting his nephew at the religious ceremony. The fated lad was married to the girl. She was of course with him for some hours during the performance of the sacred rite. She saw his features, she was delighted to find that she was the bride of a Cupid born! What girl will not feel as proud as she did? They retired for the night. Next morning she was surprised to see in the place of her husband, a dark and rustic person. She recoiled, she told her parents that there was some fraud, that she was being sacrified to some deep laid plot. The father could get no information from the substitute. He was obdurate. At last, to save further trouble he decided that the *saptapadi*, the completion of the marriage ceremony should be withheld until he had fed every man in the city of Benares. Hundrends of people were invited to dinner, they came, they ate to their satisfaction, they showered blessings on the girl and her parents. At last as the sun was going down, there came two guests who could with difficulty be persuaded by the agents of the girl's father to accept a gratuitous dinner. They were reluctant. Being of high parentage, they did not like to mix with ordinary people in a free-kitchen banquet. The poor bride had assigned to her the task of serving some dainty to each of the guests to enable her to identify her husband. She was tired, but her ardour had in no way abated. As she came to put the dainty in front of the Bania lad, she stood surprised. She looked, looked again, looked once more, into that lovely face! Her hair stood erect on her body. Her heart throbbed. She looked appealingly at her father who was near her and bowed. "That"—she said—"is my dear husband. To him was I married last evening, and to no other."

The plot succeeded, reconciliation followed. The other party was made to explain the mystery and to confess that the original bridegroom out of sheer pity for the son of the Bania, gave up the bride whom he had never seen.

The uncle, the boy, and the new bride left the city after the completion of the ceremony and travelled homewards. They halted somewhere on the banks of the Ganges. That was a Tuesday of the month of *Shrāvan.* The bride who was now very rich although she did not know it, had to perform her *vrat.* She had to worship the goddess. As there was no temple near by, she erected one of sand and water, made beams of clay and sand. She made lamps of the same materials. She collected the requisite leaves and flowers, and worshipped the deity in due form. It took such a long time for a single-handed girl to go through the whole *puja* that the day was nearly gone. They therefore hurriedly left the place. Going forward some distance she was reminded that she had yet to extinguish the central pair of lamps. She turned back, her uncle-in-law remonstrated, she begged to be excused. She said she could not possilby violate the tenets of the *Shāstras.* But said the uncle: "There are tigers there, there was no house, where will you sleep for the night." "Let me go—whatever may happen" she entreated—"pray let me go." They returned. To their amazement they saw a fine temple topped with a gold cupola. What could that mean? Had they lost their way? No, *that* was the tree they passed, *that* was the landmark they remembered perfectly well. What could the miracle mean then? Yes. It was the same spot and Vishwakarma, the architect of the goddess, had under order speedily erected a gem of architecture for the reception of her devoted guests. They entered the temple, the bride recognized her own lamps and other arrangements, she bowed, she extinguished the central pair of lamps by firmly pressing the flames with a flower, threw the flowers and leaves into the Ganges. Next morning they resumed their journey and came to a town also on the banks of the Ganges but lower down the stream. They halted under a tree, but alas! It was the fated day—the last day of the 16th year of the boy's age. He was suddenly taken ill and he died! The girl lost consciousness. She did not know what to do. The uncle lifted up the corpse, took it to the sacred river and threw it into the stream. Heaven and earth seemed breathlessly silent. The bride was hopelessly staring at the dear remains of her lord. She was crazy.

But lo! Something was floating down the stream which rivetted her attention. She stood erect. She was looking intently—not at the corpse but at a heap of flowers and leaves coming down the stream. "Oh!"—shouted the girl —"My goddess has come!" She had hardly uttered these words, when the flowers reached the dead body and passed over it from head to foot, and, curious to behold, the young Bania came to life and began swimming towards the party. All joy! The uncle threw himself into the stream to help his nephew out. "My husband! My lord!" shouted the girl and swooned. With difficulty she was brought to her senses; and taken to her father-in-law's home. There, it was found that through grief and endless crying the poor old man had lost his eye-sight. The bride however touched his eyes with the washings of the image of her goddess and his sight was restored to him. The Bania, his wife, their son, the new bride. and the uncle all lived long in happiness and plenty. Such is—says the story—the power of the goddess Mangalā-Gaur.

**Mauni Amāvāsya.** In Bengal the Mauni Amāvāsya has a folklore, possibly a varient of the Somavati (which please see) it runs:—

There lived in a village two women friends. One of them was a Brahman widow and the other a milk-maid. The former had a little daughter. The latter had her husband alive and a goodly family. She was self supporting and happy; but the Brahman woman was very poor. One day, a woman came to her house to beg and while accepting alms at the hands of the Brahman girl remarked "What a pity that such a pretty little girl should be destined to be a widow." This remark surprised the mother who overheard it. She begged of the beggar to explain herself. The latter added "If any one possesing the merit of having fasted on seven Mauni Amāvāsyas, transfers the same to your child, she will have her husband brought to life again; but the donor will lose the whole of her family." On the hostess enquiring if there was any remedy against the latter evil, she was told that, a disgusting rite would have to be performed." On getting further details the Brahman woman thanked her guest.

She knew that her milk-maid friend had acquired the requisite merit and would gladly transfer it to her daughter, but the horror of the disgusting rite was too much for any body! At last by performing menial service in her friend's house she induced her to undergo that ordeal!'

In due course, the Brahman girl was married, her husband died on the day of the nuptials, and was brought to life by the generous milk-maid. But on returning home she was faced with the anticipated calamity, and found all her people lying dead! The horror of the promised rite stood before her! She could not, under the circumstances, avoid it. She had to take a potful of curd to the jungle and pour it over the head of a Muni (Saint) who had leprous sores all over his body! One could stoop even to that, but the climax came when she had to collect the stuff again! Poor thing! For the sake of her own family sacrificed in order to oblige her dear friend of the priestly tribe, she did even that! But lo! the moment she finished her self-imposed revolting task there rose from the leprous body, God Nārāyan himself refulgent with the jewels and symbols peculiar to him. He said that he was merely trying to ascertain the depth of the faith and devotion of the two women, and restored to life the whole of the milk-maid's family. Through the blessings of that Lord, both the Brahman and the milk-maid's family thenceforward lived a happy and prosperous life.

**Mulā Shasthi.** Mulā means a radish and the sixth day of the bright half of Agrahāyan (November-December) is named after it, as the story tells. This is observed in Bengal:—

There was a Brahman who had lost his wife. His daughter-in-law used to cook his food for him. On the sixth day just named, he felt a craving for animal food bought some venison, and asked his daughter-in-law to cook it for him.

The girl in order to be sure of making it palatable, asked a maid-servant to taste it, but the servant was a low class woman. She stealthily ate the whole stuff. The daughter-in-law was alarmed. She asked the maid to replace it. The wicked woman brought the flesh of adead calf. The daughter-in-law could not cook it in time for the meal and had to contrive a scheme for evading the anger of the old father-in-law. She asked the servant to throw water over the floor, and while trying to serve the dinner slipped and fell down upsetting the curry. The device succeeded. As the curry was spilt and as the low caste woman had to sprinkle water over the face of the girl as if to bring her back to consiousness, the whole dinner was polluted. The daughter-in-law revealed to her husband the theft and subsequent trick of the servant. He discovered that beef was brought into the house and that the whole affair required purification. They all had to fast. It was the sixth day. The daughter-in-law performed the *Shasthi Puja* to expiate her sin, and offered plantains and radishes to the goddess. She sprinkled over the dead calf, the sacred water with which she had washed the image. It came to life again, and the whole affair ended pleasantly, and all the people adopted the *Vrat*,

**Nāg Panchami.** *Nāg Panchami* is the fifth day of *Shrāvan* (July-August) sacred to the snakes, chiefly cobras. There are two stories in existence. One says, that there was a Brahman. He had seven daughters-in-law. All of them except the youngest went to their parents or paternal and maternal relations to enjoy holidays. The youngest had lost her parents. She had no near relation who could take her home for a few days. She was a devoted girl. She said, that *Nāg*-king or *Shesha snake* was her relation and protector. Shesha the thousand hooded snake on whose coils sleeps Lord Vishnu, was moved to pity. He assumed the shape of an old Brahman and went to claim the girl as his niece. Her father-in-law wondered where the uncle had been up to that time, as he was not known to him and had never even been heard of. He appealed to the girl. She was so tired of living under the strict regime of her mother-in-law that out of necessity, she allowed him to pass as her maternal uncle. He took her to a rat-hole, and there resumed his original reptile shape. Asking her to ride on his hood, he took her to his abode. She lived with the *Nāg* and his wife. The *Nāg* had given strict instructions that none of his family should bite her. Days passed, on one occasion, the wife of the *Nāg* was about to give birth to a new brood. (The birth of reptiles from eggs does not seem to have been recorded in this story.) As soon as the little reptiles came out, they began creeping all over the place. The girl was asked to hold in her hand a heavy brass hanging lamp. She got frightened and dropped the lamp. It injured and severed the tails of some of them. In due course, the girl was restored to her husband's parents. There came the month of *Shrāvan* (July-August). On the fifth day of the month, she drew on a low stool the figures of snakes (Nāgās) and worshipped them. Curiously enough, that very day the snakes who had lost their tails asked their mother why they were deformed, and were told of the accident of the lamp falling on them at the time of their birth. They were very angry with the girl, and went in a body to avenge the injury. They had just reached her home, and were in hiding to watch an opportunity to bite. But her prayers to God for protecting her reptile brothers, as she affectionately called them moved them to tears, and they desisted from carrying out their design. They partook of the milk and the parched grain she had kept under the stool as an offering, and left in the cup a fine jewelled necklace. She became rich and happy.

The second story of the Nāgā's Day, says that there was a farmer. He was ploughing his field. The ploughshare accidentally entered a hole in which there lived some young hooded cobras. They were crushed to death. Their mother returned. She saw blood on the plough-share and went to the home of the farmer. There she bit every member of the family and killed them all. But her wrath was not appeased, as she heard that the farmer had a daughter still living. She went to the daughter's house. The girl was engaged in the worship of *Nāgoba* or the chief of snakes meaning *shesh* the thousand hooded cobra. The vindictive reptile mother had to wait until the girl finished her prayer. In the mean time she dipped herself in the sandal-wood paste which was lying near the stool on which the figures of nine *Nāga-kuls* or snake families were drawn. She drank the milk and ate the parched grain placed before the stool as offerings. She was satisfied and cooled down. She then stood before the girl and on the latter reopening her eyes after prayer, asked her whose daughter she was. On being told, she confessed that she had killed that family. The girl prayed that they may be restored to life. The snake-mother gave her some nectar. She ran up to her father's house, put a drop of the nectar in the mouth of each of her relations and restored them to life.

Since that time it has been ruled that on the fifth day of *Shrāvan* there shall be no ploughing operations, no vegetables shall be cut or sliced, no food shall be cooked and no cooked food shall be eaten. Nagoba should be fed with milk. That rule is still observed.

**Narali pornima.** *Nārali pornima* or *Rākhi pornima*, full moonday of *Shrāvan* (July-August) is celebrated in three different ways. In the Bombay Presidency all along the western coast of the Konkan, great fairs are held on the sea shore. The ocean is worshipped and cocoanuts are thrown into it as offerings, hence the name *Nārali* from *Nāral*—a cocoanut, cocoanut-day.

A *Rākhi* or amulet made of silk thread, silver wire, gold wire, corals, pearls, jewels and gold beads according to means, is tied round the wrist of brothers by their sisters as a charm protecting them from evil during the ensuing year. Hence the name *Rākhi* from *raksha* to protect. Those who have the privilege of wearing the sacred thread, and are accepted as twice-borns change them on this day, or on the previous day according to the position of the moon at the constellation *Shravan*. It is observed as a gala day.

**Natāi Vrat.** This *Vrat* is observed in Bengal. There was a merchant. His first wife died leaving him two good looking and amiable children, a son and a daughter. He married again, and had two more children by the second wife, but they were rather dark and peevish like their mother. He did not like them, he preferred to bestow caresesses on the elder ones, the second wife got jealous and did her best to ill treat them. Her husband's presence in the house, came in the way of her wicked plots. She had acquired great influence over him and compelled him to go abroad. He was advanced in age, and was unwilling to leave his children by the first wife, to the mercy of the second. But she overruled him. At last, he made a private arrangement with a confectioner and a milkman to supply his pets with whatever they needed. He advanced sufficient money for the purpose, and added that he would make up the difference on his return, if there happened to be any. As soon as he left the village, his wife dismissed the cowboy and compelled her half-children to take up his work. They had to follow the cattle to the grazing plot, to watch them all the day, and to feed themselves with the miserable food she gave them. Seeing however that they were not reduced in strength, she suspected that her husband must have made some arrangement to feed them during his absence. She therefore asked her own children to go with them and watch them. They did so, but returned quite pleased. When questioned, they said that their brother and sister were so very good, that they took them to a confectioner and a milkman and treated them to dainties which they had never tasted before! She was annoyed, and instead of thanking the elder children for the kindness, she began absuing them for stuffing her pets with indigestible food. She sent for the confectioner and the milkman and told them that she had received a letter from her husband. It says that his ships were foundered, his commodities destroyed, and he has become a bankrupt. She was therefore not in a position to spend extras on feeding their children and would not be responsible for any debts, any of them might incur. This step naturally resulted in the elder children being half starved. They were also ill treated with greater vigour. The result was that they grew weaker and weaker. Exhausted, fatigued, they over-slept one afternoon. The cattle went astray! They dared not return home without their charge, and entered an adjoining village to seek shelter. They sat under a tree behind a hut. That was a Sunday in the month of *Agrahāyan.* The residents of the cottage were about to perform the *puja* of goddess Natāi, as they had fasted that day. They saw these helpless children, called them in, and as they also had fasted, induced them to perform the *puja.* The result was, that the goddess was pleased. Their father returned quite safe, and immensely rich. The wicked step-mother told him that his children by the first wife were devoured by a tiger. He could not believe the story, went in search, and found them in the house in which they were given shelter. In the meantime the wicked woman took some of his newly acquired cash and jewels and was going to bury them in a secluded spot, but it was a dark night and in her hurry she fell into a well and died. The merchant, found the missing jewels and cash in the well, returned home, got his children married and lived happily performing the *puja* every year.

**Navānn-Pornima.** The full moon day following the Dasara in called by this name which means the full-moon day on which the new harvest food has to be tasted. On this day the family gods are offered a special worship at which Laxmi the Goddess of Wealth presides. Fringes and wreaths made of the grains of rice intermixed with the flowers known as bachelor's buttons, are tied at the top of the main entrance of the house. A sort of porridge made of the new rice is offered to the gods, and then eaten as a special dainty of the day.

**Navarātra.** The first day of *Ashwin* [September-

October] is reserved for the performance of *Shrāddh* of a maternal grand-father by his grand-son and is called *Mātāmaha Shrāddh.* That done, the great Navarātra ceremony begins on the same morning. *Nava* means nine and *rātra* means night. The nine nights are sacred to Devi or Goddess, whose ten manifestations and several exploits are described in the Devi Māhātmya of the Mārkandeya Purāna. It says that the history or the *Purān* was related by Saint *Medha.* Thus, there was a king named Suratha. He was defeated by his enemies. He left his his capital and went to a jungle for *Shikār.* He came across the cottage of Rishi Medha and related to the saint the history of his defeat through the breach of trust of his minister. The saint offered him hospitality, but the king was so restless that he wandered about in the locality. He met a Bania named Samādhi. The king asked him why he had left home to live the life of a recluse. The Banja explained that he was born rich, but was turned out by his own wife and sons, and yet he felt the separation from his kith and kin. The king expressed surprise at his affection for people who did him harm. Then both went to the saint and asked him to explain the curious phenomenon of a man feeling affection for his enemies. The saint in reply explained that it was the unfathomable work of Mahā Māyā the great goddess who was born of Vishnu's body. Her exploits were many, but he would describe a few for illustration. At one time, from the wax in the ear of Vishnu there rose two demons named Madhu and Kaitabha. They annoyed Brahma while Vishnu was asleep. Brahma prayed to the Goddess Mahā-Māyā to wake him up. She did so, but even after fighting with the demons for 5000 years, he was unable to conquer them. At last, through the Goddess Māya's power, they asked Vishnu to name the reward he desired to have for having fought bravely. He accepted the offer, and asked them to die! They were thus taken in! At this moment the earth was covered with water. Seeing the deluge, the demons asked Vishnu to kill them where there was no water. Vishnu lifted them up to his waist, and there killed them. Goddess Māyā who thus ensured success had ten heads and ten feet. She was very dark, and was therefore named Mahākāli: This was the first incarnation of Goddess Māyā. In the second *avatār*, it is said that a monster half man, half buffalo, named Mahishāsura arose. He defeated all the gods, and Indra their king, was obliged to run away from heaven. He went to Brahma with the gods. Brahma took them to Vishnu and Shiva. They related their grievances. Vishnu and Shiva became very angry and flames issued from their mouths. All the gods emitted flames. From these flames issued a woman. She rode a lion and killed the buffalo giant. This incarnation is called Mahālaxmi. The third incarnation is called Mahāsaraswati. When demons Shumbha and Nishumbha conquered gods, they went to the Himalaya mountains and offered prayers unto goddess Devi. They saw Pārvati the wife of Shiva coming there to take a bath in the Ganges. From her body issued forth a beautiful young woman. This is the third *avatār*. Shumbha deputed Sugriva to induce her to marry him. He returned unsuccessful. Demon King Shumbha sent his army headed by Dhumralochana. She killed most of the demons and the remnants were destroyed by her charger the lion. Then followed two demons Chanda and Munda with their immense army. They saw the goddess seated on a lion. They attacked her. She was so angry that her face turned black with rage. From her forehead issued forth Kāli—who looked dreadful with her necklace of human heads, and her dress made of tiger's skin. She was black, her protruding tongue and her eyes were red as fire. She began devouring the army of the demons, with their horses and elephants. Seeing this dreadful carnage, king Chanda came forward, and Munda followed. She beheaded Chanda and brought Munda down to dust with her javelin. She took the heads of these two demons to the Goddess Devi—who honoured her with the title of *Chāmunda* (from Chanda and Munda) and added that she would be worshipped under that title.

When Chanda and Munda were thus destroyed with their armies, Shumba and Nishumbha came forward with their forces. Devi, her lion, Kāli, and Chandika were supported by all the Gods. Their *Shaktis* or powers issued out of their bodies in the shape of women. Brahman's *shakti* was riding a *Vimān* carried by a pair of swans. Shiva's *Shakti* was riding her husband's bull, Kumār's was riding a peacock, Vishnu's was on the shoulders of Garud, and so forth. From the body of Devi issued a *shakti* named Chandika. She was a terrible figure to look at. She asked Shiva to carry her message to the demons asking them to return to the nether land. They defied the goddess, they fought, many of them were killed, and the rest ran away. One Raktabij however came forward; each drop of his blood producing a fresh demon like himself. When all the *shaktis* of the gods attacked him, countless demons rose from his blood. The whole battle-field was full of these cannibals, and the gods were alarmed. At last, Devi asked Kāli to drink the blood that issued from the wounds inflicted by the goddesses on the bodies of the demons. Devi then speared them, and Kāli drank every drop that came out. As no drops of blood could thus reach the surface of the earth, no new demons arose, and their number was speedily reduced. At last they were all killed with their chief Raktabij. The Goddesses drank so much blood that they got intoxicated. At last Shumbha and Nisumbha were both killed by the Goddess. In the fourth manifestation, Devi became Nandā or the daughter of Nand. When Demon Kausa held her by her legs to dash her on a stone to kill her, she escaped from his hands and shouted that his real enemy Krishna was already safe in Nanda's house. In the fifth *aavtār* she was called Raktadanti because she crushed with her teeth another demon. In the sixth manifestation, she protected people from a famine extending over a hundred years, and was called Shākhāmbari. In the seventh, she killed giant Durgam and was named Durga. In the eigth, she became Mātangi and in the ninth Labhramāri when she destroyed demon Aruna who had violated the wives of many Gods and Kings.

On the first day of the month of Ashwin, a water pot is placed on an alter. The eighth day is observed as a feast, and on the ninth, the sacred fire is kindled.

Animal sacrifices are offered to her. She likes them much. An unmarraid girl is worshipped. When the moon arrives at the constellation called *Mula*, she is invited to come, and when at the constellation *Shravan* she is allowed to return so her heavenly abode. On the Vijaya Dashmi day, she is worshipped again before finally bidding her good bye. During the nine days of the *Navarātra*, her devotees either fast or take only one meal. If they are unable to do so, they observe the fast for seven, five, or three days, at least. The recitation of the *mantra* is performed. Brahmans are fed, and given cash and clothes. The *puja* is performed in the right royal fashion. The unmarried girl selected to represent the goddess, should be healthy, beautiful, and free from eruptions. She should be of the same caste as the devotee. It is advisable to worship nine girls simultaneously on the fifth day of the month, when the Goddess Lalita is specially worshipped. [For falklore see under Lalita Panchami.] On the tenth day all books, arms, and instruments are worshipped, and all men cross the boundary of the town.

The origin of the Navarātra is thus given. When Rāma found that as soon as he cut off any of the heads of Rāvan, they came back life again, all the gods became alarmed at this phenomenon and prayed to the goddess Devi who was asleep. She awoke at mid-night of the first day of Ashwin, before the moon rose above the horizon. She blessed Rāma, and said that he would soon be able to kill Rāvan. The gods were grateful, and decided that they should fast and worship the Goddess until the demon was killed. They performed the *puja* in the best possible manner. On the eighth day, Rāma did kill Rāvan. The Goddess appeared before the gods and they ignited the sacred fire on the 9th day, and offered animal sacrifices. On the tenth day when the moon reached the *Shravan* mansion, Rāma started back triumphant for his capital, and therefore this day is called Vijayā-dashami from *Vijaya* success, and *dashami* the the tenth day. Before taking his seat in the heavenly vehicle, Rāma worshipped the *shami* tree [*Prosopis spicigera*], and then crossed the boundary of Ceylon.

## DASARA.

*Dasara* does not exactly form part of the *Navarātra puja*. It immediately follows that worship. In the Rajput and Maratha states this is a grand holiday. It is pre-eminently the most important day of the year among the ancient ruling families of these tribes. Early in the morning, all the elephants and horses are washed, groomed, and caparisoned in accordance with the rank of the owner. In the front quadrangle of the palace of a Māhāraja, the principal state officers and hereditary dignitaries assemble to take part in the *puja* of the *Gādi* or *masnad*, or throne, on which the Mahārāja sits on state ceremonies of a religious type as distinguished from the Durbars in which chairs and sofas are requisite, and European officers are invited. The *gādi* is a separate thing altogether which no one with shoes on ever approaches. It is always made of the best material and the silk cushions are lined with gold cloth. It is most scrupulously guarded night and day from evil eyes and missiles of witch-craft. Excepting those who are really trusted by the Mahārāja none are allowed to approach it. After the *puja* of this emblem of royalty, the elephants, horses, palanquins, charriots, *haudās*, armours, arms, and the state-flag are all worshipped. As each animal 'march passes' the standard it turns towards the Mahārāja and makes a *salām* or a signal to that effect. A horse neighing or an elephant making a peculiar sound at this moment is considered a good omen. At the end of the "march past" Brahmans are paid cash or presented with dresses and the morning Darbār is dissolved. At about three o'clock in the afternoon the whole army of the state, consist ing of artillery, cavalry, infantry etc., is ready in full dress to take part in the great procession. The elephants, about a hundred in number, are arranged in front of the palace according to the ranks of the *Sardārs* who are privileged to ride them, the palace officer and his assistants are busy calling out the names under which each of the animals has been registered, and despatching them to the residences of the *Sardārs* for whom they are intended. All arrive at the palace in good time with their mounted orderlies and silver-sticks or *chobdārs*. The whole army is arranged; some in front of the palace for the procession as orderlies and some on the "*Dasarā-maidān*." which means the place where the sacrifice takes place on the *Dasara* day. The route is duly lined with soldiers, and policemen. All private traffic is suspended, but there is not much of it, because every body is seated somewhere on a vantage ground or on the road side to see the gorgeous spectacle. When everything is ready, the 'standard-bearers,' elephant is brought forward and placed in front of the main entrance of the palace, closely guarded. He carries in addition to the standard, the *danka* or war-drum. Silence prevails for a few minutes; all standing expectant at the near approach of the Mahārāja. As soon as the Mahārāja's elephant issues out of the chief gate, the war drum is sounded by command of the Head of the Army who salutes His Highness. This royal salute is a signal. The few selected *Sardārs* who are privileged to take their elephants inside the gate to wait on the Māhāraja, come out one after another, the rest who had to wait outside the quadrangle joining the procession in rank and file. For about a mile or two this pageant goes in full swing followed by spectators of all castes and creeds. At the boundary of the city, the Agent to the Governor General, or the British Resident at the Court, has his camp in tents carefully arranged and suitably decorated with flags and pennons. On the Māhāraja approaching the spot, he receives a salute from the British officers and responds in a graceful manner. The Māhāraja then proceeds to the *shami-tree* (*Prosopis spicigera*) under which arrangements are made for its *puja*. The tree is specially held sacred on this day, as the Pāndavas of old, once tied their arms to the branches of a specimen of this species. Whatever the case, a *Shami-tree* is absolutely necessary for the chief worship of the Dasara-day. Here, the King and the chief *Sardārs* get down from their *haudās* and sit on the carpets, spread all round the tree on a masonry plat-form. At the end of the worship, the Mahārāja cuts with his own sword a calabash fruit *(Cucurbita pepo)* as a sacrifice in place of the animal that was cut down in olden days. The *Shami-tree* has all round it branches of the *āpta (Bauhinia tomentosa).* They are *looted* by the *Sardārs* and the leaves are called 'gold' for the time being. This done, the Mahārāja rides his elephant, and so do the Sardārs. A royal salute accosts His Highness, and before he turns back, a buffalo is sacrificed. On its return journey the whole procession is greeted with bon-fires and fire works intermixed with shouts of "*Sriman, Mahārāja, Vijayi Bhava*"; "May success follow Mahāraja"; or "May he be successful." On arrival at the palace another Durbar is held and *Khillāts* distributed according to rank. In private families, when a husband returns home, his wife receives him at the door, waves round his face a cupful of water with a few grains of rice in it and throws it away to take off the effect of the evil eye. He offers a leaf of the *āpta* with a coin to his family gods and takes a seat specially arranged for him. His wife then comes forward with a silver tray holding a lamp and waves it round his face. He drops a necklace, a ring, or a coin according to his means. The *āpta* leaves are then exchanged among friends and relations with good wishes for the forthcoming year. Among the Marātha chiefs this was considered the most auspicious day for starting on a militant expedition against restive *Sardārs*; and many of the historical expeditions will be found to have started on the *Vijaya* or success day. *Dasara* is also considered a very auspicious day for beginning the educational career of a boy. For this purpose, after worshipping all the books, manuscripts, and *daftars*, containing family documents as representing goddess Saraswati who presides over learning, the priest ceremoniously initiates young boys of four or five, by drawing a symbol of that Goddess on a slate and showing the A B C of the local alphabets. He gets his fee and a dress. A feast follows in which relatives and caste men take part.

**Panchak.** The five constellations from the second half of *Dhanistha* to the first half of *Ashvini*. During this time the sun is at these houses of the stars, certain things and actions are forbidden.

**Parashurám Jayanti.** Parashurám was the son of a Kshatriya princess married to a Brahman named Jamadagni. His mother, Renuka, went to her sister's house who was the queen of King Sahasrārjun. She was not respected. Her husband was annoyed with her, and at his command Parashurām killed his own mother. The father was pleased. Parashurām subsequently asked his father to bring his mother to life. It was done, and she became a martyr, or goddess. It is said that the Kshatriyas killed Jamadagni, and in retaliation, Parashurām carried on 21 expeditions against that tribe. He was defeated by Rāma the hero of the Rāmāyan. He supplies an example of the animosity perceived against the mother's tribe by a half caste. His birthday is observed as a fast on the 2nd moon of *Vaishākh* ( April-May ), specially by Brahmans whom he helped, when there was a keen rivalry between the ruling race and the priestly tribe.

**Phāg.** The Holi Holidays or the licentious songs sung during the Saturnalia. ( See *Holi* ).

**Phalgu.** The vernal festival commonly called Holi ( which see ).

**Phālgun.** The last month of the Hindu Calender. (For folklore of the holidays see *Holi*).

**Phalguni.** The name of a pair of constellations (a *Al Zubra,* Pichorion, Frons and (b) *Al Serpha,* Asphulia, St. Amoris, in the Arabian, Greek and Latin Languages. It is also the name of the day of the full-moon of the month of *Phlāgun,* the day on which the *Holi* is celebrated (see Holi for folklore)

**Pithori.** High class or twice born Hindu mothers worship the goddess Pithori on *Amāvāsya* or the last day of the month of *Shravān* (August-September).

In the *Bhavishottar Purān* Indrāni, the wife of Indra, the King of the Gods, asked Pārvati, the wife of Shiva, to describe the *Vrat* which would grant the blessing of a son to a sonless woman, and would thus help her to ensure happiness in Heaven to her ancestors (through the *Shrādh* ceremonies the son would perform). Pārvati replied, says the *Purān*:

" There lived in ancient days a very rich Brahman named Shridhar. His wife Sumitrā was very faithful and very obedient. Shridhar's eldest son was named Sankar. His wife was named Videhā. She gave birth to many children but they were short lived. On one occasion, it was a stillborn son, born on the day of the *Shrādh* ceremony, Shridhar was performing. Sumitrā, the mother-in-law, was much grieved at the unfortunate coincidence which interfered with the *Shrādh*, and abused her daughter-in-law. The attack of the mother-in-law exasperated Videhā, and not knowing what would follow, she left the house with the corpse in her arms, to commit suicide. She wandered into a forest. There, she saw a beautiful hermitage on the banks of a river. It was occupied by a woman, who repeatedly looked at Videhā and said to herself 'Why has this good-looking woman come here?' She then turned towards her and said 'Oh auspicious lady (married) this place is haunted by the ghosts, *Jhotingas*, *Yakshās*, and *Vetāl*. They will devour you. Do quickly go back.' Videhā replied 'Oh fair-eyed, I am so distressed: pray tell me how I can be saved and made prosperous. She was advised to pray to the sixty-four *Yoginis* or Devis who visited the hermitage at midnight. 'They will,' she assured her, 'grant long life to your children.' She was advised to hide herself among the *Bel*, *Ægle marmoles* leaves 'When the Devis will,' said the woman living in the temple, 'enquire if there is an *Atithi* or a guest entitled to hospitality, come out and present yourself before them.' Videhā felt assured of good luck and hid herself in the leaves as desired. At this time various ghosts entered the hermitage. They smelt human flesh and enquired of the keeper. They asked her to account for the smell of a human being. While the enquiry was thus proceeding, and the keeper was being repeatedly pressed to speak the truth, the sixty-four Goddesses arrived and they began worshipping the goddess of the hermitage. The ghosts ran away. As soon as they finished their *puja*, they enquired if there was a guest deserving hospitality. At this moment Videhā came out of the *Bel* leaves and said, 'Mothers: I have just lost my child and am in mourning. I offer myself as the *Atithi*. Seven children were born unto me, one after another, but they all died soon after birth. I am a miserable, distressed creature. It is my good luck that brings me to you. I therefore beg of you the blessing that my future progeny be granted long lives.' The Goddesses pitied the poor woman and gave her the remnants of the offerings of eatables presented to the deity, They then told her that they already knew that she was the daughter-in-law of Shridhar and the wife of Shankar. 'May you,' said they, 'in this mortal life enjoy all the happiness possible as a mother and a grand-mother of many children. May you after completion of your term of life, be equally happy in Heaven. You will soon regain your eight sons. Return to your house.' The Goddesses then disappeared. But hardly had they become invisible, when the eight sons of Videhā came to her. She was overjoyed. She left the hermitage with her sons and went back to her town. Shridhar Brahman, his son Shankar, and his relations all received Videhā and her sons with joy. Many festivities followed. All felt very happy. The Brahman guests began singing the sacred hymns of the *Vedas*. Musicians began all sorts of entertainments, women came dressed like butterflies and performed auspicious ceremonies. Dancing girls were in full swing, and singing reached a high pitch. In the midst of these excellent accompaniments Videhā performed the *puja* of the Sixty-four Goddesses. Such—says Pārvati to Indrāni, is the power of the Pithori *Vrat.* If a woman worships the Goddesses she gets sons, grand-sons and wealth. She should first of all pray unto them, pay obeisance to them and worship them full of faith. Women who worship the Pithori Goddess become very lucky. Good fortune follows them wherever they go."

The woman who has to worship the Pithori, observes a fast on the day sacred to the sixty four goddesses. In the evening of that day she bathes and puts a picture before her reclining against the wall facing the East if possible. She then puts near it a branch of the *Vat-Ficus Indica*—and a pot full of a preparation of milk and sugar—near the picture in front of these are arranged carefully the offerings, she wishes to make—most of them consist of betel leaves, betel nuts, cocoanuts, plantains and other fruits of the season. From the time she comes out of the bath she must not speak a word. She performs the *puja* as usual, and at the end, places a cake over the pot of milk and sugar, holds it over her head and says, *Atit kon?* Her children respond to the call and take the food from behind. They are then given a good dinner with the other members of the family. In olden days elaborate scenes were painted on the wall with sandalwood paste or on a piece of silk cloth with an indelible ink but since the introduction of printing, they are being lithographed and sold at a nominal cost: thus saving the trouble of drawing them but losing the variety due to individual propensities or capabilities of the worshippers.

Panel 1 of the picture worshipped, shows Ganesh or the God of success and his two attendants Riddhi and Siddhi who represent Prosperity and Success. He has to be worshipped at the beginning of every *Puja* of any God or Goddess. Panel 2, contains Shiva and his wife Pārvati with the sacred bull Nandi and an attendant. He is the Bhutanāth or the ruler of all the ghosts and evil spirits including Kāl the god of death. Panel 3 represents Krishna who was the (eighth) surviving son of Devaki. This *puja* has possibly been suggested by the events preceding Krishna's birth, the death of the first five children of his mother, at the hands of their maternal uncle Kansa. Krishna's childhood has therefore been depicted in this and the next panel. Here he is shown playing his flute with the avowed object of calling in cows but really of inviting the milkmaids of his town to frolics and flirtations. Panel 4 shows, how he used to steal butter while his adopted mother Yashoda was churning. Panel 5 shows, the Goddess Gauri and her maid. She is the emblem of chastity. Panel 6 represents, the entrance of the house occupied by the 64 fairies with a band of musicians and a few boys. Panels 7 and 8 show grinding and pounding corn, the domestic pride of a good house-wife. Panel 9 represents the river on whose banks stood the hermitage of the fairies. The ubiquitous priest, the usual bathers, and the playful boys are all shown. Panel 10 shows the most important scene. Here is the once bereaved mother still on her sick-bed following accouchement, as is shown by the presence of the fire underneath. She has two babies in the cradle and half a dozen boys brought to life again through the blessings of the 64 fairies. It is the highest goal of ambition of a Hindu woman. She is all happy. The next panel, 11, shows that she is now very rich as she could keep an elephant, and a milch cow (panel 18). But in the back ground of this panel, there lies the temple of Shiva surrounded by ghosts and evil spirits, for she is the lord of them all. That is where the story began, a haunted temple. At panel 13, our devoted heroine has been worshipping the 64 fairies. She has just held over her head the pot containing food and says "*Atit kon?*" or "*Koi atit hai?*" Is there any guest expecting hospitality? Just behind her stand her children who reply "Yes, mama, I am; and I too, etc." At panel 14, the pancake is being prepared by a cook and at panel 15 our lucky heroine the proud mother of 8 sons has been worshipping the sacred *tulsi* plant, *Ocyumm Sanctum.*

**Povati-Pornima.** The day of full moon of the month *Shrāvan* (July-August). It is called so because, a new sacred thread (*povte*) is thrown round an idol, then taken and worn as a blessing from the god symbolized in that idol.

**Probodhini Ekadashi.** (See Ekadashi).

**Prodosh.** The twelfth day of each half of the lunar month which is observed as a fast by the followers of Shiva.

**Puja holidays.** In Bengal, the Navarātrās are called *the* Puja Holidays, being the largest and the most important local festival. For folklore, see Navarātra.

**Rákhi-punam.** See *Nārali Pornima.*

**Rāmanavami.** On the first of *Chaitra* (March-April begins the *puja* of the birth of Rāma the seventh incarnation of Vishnu. Every evening *Kathas* or sermons are delivered by professional *Kathaks* in all temples dedicated to Rāma until the ninth day, when as soon as the sun reaches the meridian, the birth is celebrated with great eclat. In the *Kathās* prominence is generally given to stories from the Rāmāyan.

**Rangapanchmi.** The fifth day of the dark half of the month of *Phālgun* (February-March), on which people throw colour, etc. about. See Holi for particulars.

**Sādhan Dvádashi.** The twelth lunar day on which the first breakfast is taken after observing Ekādashi, is called by this name.

The story runs, that once upon a time there lived a pious king named Ambarish. He always fasted on the *ekādashi* or the 11th lunar day, and distributed food and alms among Brahmans on the twelth. Thousands of Brahamans were fed and feasted, and given presents including horses and elephants. On of these days, Rishi Durvāsa came to him as a guest. Durvāsa was notorious for being a very irritable saint with a very sharp tongue. He quickly lost his temper at the slightest want of courtesy and wickedly cursed alleged offenders. His curse was considered potent and his punishment was cruel. Pious King Ambarish received him very courtiously and offered him a seat on his own throne, worshipped him and touched his feet in humble submission. He then solicited the Rishi's company at breakfast. The saint consented and left the place for a bath in the river Jamna. But he took such a long time to finish his oblations, that the period for breaking the fast had nearly expired. The King found himself in a curious position. The irritable vindictive Brahaman on one side, and his own sacred vow of observing the details of the fast, on the other. As a good host he could not take his food before feeding the Brahaman, and as a religious duty he could not neglect the observanace. What then could he do? He thought of a device. He said to himself, that a sip of water from the washings of the sacred image he worshipped, would break the fast, while taking such a sip would be taking no meal. Waiting however until the last moment, he held in the hollow of the hand that little water. As the *Rishi* did not reach the palace in time, he most unwillingly took the sip. But the moment he did so the irreconciliable Brahman stood before him like a ghost, and demanded explanation for having broken the fast before feeding him.

Terrible was his rage, it seemed as if fire flashed out of his eyes as he angrily stared at the king. The poor mortal of a king trembled, supplicated, apologised and lay prostrate in servile submission. But the uncompromising conceited Brahman could not be appeased. He moreover loosened the knot of his hair as a mark of extreme rage, and out of the long hair that touched his knees he created a female demon. With wild eyes, open jaws and terrible nails like the paws of a lioness, she sprang at the king to tear him and to eat him piecemeal!

But halt! There rose in heaven the protecting all powerful, invincible *Sudarshan* of Vishnu, the powerful missile, against the monster and burst into flames like a twentieth century bomb and reduced her to ashes in the twinkling of an eye! God Vishnu the Protecter had deputed this all powerful weapon to protect his devotee. As soon as the cannibal was destroyed, the divine missile ran against the mischievous Brahman and began to burn him! But he was a tough Brahman and the process was slow! He ran up to Brahma and begged protection. Brahma the Creator, said that he had no power to interfere with the all pervading Vishnu. The Rishi then went to Shiva but he also pleaded inability to intervene; on the contrary he reminded the priest that he himself owed his cure from the burning *halāhal* to Vishnu, when he drank it once upon a time. Scalded all over, the offending priest went to Vishnu and touched his feet, earnestly begging to be protected. God Vishnu reminded him of his determination to protect every one of his devotees from harm, and said that he could not consistently withdraw the divine missile or prevent its fire from burning him. The only course left was to apologize to the pious king for foolishly attacking him while he was in the discharge of his religious duty. The crestfallen priest was obliged to go back to the king who received him most generously and prayed to the divine fire to retire. It did so, leaving the Brahman free!

Such is the power of Vishnu, the Protector and such is the merit of observing the *Sādhan Dwādashi Vrat*.

**Sampat-Shanvār.** Every Saturday in the month of *Shrāvan* (July-August) is called *Sampat-Shanvār* or wealth-giving Saturday. The story runs, a poor Brahman lived in a certain town. He had three daughters-in-law. Once on a Saturday, in the month of *Shrāvan* (July-August); he left at home his youngest daughter-in-law to look after the cooking and went out to work in the field with all other members. He instructed her to prepare the meal and the articles of worship in the prescribed fashion. She was a charitably disposed good girl. In the absence of the members, there came to her house the god Shani or Saturn assuming the shape of a man suffering with leucoderma. He begged to be anointed with oil and pounded balsam seed. He then asked for warm water to bathe, and finally begged that he may be given a hearty meal. The charitable girl granted to the beggar all his desires. He took his meal and pushed the leavings of the platter into the eaves of the hut. After he left the house, the family returned and found everything ready except food, which proved insufficient. On enquiry, the Brahman learnt that his daughter-in-law fed a poor recluse. On the following Saturday, he left the eldest daughter-in-law in charge of the hut, and went out as usual. Saturn came as a leper, and begged to be bathed and fed, but the girl turned him out, saying that she had no food to give him. "Be it so" cursed the irritated god and left. On returning home, the father-in-law found that nothing was ready, and that the food prepared by his daughter-in-law had mysteriously disappeared. On the third Saturday, the second daughter-in-law was left behind. Saturn came again, and was turned out. He levelled a similar curse and disappeared. The same result followed. On the fourth Saturday the youngest daughter-in-law was again placed in charge of the kitchen. The god Saturn this time appeared as a leper with ugly sores. He begged in the same way and his request was granted with good faith. He again pushed the leavings of his platter into the eaves and left. On returning home, the family found the house full of good things and nice dainties, and wondered how could they be prepared with the scanty supply they had in store. The girl was asked to explain the miracle. She gave the history of the leper-guest. It was clear to the Brahman, that the god Saturn's blessings made him rich. He began examining his house and admiring its new contents. To his surprise, he found something shining in the eaves of the hut. On taking the two bundles out he discovered that they contained most valuable gems! These said the girl are the leavings of the recluse! May the god Saturn bless the reader in the same way.

**Sankata Vrat.** A certain king in Bengal had no child. He married seven wives one after another, but they all proved barren. At last an ascetic offered him a drug on condition that if by virtue of his potion his seven queens presented him with seven sons he should give away the most beautiful of the lot to the holy man. Of the seven queens six senior ones were jealous of the youngest, because she was a favourite of the king. They took the medicine without giving her her share. When the omission was discovered they pleaded forgetfulness. Some one advised the youngest queen to drink the washings of the curry stone over which the drug was pounded. She did so. All gave birth to sons in due course but the youngest wife's child looked like a conch shell! When the king saw the conch shell he felt disgusted and deserted the mother of that monstrosity. She went to live in a cottage. The queen held the conch shell near her breast like a child! She was so simple and loving. During her sleep the shell sucked her milk unobserved and grew bigger and bigger. One night she pretended sleep and watched. She then saw a baby coming out of the shell! She caught hold of the boy and broke the empty shell. But the child remonstrated. That reminded her of the King's promise to the holy man! She took him to the king. He was pleased to see so beautiful a prince. At the end of twelve years the asectic returned, and claimed that very boy as his share, because all the others were ugly. There was no help! The queen was advised to observe the *Sankata Vrat* to regain her son. It consisted of a fast on Fridays with meditations. The holy man took the child to a Kāli's temple in a forest. He took a bath in the adjoining river and leaving the prince in a hut, entered the temple alone to propitiate the goddess, telling the boy not to open the south entrance of the cottage. But as soon as the ascetic left, the boy, out of curosity, did open the door! He was horrified to see a number of human heads floating over a tank full of red fluid! The lifeless heads laughed at him! When questioned, they said that they were all princes like himself, and that the wicked ascetic had sacrificed them to his horrid goddess. He had the same fate awaiting him. He was advised by one of the heads to ask the ascetic to show him how to bow unto the goddess when he would himself be told to do so, and to chop off his head as soon as he did so! He was asked to sprinkle that fellow's blood over them (the heads). That, he was assured, would bring them to life again. The assetic returned to the hut and found the prince deep in meditation. He had already sacrificed 107 princes and this boy was the last the 108th to complete this offer. He was so overjoyed that he forgot to follow the *modus operandi* of the *puja* and thus offended the goddess! He took the prince to the temple and asked him to bow down to the goddess falling flat on his face as is done by devotees. The prince pleaded ignorance as he was tutored, and asked the man to show him how to do it. While the wicked man was in that posture, the prince severed his head with one stroke of the sacrificing knife, which lay near. He then bowed unto the goddess, sprinkled the ascetic's blood over the floating heads, and brought them to life. His reputation reached the king of the country in which the temple was situated, and he was sent for. The king married him to his own daughter. He then returned to his father with his blushing bride, and his 107 princely friends. He was well received. He explained how he succeeded in killing that wicked ascetic through the help of the goddess *Sankasthi.*

**Sankrănt.** The last Tuesday in the bright half of every alternate month of even number, that is 2, 4, 6, 8, 10, 12, is called *Mangal-Sankrănt.* If observed as a fast ending in the worship of the goddess presiding over it, it has the power to wash away the sin of touching a Brahman, a conch-shell, a cow or a copper basin during a woman's recurring monthly illness.

A certain woman did not observe the fast, and suffered terrible illness. She was also transformed into a conch-shell, a cow, a copper pot, and earthen pot by turns. One of her daughters-in-law gave away to her the merit of the fasts she had herself scrupulously observed, and the old woman recovered. A priest explained the ill effect of the non-observance of the fast, and the good effect of the daughter-in-law's benevolence. Women in Bengal therefore observe this fast to evade the terrible calamities.

**:ankrant Sodo.** There was a Bania with only one daughter. She was married while she was a girl of eight. Her aunt had some hand in the matter and it was suspected that she was given away for a consideration to a *dakait*, because she was good-looking. The parents felt disgraced and would not refer to the subject again. Time passed and her father got seven sons one after another. But the father died. The boys were obliged to take up his business. They loaded seven boats with commodities and started on a voyage. Accidentally they happened to put up in the house of the *dakāit* family. The thieves were five brothers. They cunningly gave wet faggots to the guests in order to delay the operation of cooking their food, so that they might be overtaken by night and be induced to sleep in their house, giving them an opportunity to murder them. The *dakāit* brothers left home under some excuse or other to avoid suspicion. The daughter-in-law of the house discovered that the guests were her brothers and disclosed to them the plot. The brothers ran away. She then set fire to the house. When her husband and his brothers returned she told them that the guests had burnt the house and misdirected them in pursuit. They were asked to go to the south. They ran, they tumbled, they fell, they got themselves injured, their progress was delayed, the merchant brothers escaped. During their absence, their mother performed the *puja* of the Surya Deva (Sun God.) The offerings consisted of boats made of the -fresh sheaths of the plantain tree, adorned with flowers and surmounted with a lamp. Her daughter learned the process, followed it, and the sin of committing *dakaities* was washed off! The two families were reconciled, and lived in peace.

**Saraswatipujan.** To worship Saraswati, the goddess of learning after the invocation of her spirit or influence upon books and writings, observed in the month of *Ashwin*

(September-October), when the moon is at their *Mula*-Constellation. See Dasara for particulars.

**Saturn,** worship of the. See Sampat Shanvār.

**Satya Nārāyan.** Once upon a time, Saint Nārad the son of Brahma, came down on the earth from Heaven. He saw that the people of this planet were born, reborn, and born again in accordance with their *karma* or action in the previous birth, and that they suffered pain in proportion to their sinful and good conduct during each transit. Seeing this the Saint returned to Vaikunth, the abode of Vishnu, the Protector. There he saw the fair complexioned, four-handed God with the conch, wheel, mace and lotus in his hands and the Vaijayanti necklace round his neck. Seeing the God of Gods, Saint Nārad prayed. He said, "He whose form is incomprehensible to the mind and difficult for the language to describe, He who is Omnipotent, He who has no beginning, no middle and no end, He who has no quality and quantity, He who without possessing these qualities himself is able to create, protect, and destroy, He who is the beginning of everything, He who destroys the misfortunes or pains of His devotees, unto Him do I bow." Hearing this prayer God Vishnu said "Oh fortunate Nārad, what brings you here, What are your wishes? Tell me all this." Nārad replied," Oh Lord! The residents of the planet Earth have been steeped in the ocean of sin. The dead are born again in different forms, commit sin again, and are again doomed to a fresh birth equally sinful; therefore oh God, as you are so kind to me, pray tell me the simplest plan to relieve them from this cycle of births and deaths."

Vishnu replied, "You put this question to me with the charitable object of relieving the misery of the people. It is very creditable to you. I tell you what will meet your wishes. Listen, in Heaven and on Earth there is a very sacred and very rare *vrata*. I disclose it to you out of love for you, dear child. If people perform the Satya

Nārāyan *vrata*, they will be blessed with a happy and prosperous career and will also get seats in Heaven." Nārad said, "Oh Nārāyan ! What is the effect of this *vrata*, what is the process, and who performed it before, and when should it be performed?" God Vishnu replied, "This *vrata* gives relief from pain and distress and grants a copious supply of food and wealth. It also bestows long life to the husbands of married women, gives them children, and grants success in every undertaking. It may be performed on any day when the devotee feels inclined to do so, whenever he has faith and devotion enough. It should be performed in company with relations and Brāhmans at sun set. God Nārāyan (myself) should be worshipped and to him should be offered a pie made up of one and a quarter *seers* of flour or one and a quarter of any measure, mixed with sliced plantains, *ghi*, milk and sugar. But every one of these ingredients should be "one and a quarter" in measure or weight. This *katha* (history) should then be read aloud, and all the Brahmans, relations and guests should be fed. The worshipper should also partake of the pie. He should then dance. The place to perform the *puja* should be a sacred place like a temple, or the banks of a river. Finally meditating on the eternal qualities of the real Nārāyan he should return home. I assure you, that during this Kali Yuga or Iron Age, this is the easiest way of attaining success in everything. This *puja* was for the first time performed by a very poor Brahman a resident of the beautiful city of Benares. He was hungry and thirsty and used to go about begging. Seeing this the Protector of the priests, assumed the form of an old Brahman and asked him why he wandered in such a painful state. The poor vagrant explained his miserable state and prayed that he be shown the way to get out of the clutches of poverty. The All-prevading God in the form of the old Brahman replied "Vishnu who is Omnipresent will grant your desires, if you worship him through the Satya Nārāyan *vrat.* It relieves a man from distress of every kind. He then explained the process and disappeared. The poor beggar was so anxous to perform the *puja* that he had no sleep that night. The next morning he got up from his bed and vowed that he would that evening perform the *puja*, and left for begging. He got lots of money, with which he made the necessary preparations, invited his relations and friends and performed the *puja*. The result was that the good Brahman became rich and was freed from all anxieties. He therefore repeated the *puja* every month. He enjoyed a long and prosperous life and in the end reached heaven safe free from all sins. He who does so will be equally blessed. On one day a hewer of wood who was collecting fagots, saw that this Brahman devoutly performed the *puja* and asked him after reverential salutaions what it was? What was the effect? The Brahman described the *vrata*, of the real God, and added that he had become fabulously rich through the performance of this worship of the All-prevading God.

The fagot-bearer partook of the pie given to him, drank fresh water and resumed his journey to the city with the fuel on his head. He meditated on God Satya Nārāyan and vowed that he would that day spend the proceeds of his fuel on the worship of that God. As he entered that charming city he went to the Richmen's Row, and got double the price! He was so glad. He bought excellent plantains, good sugar, fresh *ghi*, fine milk, and first class flour. Each of these weighed one and a quarter of the measure selected. He performed the *puja* in the presence of his friends and relations in the right sacred way. He got money, grain, sons, and was happy all the days of his life. Hereafter he reached heaven.

Another instance may be added. There was an Emperor named Ulkamukha. He had conquered the passions, was truthful, and very intelligent. He punctually visited temples and there distributed alms to Brahmans. His faithful wife Bhadrasila, the lotus-faced, was beautiful beyond comparison. That king one day was engaged, in performing this *puja* on the banks of a river. A Bania named Sādhu went there with many trade-samples of numerous commodities. He most respectfully asked the King what he was doing with so much devotion. The King replied " Oh Sādhu, I have been worshipping the All-pervading Vishnu whose lustre is above parallel, in the company of my relations, with the object of obtaining sons, &c. At the request of the merchant the King described to him the whole process of the worship. The Bania then returned home, postponing his tour and described in details the worship to his wife. He vowed that on getting children, he would perform the *puja*. Sādhu, the Banker, thus impressed the sanctity and the fruitfulness of the *puja* on his religious wife Lilāvati. She soon got a daughter as beautiful as the moon. She was named Kalāvati. The mother of this beauteous child reminded her husband of the vow, but (a miser that he was) he said that he would perform the *puja* at the marriage of the girl. He then left on his travelling tour. Kalāvati become marriageable. Her father the Bania sent messengers to various towns to find out a suitable husband. One of them reached Kānchannagar. From that city he brought a Bania's son. Finding that the boy was a good-looking and a well educated young man, Sādhu offered his daughter to him. He collected his caste-men and ceremoniously performed the marriage. Unfortunately for him he forgot to worship God Satya-Nārāyan even at the marriage as proviously arranged. He again left on a commercial tour accompanied by his son-in-law. He reached the city of Ratnsār situated on the banks of the river Sindhu, ruled by a king named Chandraketu. It was a fine city. God Satya Nārāyan finding that this money-grubber had sinfully neglected the vow, cursed him. He was doomed to suffer a severe penalty. Soon after this event, a thief entered the palace of King Chandraketu, committed theft and left the stolen property in the house occupied by the Banias and ran away. The police discovered the property, arrested the Banias and took them prisoners. They were handcuffed, placed before the King with the property so 'cleverly' recovered. The King without listening to the defence, hastily directed that they be chained heavily and confined in a dungeon in his fort. The Banias pleaded that they were innocent, but no one listened to them, because of the curse of the real God, when the real God was displeased. The King directed that their property be confiscated. The curse of the real God, also affected the wife of the Bania. *Dakaits* looted her house. She was overtaken by diseases, she became a beggar in the streets with her daugter Kalāvati. One day the daughter became exhausted through the pangs of hunger and entered the house of a Brahman for alms. He was performing the *puja* of the real God. She sat, she watched the *puja*, she heard the sacred book describing the *vrata*, she got a portion of the pie, she ate it, she prayed for release from distress, and returned home. The mother inquired why she was so late that evening? What did she mean by such a conduct? Her daughter Kalāvati described the *puja* she saw in the Brahman's house. Mother Lilāvati was glad, and vowed that she would perform that *puja*. She did so with the object of the safe return of her wandering husband and her son-in-law. She prayed "Oh Lord pardon my husband and my son-in-law. You are all powerful." The God was appeased, and influenced King Chandraketu by appearing in his dream. He said "Oh King! do release the two Banias from the jail, the first thing to-morrow morning. Return to them their property and cash. If thou darest disobey, thou shalt lose thy crown, thy wealth, and thy heir-apparent in the bargain!" Saying so to the King in his dream, the god Sataya Nārāyan became invisible. Next morning the King held a *Darbār* and there related his dream: His Majesty then directed the immediate relase of the two Banias. They were brought to the presence of the King. They were so terrified that they began shivering and could not utter a word. The King therefore addressed them thus. He said, "Banias! it was your misfortune that dragged you into the prison. Now, you need not be afraid. You are free. Their shackless were forthwith removed, they were bathed and dressed, and were allowed seats in His Majesty's august presence. They were given double the amount of the wealth that was confiscated, and were requested to return home. The Bania distributed most liberally cash among Brahmans and started in a boat. But to test his devotion, God Satya Nārāyan assumed the form of an old Brahman ascetic, and asked him what his boat contained. The Banias were so arrogant that they began jeering at the old Brahman and enquired "Oh Sanyāsin! (ascetic) why do you put such a question? Do you covet our wealth? Our boat contains merely old leaves and creepers." Hearing this the real God said "May it be so", and walked on. He then went further on and stood on the beach. After the departure of the ascetic the Bania came out to wash himself but was alarmed at the water mark on the stern of the vessel sinking low! Why has she become so light! He examined the contents, and finding that there was nothing but leaves and creepers, he fainted! When he regained conciousness he was very depressed. His son-in-law said that it was the curse of the ascetic that had effected the transformation of his gold into leaves. That showed his power to do what he liked. Let us therefore prostrate ourselves before him. Hearing this the Bania forthwith took himself to the ascetic and said: "Oh Lord, I told you a lie, pardon me for it," and repeatedly bowed. The Brahman-shaped God said: "Oh you wicked! Do not cry. Listen to me. You have turned yourself away from devotion and this is the result. The Bania, prayed and prayed and prayed! He said, "Oh God. Through your illusion even Brama feels confused and forgets what your power is. What then of a foolish mortal like me? What power do I possess to realize your Omnipotence. Be gracious to me. I will perform your *puja.* Give me back all my gold. I lay myself at your mercy. Protect me." Hearing this "the Lord was pleased, and granted him all his desires and disappeared. The Bania then returned to his ship and was glad to see that she was full of money! He then performed the *vrata* and returned home. As he approached the city, he showed the pinnacles of its palatial building to his son-in-law and said, "Look! look at my Ratnapur!" He then deputed a messenger to his house, who told his wife, that her husband and son-in-law were at the port, loaded with riches. She was very glad. She immediately performed the Satya Nārāyan *puja* and left for the ship telling her daughter to follow as quickly as possible. The girl also finished her *puja* quickly but in her haste she forgot to eat the propitiatory offering—the pie. God Satya Nārāyan was angry at this neglect and sunk the vessel with the wealth and the younger Bania. Such a slip between the cup and the lip brought extreme prostration, and the girl cried until she fainted. Seeing this the senior Bania and his crew who were on the beach wondered why had such a thing happened. The wife of the Bania said that it was possibly the displeasure of some God that brought about so sudden a change. She embraced the daughter and began crying bitterly. The daughter took the wooden sandals of the husband and prepared herself for death as a *sati.* At this stage it occurred to the Bania that this must have been done by God Satya Nārāyan. He then called all his cognate together and in their presence vowed that he would perform the *puja,* if every thing came right again. He bowed repeatedly to the God. The Lord that prevades the universe was pleased and said in an echo, "Your daughter neglected the duty of eating the propitiatory offering in her haste to see her husband and therefore I have made things invisible. If therefoie she goes back to the house, eats the pie and returns to the post, she will get her husband back." Kalāvati heard this voice, returned home, partook of the pie and quickly returned to the scene. She was surprised to see her husband there. The Bania was delighted. He worshipped Sataya Nārāyan on the spot, and then returned home along with his friends and relations. Since then he repeated the *puja* on all full moon days and sacred days of sorts. He devoted himself to the real—God, enjoyed long the blessings of mortal life, and in the end attained heavenly bliss.

One more fable. There was once a King named Angadhvaj—very just and very kind, very anxious to protect his subjects. He also was made to suffer for disregard of the pie. One day he had gone to the forest on a shooting excursion. He killed many lions and tigers and sat under a *vat* (*Ficus India*) tree for rest. Some cowherds were engaged in this *puja* on the very spot. The King saw that, but through conceipt, did not go to take part in the worship. Not only that, he did not bow unto the Lord. But the humble cowherds went to the King bowed to him, placed the pie before him and resumed their work. The result was that for this gross insult, the King was made to see his hundred sons disappear at once. His wealth was lost, and his graneries were destroyed. He realized that he had himself to thank for all these misfortunes. He therefore went to the cow-herds, there worshipped Sataya Nārāyan, and partook of the pie with them. The King thereupon regained his lost sons, and his lost wealth. He enjoyed happy life and in the end had a comfortable seat in heaven.

He who perform this *vrata* with real devotion, he who attentively hears this desire-granting story, gets by the grace of the God Sataya Nārāyan, wealth, grain, etc. A beggar becomes a millionaire, of the prisoner—the shackles fall, to the one troubled by fears, there is immediate relief, Worshippers of this God get whatever they wish and there is no doubt that they reach heaven after death. This worship grants every desire. Some call the God, Kāl, some call him Ishvar, some name him Sataya-Nārāyan, some Satya Dev. God assumes all these forms and grants them their desires. In the *Kali* or Iron age, God will manifest himself in the shape of this worship. He who reads this *puran* repeatedly or listens to it has all his sins washed off. This is true. (*Reva Khand,* Chapt. V.)

**Saubhāgya Tritrya.** The third day of the light half of *Bhādrapad* (August-September). For folklore see Haritālika.

**Shanvār.** See Sampat Shanvār.

**Shasthi-Ashoka.** It falls on the 6h day of the bright half of *Chaitra* (March-April) There lived in a hut a sage in an Ashoka *(Jonesia ashoka)* ferest. One morning he saw a very beautiful baby lying in front of his hut. After meditation he understood that a wild doe left the child there after giving her birth. He took her to his hut and nursed her there. When the child was alone, the doe would come and suckle her. Gradually the girl grew to marriageable age. The sage sought in vain for a proper husband for the girl. At last he promised her that he would give her in marriage to the first man whom he would see the following morning. Luckily, he met a Prince at his door, who had gone there for hunt ; but who owing to a heavy storm the previous night, was compelled with his companions to take shelter in the vicinity. Then the sage explained the history of the girl to the Prince and offered her to him as his adopted daughter. He gave her some *Ashoka* flowers and seeds telling her to keep the flowers dried up and to eat them on the *Ashoka Shasthi* day in the month of *Chaitra* (March-April) and secondly to throw the seeds on the way from his hut to the palace of the king. Trees would, he said, grow out of the seeds, and form an avenue. When in trouble, she might return to him through that avenue.

The girl strew the seeds as instructed. After some years Ashokā (as she was called) became the mother of seven sons and one daughter. The sons were married. In due course the father and mother-in-law of Ashokā died. The day for the *Shrādh* ceremony was fixed on the day of *Ashoka-Shasthi.* In the evening Ashoka's daughter-in-law asked her to take her food but she remembered that to be the *Ashoka-Shasthi* day. Her daughter-in-law gave her some boiled *mug.* (*Phaseolus Mungo*). Then all of them went to sleep. On the following morning Ashoka's sons and their wives and children were all found dead. Ashoka hurried to the sage through the Ashok avenue and told him of the sudden death of her whole family. After contemplation, the sage found out that the *mug* (*Phaseolus mungo*) which his foster daughter ate was boiled on fire produced from a cowdung-cake. There was a grain of rice which got mixed with her *mug* diet, and that displeased the Goddess Shasthi. Hence the calamity. To ward it off he gave her some water and instructed her to sprinkle it on the dead bodies. He further asked her to worship Shasthi on the *Ashok* day. Take, he said, 6 Ashoka buds with 6 grains of *mugs* and eat them with curd.. After listening to verses from the *Purans* Ashoka bowed unto the sage and returned home. She did as she was told. As soon as the water was sprinkled on the dead bodies, her family came to life again. From that time the *Puja* became popular.

**Shasthi, Am-Shasthi.** It is the mango grove, goddess of infantine mortality. There lived a Brahman with three sons and three daughters-in-law. One of the latter used to eat food stealthily and to accuse a black cat of the theft. But the cat was Shathi's charger. After a few days the daughter-in-law gave birth to a son. As she was sleeping with the babe at night he disappeared.

Her six more sons and one daughter also disappeared on the night of their birth day. People accused her of being a witch. She over-heard the remarks, left her house in disgust and went to a mango grove. She was crying helplessly. At this moment there appeared the Goddess Shashti and asked her the cause of her grief. Out of shame, she hesitated, but the goddess knew everything and told her so. She added that, that was a punishment for stealthily eating something and falsely accusing her black cat. She supplicated and begged to be informed how she should atone for the crime. Mother Shasthi said: "There sleeps my cat in a dead swoon: Go there with a pot of curd, throw it over the carcase and lick it with your tongue." (Horrid!) The poor woman did so. Mother Shasti gave back all her children which the cat had carried to Her. She said "Go thou home with thy children and put a mark with the curd on the forehead of all of them. Never steal again and never blame my cat. Make an image of a cat with rice flour mixed with water on the 6th night of the bright half in the month of *Jestha* (May-June). Then worship me and the cat along with a charm to be made up of threads. After the worship tie the charm to the right arm of your new born child. Then after hearing verses from the holy scriptures, take fruit and milk diet. Don't eat rice on that day. Never slap a child with the left hand and never curse it. Never kick a black cat and never accuse it falsely. If you follow my instructions all your children wil live long." The daughter-in-law returned home accompanied by her lost children. She described her visit to Shasti in the forest to her mother-in-law and sisters-in-law and taught them how to worship the goddess. This is how the *puja* was introduced.

**Shayana-Ekādashi.** The eleventh day of the waxing moon of the month of *Asāhdh* (June-July). It is the day on which Vishnu goes to sleep.

**Shilā Saptami.** *Shila Saptami.*—The seventh day of *Shrāvan* is sacred to water nymphs. There was a king, says the fable. He built a large tank for the public. But there was no water. He worshipped the water-nymphs. They told him that he would have to sacrifice his grandson. He consented. He was very sorry, but the good of the public demanded such a sacrifice and he yielded. He dared not ask his daughter-in-law her permission. So he sent her away to her father's home. In her absence, he took the child to the empty tank, there worshipped the nymphs again, placed his grand-son in a cradle and left broken-hearted. To the surprise of the city the next morning the tank was full of water. After some days the daughter-in-law returned. She first went to see the tank. It was the seventh day of the month of *Shrāvan.* She worshipped the nymphs and offered them flowers &c. In doing so she entered the water, and prayed that any member of the family that may have met his or her death by drowning might be restored. Curious to behold she felt a drag at her feet. On examination it was found to be the prince, her lost child! She lifted it up and took it to the palace. In the meantime runners had informed the king that his daughter-in-law was returning home with the sacrificed prince restored to her bosom. He ran up to receive her and thenceforward heaped on her great honours.

A branch of the Indian fig *(Ficus Indica)* and seven pebbles are worshipped on this day, along with the picture of Jivantika. Cooked food of various kinds, mostly sweets are distributed among friends, relations, and caste women. (Compare of Bengal.)

**Shimga.** Holi festival, for folklore see under Holi.

**Shirālshet.** The name of an ancient Bania or corn chandler, who rose to become a king, and reigned about an hour and a half. An earthen image of him is made and worshipped with festivities, by Marātha women, on the sixth of the light half of the month of *Shrāvan* (July-August). After the women have danced around it, it is thrown into a well or tank.

**Shivaratra.** The *Shivaratra* is also a day of fasting in honour of Shiva. It falls on the 13th day of each half of the month and is a full day or 24 hours fast day. *Mahāshivarātra* which falls in the month of *Māgh* (January-February) is considered specially sacred. A full discription thereof appears below.

In the mountainous tract of the province of Pratyant there lived a *Vyādha* or *Shikāri* named Lubdhaka. He was very fond of animal food. He lived on the frontier and got his livelihood by killing animals. He was black and bulky. He wore a chain armour and leather gloves. He had a bow and was always thinking of nothing but game. On the *Shivarātra* day his creditor got him arrested and confined him in a Shiva's temple. He thus had the good fortune to see the image of the God, was obliged to remain without food, and could hear the words "Shiva" "Shiva" repeated by the devotees that visited the edifice. Some of these pious people subscribed the sum demanded by the creditor and released him. As soon as he recovered his freedom he started for *shikār*. He went to the South. He entered the forest and heartily laughed at the foolish people who chanted "Shiva, Shiva!" In the city wherever he went, he heard only one word Shiva, Shiva!

"Shiva, Shiva!" he began repeating mockingly. He followed the tracks of antelopes, hogs and other animals. He was hungry. The day was gone, he could secure no game! He therefore went to a tank and hid himself in the branches of a *bel (Aegle marmelos)* the trifoliate tree sacred to God Shiva. Under it was a hidden (*Gupta*) *lingam, i.e.* Gupteshvar. In order to remove all obstacles to his sight and his movement he began plucking the leaves and throwing them down. They fell on that sacred emblem. He had, it will be remembered, to fast during the day. While he climbed, he could hear and repeat the name of God Shiva, and he dropped the *bel* leaves on the *lingam.* All these unconcious acts, added to his credit. His sins were being reduced in proportion, although he was such a low caste vermin eater that the very stink of his body warned all game of his obnoxious presence and they instinctively ran away from him. Thus the first three hours of the night passed. The *Shikāri* was mocking at the people of the town by again and again repeating "Shiva, Shiva." He continued plucking up and throwing the *bel* leaves at the *lingam.* The result was that one-fourth part of his accumulated sins had disappeared. At this time there came to the tank opposite, a doe big with young. She could hardly run owing to the delicate state of her health. The *Shikāri* spied her, bent his powerful bow and aimed his arrow! The fatal moment came, but lo! the four-footed quadruped, the antilope saw him, and began speaking to him in his own human tongue! Surprised at the phenomenon he withdrew the arrow, and held his breath!

The doe said:

"Hold! Oh, *Vyādha,* Oh destroyer of all creatures! Tell me why you want to take my life?"

The *Shikāri* replied:

O antelope! I have been starving with my mother and my family. We are very hungry and therefore I want to kill you for your flesh. I have killed thousands of animals but never came across one who could speak with human voice. Who are you, where were you born, and how did you come to this tract?

The doe replied:

Listen, Oh chief of *Shikāris.* I am telling you my own history I am an *apsara* or celestial fairy of the Court of Indra the King of Gods. I was very beautiful, quite young, and plump, but conceited. I married a demon named

Hiranyākshya. I was so fond of him and enjoyed his company so well that I neglected my duty of dancing in front of Shiva at stated times. That irregularity brought on the displeasure of the God and he cursed me. He said :—

"Rambha! You have been going astray! Tell me with whom have you been misconducting yourself? I confessed that I was in love with a *Daitya* a Demon! and being exhausted I felt too tired to leave the bed! Shiva said :—

As you are enamoured of a Demon in preference to Gods, and demi-gods, you are a shameless girl! You shall go about nude in the jungles born as a doe and that wicked demon who dare seduce a celestial damsel, shall become a black buck and follow you night and day. This shall last for twelve years. At the end of the period a *Vyādh* will aim an arrow at you while seated near my emblem. You will then recollect what happened here and at the sight of my emblem you will attain freedom, from that low birth! The doe proceeded; oh *Vyādh*, I have a young one in my womb. I have hardly any flesh on my body. You will get no food out of me as I am in a very delicate state of health. Another doe will soon come here. She is young and fleshy, she or the black buck which is also expected, will satisfy your hunger. If you do not like this proposal, allow me to simply drop the young one, and to hand it over to my friends. I will then return myself to offer you what flesh I possess.

The *Shikāri* after some hesitation asked her to swear that she would keep her promise and allowed her to go. He was alone again. He began involuntarily repeating the word "Shiva, Shiva," and throwing the *bel* leaves over the *lingam*. He had no sleep. At midnight he saw another doe who was quite young. She was looking out for her mate. She was restless. The *Shikāri* aimed his arrow! But alas! She also began speaking with human voice. She said to herself. "Oh these cruel *Shikāris*! One of them killed my sister this morning. What is the use of living in this sinful world! The sooner this fellow kills me the better. She then addressed the man and said:—

"Oh *Vyād*! only one word! hold please! Have you seen another doe passing this way?

The man was simply astonished. He thought that the one he allowed to go away, has possibly returned to keep her promise, or this might be the other one that was to follow her.

He replied. "Oh *Mrigi* (doe). That one has gone home. She is true to her word and has therefore sent you perhaps, to die in her place. I am tired of waiting, and am very hunry. Take the name of your God, and be prepared for death!

The doe was in tears and said: "Oh *Vyādh*! Do not kill me. There is no flesh in my body. I am burning with love. If you shoot me I shall lose my life, but you will get no food. On the contrary, you will have committed the sin of killing a female during the breeding season. Do not do that, I prostrate myself before you, I beg for my life! A strong, big, young, fleshy black buck will soon be here. If you kill him you will get sufficient food to feed the whole of your family.

Ludhaka, the *Shikāri*, began hesitating. How was he to trust, he thought, these animals. He then asked her to swear that she would positively return. She did so, and was allowed to go.

The *Vyādha* was again left alone. He began repeating "Shiva, Shiva" and plucking up the leaves. They fell on the *lingam*. The result was that half of the sins he had committed during his life, vanished. He had no sleep. A young healthy well developed black buck came to the tank. He was very active, he was in search of his mate. It was the breeding season. The *Shikāri* bent his bow and aimed his fatal arrow! The buck saw him and thought that this wicked man must have killed his dear little wife—his mate—and said aloud.

"Alas! I shall now have to die of pain due to separation from my beloved! Oh God! What sin have I committed to deserve such punishment? In this world there is no happiness like that of the company of a wife! Be he in his house like a man, or be he in the jungle like myself, a male is happy only when he is in the company of his wife. No man can attain religious, moral or worldly happiness without a wife! If his love, his wife, is by him, a man will be happy even when living in the open air exposed to the elements, but without her, even a palace to him is worse than a forest. The wife is the helpmate of the husband in the performance of all duties, in this world. Even in travels, a wife is the only really trusted friend a man has. The wife is his confederate, his source of all happiness. To a man in distress there is no soothing remedy that would surpass the tender affections of a wife. He who has no loving and amiable wife in his house, need not seek a place in the midst of a forest for torturing himself out of penance! His house is in itself a desert! I cannot live without my dear mates. They are so loving!" He then turned to the *Shikāri* and said "Oh *Vyādh!* Have you seen two does passing this way? Have you killed them? Tell me the truth."

The *Vyādha* replied:

Yes I have seen them. They have both sworn that they would return if needed. Have they sent you to me to be killed?

The buck said that his favourite mate was in season, that he would grant her conjugal happiness and return to the spot, that he had hardly any flesh worth eating. He repeatedly promised to return, and swore that be would keep that promise. He was allowed to pass on.

The *Vyādha* was alone again. He had no sleep. He

was repeating the name of the God and throwing the leaves down. All his sins were destroyed. He was freed at sunrise. There came another doe followed by her young ones. The *Shikāri* was very hungry. He again aimed his arrow. The doe said:

"Oh pure-hearted *Vyādha*! Hold! I am not fit to be shot at. What does your religion tell you, listen:

"If a king who has come out for *Shikār* sees game sleeping, suckling, ill, or a doe followed by her young ones, he shall not kill them."

If you in defiance of the text wish to kill me please allow me to go home and hand over my tender charge to my relatives and friends. I will then return to you, I swear. The *Shikāri* went home. He was kept thinking of his own cruel deeds in killing life. On reaching home he was surrounded by his hungry children. The whole family was disappointed. There was not a morsel in the house! He was all absorbed. He did not know what to do unless the honest animals returned to be killed as promised.

The black buck went home. He saw that one of his mates had given birth to a young one. He granted conjugal happiness to the second one. He then addressed his family thus—"You had better stay at home. Protect your young ones from the *Shikāris* and the carnivorous animals that frequent the forest. I am bound to keep my promise. I came simply to perform my husband's duty to the second wife. He who disregards his wife at the breeding season commits the sin of killing his own future progeny. Sons help a man in attaining heaven by performing religious duties. They serve to raise the reputation of the family in this world. It is therefore the duty of every man and woman to protect his children. A man without a son will not go to heaven after death. Every one should therefore try to leave a son behind him. I must go to the *Shikāri*. I must be true to my word. It is my duty to do so. All religions inculcate Truth. Truth is the foundation of all religions.

The females replied:—"We shall follow you. It is our duty to die with our husband. We do not recollect a single instance of your displeasing us. Oh! dear husband. In the dense forest, in flooded streams, at the confluences, at the steep crags, or in deep vales, you have been our protector. There is no use living after you are dead. Of what use are widows? Fathers mothers, and brothers can only give to their daughters and sisters a limited support. A husband is the only one who gives his all-in-all to his wife. A widow even when rich and when she has many sons to look after her, is a despicable being. No one will respect her. Widowhood is the greatest calamity that overtakes a woman. Those who die before their husbands are lucky. No *vina* (a stringed instrument) without wires, will give music, no cart can go without wheels, and no woman can be happy without her husband even if she has a hundred sons. Even a penniless, vicious, old, sickly, maimed, lame, stupid, leperous, and miserly husband takes a woman to heaven! Women have no religion beyond devoted attachment to their husbands."

The black buck hesitated. If he were to keep his promise, the whole family would be destroyed. If not, he would be doomed to perdition for breaking it! Truth must prevail. One must keep his promise even at the loss of his wives, sons, or his own life! He therefore went to the *Shikāri* with the whole of his family. On reaching the place he offered himself to die first. But his mates the does would not allow that. They wanted to die first. It was a pathetic scene. The *Shikāri* was moved. He refused to kill any of them. He said that he did not care for any meat. Whatever may happen he would kill no animal. It is a great sin to destroy life. He thanked the buck and said that his behaviour towards his four-footed family was a lesson to him. He threw away his bow and arrow and became religious. The buck told him that he was doing his duty in keeping his promise, but the *Shikāri* repeated that he was taught a good lesson by a beast (buck). He broke his bow and threw it away.

But lo! We hear the sounds of the celestial drum announcing the arrival of *Vimāns* or palanquins for the conveyance of the saintly! There is the crowd of the *pālkhi* bearers of heaven, and the usual shower of flowers! The messengers of Shiva arrived, and addressing the *Shikāri* said that they were deputed to take his purified soul to Shivalok—or Shiva's abode. The black buck, his family and the *Shikāri* were thus taken to Heaven! The buck was given a separate place in the sky. He was turned into a consellation named *Mriga* after him.

Shiva said: "Oh Pārvati, you can even now see in the sky the path (the milky way) by which the does went to their constellation. Behind it are the two other stars called Lubdaka, or *vyādha*. The group of three stars below that is called the contellation of *Mirga-Shirsha*. In front of it are the two stars where the young ones of the antelopes dwell and behind it is the third doe. Such is the origin of the *Mrigarāj* that shines in the sky. Note well that the *shikāri* had no intention of performing the *puja* or observing the fast, and yet he could obtain the fruit. What then would be the reward for those who devotly fast and devotedly worship me! Even Brahma cannot describe that bliss!

[Linga-purān: Shivarātri Vratkatha].

### DISSERTATIONS.

This is evidently a folklore based on the shape of the *Nakshatra, Mriga Shirsha* the fifth mansion of the moon. It consists mainly of three stars. Its longitude is 63 latitude 10.s. The principal star of the asterism according to Colebrook and Burgess is Orions according to Bentley 113, 116, 117 Tauri. The *Sidhāntās* mention the star Lubdhaka (the Hunter) as its Yog-tara or principal star. But

Lubdhak is the star Sirius. In the Ratnamāla the constellation of *Mriga Shirsha* is figured like the head of an antelope. Literally its name indicates the same thing *Mriga*, antelope, and *shirsha* head. The ninth constellation of the Chaldian zodiac is called, Dhanus and represented like an archer (literally *dhanu* a bow). This heavenly archer is possibly the hero of our tale, Lubdhak or Sirius. The next one is the Chaldian Goat but a goat is not very different from an antelope in crude outlines. The archer and the antelope are both together in the Chaldian zodiac. The three stars mentioned in the *purān* are called Al-Hekah and are placed in the head of the Orion according to Ulug-Begh the chief monarch of the Tartars, who was devoted to the study of Astronomy. It will thus be seen that this mythological story has for its basis, the heavenly phenomenon of the fifth mansion of the moon known as *Mriga Shiras* and the sign zodiac called *Dhanus* (bow), and that the *Yog-tara* or chief star Sirius, is the Lubdhak or hunter of the story. Why this particular day should be selected for the fast, it is not clear unless we divine that the darkest night of the month of *Māgh* (January-February) is the longest and affords scope for taking observations of these stars, by keeping up all the night, as *shivaites* are asked to do.

**Shrādhās.**—The second half of the month of *Bhadrapad* [August-September] is entirely devoted to *Shrādhās* or offerings to the *manes* of the *pitris*. It is a series of offerings and feasts in honour of the dead. In some families only dry food is offered to a Brahman, in others, many Brahmans are also fed. The day on which a man lost his father is represented in this fortnight by one corresponding to it for the performance of the *shrādha*. The ninth day called *Avidhava navami* is the one on which offerings are made to the souls of women who died before their husbands. It is in fact the widower's day of adoring the soul of his lost wife. A castewoman whose husband is alive is invited to partake of the dinner specially prepared, and is honoured by being fed before the males are fed, a unique privilege among Hindus. She is offered toilet perquisites and a dress or piece of cloth according to means. The younger or second wife of the widower bows to her and inwardly wishes that she may be so fortunate as to die before her lord, just as the first happy one did.

**Siddhi Vinãyak.** See Ganesh for folkore.

**Sital Shasti.**—It falls on the 6th day of the bright half of *Mãgh* (January-February). There lived a Brahman and his wife with a son and daughter-in-law. The latter had no child. After they prayed mother Shathi for one year, the daughter-in-law became *enciente.* But another year passed away and there was no issue. One day she went to the *ghãt* of a river, slipped there, fell down, and gave birth to a pumkin-shaped bag. She returned home and told her mother-in-law of what happened. The old lady went to the river and saw that a crow had torn the bag open and that little mites were coming out of it! The master of the house was informed. He took home the bag of babies. He found them to be 60 in number. When they grew to marriageable ages their mother said that she would marry her sons only to a family of 60 daughters. The grand father of the boys at her importunities went in search of a family of 60 girls. He reached a place where he saw a mother anointing her 60 daughters with turmeric on the bank of a river. He found that she was a Brahman by caste, and that her 60 daughters could not be married because she could not afford to pay the dowry, etc.

He arranged the nuptials of the girls with his 60 grand-sons.

The *Sital Shathi Puja* day came in the month of *Mãgh.* It was a very cold (*sitàl*) and rainy day. There was so much chill that the old lady could not bathe with cold water. She therefore asked her grand-daughters-in-law to supply hot water for her bath. That was against the rule. She further asked them to cook rice on that day of prohibition. They objected, stating that cooking was prohibited on the *Sital Shathi* day. But she did not listen to them, and forced them to do as they were told! She actually ate rice on a prohibited day! Oh! the sinner! the result was that the whole of her numerous family and her domestic animals were found dead the following morning! When she saw that, she cried helplessly. Her neighbours gathered round her. Goddess Shasthi also appeared before her in the grab of a Brahman woman and said " Anoint your family with cooked rice and bathe them in hot water as you bathed yourself yesterday, and they will come to life again."

Goddess *Shasthi* added angrily " Mix some curd and turmeric on the *Sital Shasthi* day and put a mark with it on the forehead of a dog to begin with and do the same to your family later on. Tie to the wrists of your sons and grand-sons the charm dyed with turmeric. Never eat cooked rice and never bathe with hot water on a *Sital Shasthi* day." Saying this the Goddess disappeared. The old matron did as she was told. All the dead members of her family came to life again. From that day the *puja* came to be introduced in Bengal.

**Somvār** or Monday is a part fast day, that is, from sunrise to four o'clock in the after noon. It is also sacred to Shiva. Mondays of the month of *Shrāvan* [ July-August ] are considered specially sacred and generally observed as fasts. Mondays of other months are scarcely so honoured. But on ordinary Mondays, no father who has a son living should get himself shaved, and fish and flesh eating Brahmans of North India as well as other high caste non-Brahmans abstain from taking any animal food on that day. It is considered a lucky thing to kill a centipede on Mondays if one happens to see it. The belief is, that taking the life of the vermin amounts to offering three *tolās* of gold to Shiva.

**Svarn-Gauri Puja.** On the banks of the Sarasvati

there was once a city called Vimala. Its king Chandra Prabhu had two queens, named Mahādevi and Vishālāxi. The elder, Mahādevi was his chief and favourite consort. Once upon a time while engaged in *Shikār*, he came across a lake full of lotuses frequented by many birds, and fairies. The fairies were performing some worship. The king asked them what it was, and was told that it was *Svarna-Gauri-vrat.* It grants wealth. The king begged that he might be taught the details. The fairies said that it should be begun on the third day of the bright half of *Shrāvan* [July-August] and continued for sixteen years. The king accepted the *vrat.* The fairies then tied to his wrist a string made up of sixteen threads. He was then told that at the end of the sixteen years, he should bathe as usual and live on one meal only on the third of *Shrāvan.* On the fourth of the month (next day) a good-natured priest should be invited with his wife. In their presence he should worship the Svarna-Gauri, and should tie to his wrist a cotton string made up of sixteen threads. He should then offer them cows, land, gold and cash. Sixteen *Vāyanās* or winnowing baskets full of toilette requites should be given to so many married women. The women should also be offered new clothes. *Apups* or sweet cakes should be placed in sixteen baskets and offered to the lady guests, Brahmans should then he fed as usual. He who performs this *vrat* as discribed, gets on well in this world and a celestial abode in Kailās in the next world. The king performed the first *puja* on the spot, and returned to his palace. While he was in the company of his favourite wife, she saw the string and was very angry. She thought it was degrading for His Majesty to wear a worthless string instead of a jewel. She cut it and threw it out of the window. It fell on a dead tree, but as soon as the tree came in contact with the sacred thread, it came to life and was all full of fresh foliage! The co-wife or second queen saw this phenomenon, took up the string and tied it to her own wrist. The result was, that through the charm thus worn she became the favourite queen. The first one was banished. She went to the hermitage of a saint, but he turned her out. She then began roaming in the forest. She met God Ganesh. She told him that she was in search of Goddess Svarna-Gauri. Further on, she saw a grove of mangoes. Going further she came to a little tank and there met the fairies, but they prevented her from approaching them, a sinner that she was. She sat herself down and fully repented for her sin. There, she saw Goddess Svarna-Gauri. She fell flat before her in obeisance. She prayed and begged to be excused, for the sin she committed in removing the charm from her husband's wrist. The goddess was pleased. She blessed her and disappeared. The deserted queen, then returned home and performed the *vrat* she had once despised. The king again performed the *vrat* and became an Emperor and in the end returned to Shiva's Kailās, the best of Heavens.

He who performs this *puja* will get immense wealth, will have all his enemies conquered, and will in the end obtain salvation. [Skanda-Purāna.]

**Simhasta.** When the planet Jupiter enters the sign *Leo* of the Zodiac, Hindus come from great distances to sacred places to take a bath. Pushkar near Ajmir, Ujjein in Central India, Allahabad in the U. P., Nasik in the Bombay Presidency, and Kumbhakonam in Madras, are some of the places selected. In Kotihar in Kashmir, there is a fountain which, it is said, continues dry for eleven years, and when the planet Jupiter enters *Leo*, the water springs out. This position of the Jupiter marks the completion of the twelve years' cycle of that planet.

**Thursday Worship.** See under Wednesday worship.

**Tortoise Incarnation** (called the *Kurma Avatār*). It falls on the full moon day of *Vaishākh* (April-May). "The churning of the ocean," says Mr. Brennand, "founded upon the various incidents of an eclipse of the sun, which took place, according to Bentley's calculation, when the Vernal Equinox was in the middle of the asterism *Bharani (Koltion, St. Connecteus)* in the year 945 B.C., on the 25th October. It gave birth to a highly coloured fable (an allegory of an eclipse) in poetical language—a pretended fight between the *Surās* and *Asurās*, the gods of Light and the demons of Darkness, and their offspring. A translation from Hesiod, given by Bentley, describes the war between the Gods and the Giants, a fiction resembling that concerning the churning of the ocean in the *Purānās*, the former being supposed by Bentley to be borrowed from the Hindu fable at a period same 200 years later, or about 746 B.C. Saturn was discovered in this eclipse of 945 B.C." (p. 122).

The Hindu story runs that the Gods and Demons, began churning the ocean with Mount Meru as their rod, and the thousand-headed snake Shesh as their rope. The earth began sinking under the weight. Vishnu therefore assumed the shape of a big tortoise and crept himself under the mountain to prop it up. The gods succeeded in churning out 14 gems and distributed them among themselves. The expected deluge was prevented.

The column of the dark shadow of the Moon, caused by its intervening position between the great luminary and the earth, supplied the idea of a mountain, the valuable discovery of the planet Saturn gave an idea of a gem, and the rest of the story emanated from the high flight of the poet's imagination.

**Trimurti.** Literally means a triple figure. It ts believed to represent the combined form of the three gods, Brahma the Creator, Vishnu the Protector and Shiva the Destroyer. It is possibly a myth based on the peculiar position of the three constellations (1) *Mriga* (2) *Ardra* and (3) *Punarvasu* (see plate). The two stars of the horns and other two of the neck of the *Mriga* or antelope form a cradle-shaped figure and the three stars of the belt of

Orion, represent the three bodies mentioned in the folkore of the birth of Trimurti recorded under *Datta-jayanti.* The nearest, and the next constellation is *Ardra* which is represented by one big star. Its name literally means a gem. Next to this constellation is the great *Punarvasu* literally a house, and is shaped like the front wall of a cottage with a doorway. Sirius the brightest star in front of Orion represents the *Rishi*, Atri, *Ardra* the gem represents Anusuya his wife. *Punarvasu* represents their hermitage, and Orion or *Mriga* the cradle with the three babies. If further corroboration is required it is not wanting. It is said that when *Trimurti* came to age, he had four dogs in attendance. They represented the four Vedas. Just near Orion we have Cannis Major consisting of four stars. In Trimurti's portrait there is usually a fig tree (*Ficus glomerata*) under which he stands. The stars of the horns of the *Mriga* constellation just above the heads of the three bodies possibly supplied the material for the construction of a tree. Finally there is a cow usually painted near him. She possibly evolved out of Lupus.

Mr. J. Offord tells us in the columns of the Journal of the Royal Asiatic Society of Great Britain and Ireland (p. 202 of April issue of 1915) that Anu is the name of the sky-god. In India, Anusuya is a female—the mother of Trimurti. This mother Anu—or sky goddess had three wandering sons born into her (*a*) Guru, the further transformation of the three babies, (*b*) the Moon, and (*c*) Saint Durvās. It has to be discovered what heavenly body this Durvās represents, but we certainly know *Guru*, Brihaspati, or Jupiter with his satellites. Guru has four dogs in attendance, and he became, (it is said in the *Purānās*) a wandering recluse. Mr. Offord adds that a cuniform tablet in the British Museum referring to the celebrated deity of the Babylonian Merodach (who is identified with the planet Jupiter) states that he possessed four attendant dogs, and gives their names. It is also possible that these represent the four largest of the planet's moons, because instances have been known of these having been discerned with the naked eye. The second son, the Moon-god, Sin, was masculine and so is he in India. There remains only the third son saint Durvās to be accunted for.

**Tripuri Pornima.** On the 15th or full moon day of *Kārtik,* [October November] Shiva destroyed the demon Tripur and the gods celebrated the victory by letting off fire works and illuminating their abodes. In memory of that day Hindus do the same every year, and call it *Dev-Divāli* or God's *Divāli.*

**Tuesday Worship.** The story in Bengal is that on a certain Tuesday the Goddess Chandi went to a poor Bania with seven daughters and assuming the form of an old Brahman woman asked for alms. As soon as the mother of the seven girls came out, she asked her if she had a son and on getting a negative reply refused to accept any thing from the hands of a woman not blessed with one! The Bania woman lay prostrate in supplication, the Goddess was pleased, and gave a flower. She said that by dipping the flower in a cup of water and drinking that fluid, she would get a son. She moreover taught her how to perform the *Mangal Chandi Vrat.* The goddess then went to the house of a rich Bania with seven sons and asked for alms, when the hostess appeared, she asked her if she has got a daughter, on getting a negative reply she said that she had taken a vow not to accept charity at the hands of people not blessed with a daughter. The scene was repeated, a flower was handed over and instructions for performing the Mangal or Tuesday fast were duly given. In course of time one got a son and the other a daughter. They were named Jayadev and Jayavati respectively. As they were neighbours, friendship between the two specially born children developed. The boy Jayadev expressed his desire to marry the girl Jayavati, but his parents were too poor to hope for such a union. Goddess Mangal-

Chandi appeared and advised the father of the girl to offer her in marriage to Jayadev. They were married. One day while crossing a river on the back of an elephant Jayadev saw his wife repeating some verses to herself, quite absorbed in meditation. He asked her to explain what they meant, and she said that the stanzas contained a prayer to goddess Mangalchandi. He inquired about the efficacy of such a prayer, and was told that Mangalchandi becomes the guardian angel of her devotees and protects them from accidents as well as from thieves and *dacoits.* In order to verify this assertion her husband Jayadev tied her ornaments in a bundle and threw them into the river! The good girl said nothing. Time passed, and one day her father-in-law bought a big fish for a feast, and on opening it, the lost ornaments were found in its stomach. Not fully satisfied with the experiment, Jayadev one day stealthily took his own babe away and placed it in a potter's kiln. The potter was surprised to see that all his attempts to ignite fire, failed. On examining his kiln, he found the babe peacefully sleeping and restored it to its parents. Then Jayadev threw it into the river, but it came out safe on its mother going to fetch water from the stream. Finally the unbeliever tried to stab his second child, but he failed. At last he was convinced of the potency of the *puja,* and of the prayer. It is said, that no harm would ever come to any one who adopted this *Puja.* (See also Manglā Gaur).

**Tuesday Worship.** In Bengal, on Tuesdays in the bright half of *Agrahāyan* a fast is observed by people who have lost their relations or are in distress. It is called *Sankasth Mangalvār* or distress removing Tuesday. The story runs that a merchant left home on business. There was no news of him for a long time. People thought he was either abducted or killed. One day a Brahman woman came to his house and advised his mother to make her daughter-in-law observe the fast and added that her own son's wife had to do so, because she had no child. She further said that the *Vrat* can only be performed conjointly by two or more married women. They did so. The missing hushand returned. But in the hurry of the moment of his arrival the wife left her plate without finishing her meal. The result was, that the goddess was offended! The man could not recognize his wife and mistook for her, the maid-servant engaged during his absence. He bestowed his affections on the menial as he thought there was only one woman in his house, his wife, and the goddess changed the physiognomy of the girls. The wife thought that she was discarded. The mother dared not speak for fear of offending her wealthy son her only support. She thought, he did it purposely or knowingly. She at last complained to her neighbour the Brahman woman. The priestly adviser explained it away by saying that the maid-servant must have stealthily eaten the food the wife left in her plate when she foolishly got up before finishing the sacred meal. She advised the old mother to direct her daughter-in-law to perform the *Vrat* again in the month of *Māgh* [January-February]. She did so, with the result that the husband overheard the prayer of his wife in which she said to the goddess: "I bought the slave girl with the proceeds of my own bracelets and you, oh, Mother! have made her my mistress and turned me into a menial. Pray forgive me." He made enquiries, was conviced of the mistaken identity, discarded the maid and accepted the ex-wife with many apologies. The daughter-in-law of the Brahman who had associated herself with the merchant's wife in performing the *Vrat* was blessed with a son followed by many other children. The merchant's wife also became the mother of many children and lived in peace and happiness. People came to know the efficacy of the fast, and adopted it.

**Tulsi's marriage.** On an auspicious day between Kārtik 11th to 15th the God Krishna is every year married to Tulsi. Tulsi, the plant *Ocimum sanctum*, was, in her former birth Vrinda, the daughter of a giant named Nemi or Kālnemi. She was married to a demon. Her husband was born of the sweat which Shiva had thrown from his brow into the ocean when he perspired at being insulted by Indra. Born in water, *jala*, he was named Jalandhar. Owing to this circumstance, he claimed as his birth-right the suzerainty of the Ocean like Neptune, and demanded back from Indra the fourteen treasures churned out of the ocean in the second Incarnation of Vishnu. They were *Laxmi*, the goddess of wealth *Kaustubha*, the Kohinur of the Gods ; *Parijātaka*, the *Nyctanthes arbortristis* flower tree ; *Sura*, wine ; *Dhanvantari*, the heavenly physician; the Moon, the Nectar ; *Kāmadhenu*, the cow of wishes or desires, granting the fulfilment of all wishes ; *Airāvat*, the white elephant of the Gods ; Rambha the beautiful damsel ; *Kālakut* the poison ; *Uchaisrava*, the seven headed horse of the chariot of the sun ; the invincible missile of Vishnu ; and the Conch shell. He claimed them as his heritage, but Indra, the King of the Gods, refused. He worshipped Brahma, the Creator, observing penance, and the God granted him the boon of freedom from death as long as his wife knew him only. He was therefore invincible, and feeling the affront given by Indra in refusing to return his patrimony ; he declared war. Jalandhar looted and despoiled Amaravati, the Capital of *Swarga*. All the Gods ran up to Shiva and Vishnu for pretection. They all went to fight the demon. Vishnu ran away from the battle field. He returned to *Vaikunta*, his abode, and deputed Laxmi, his wife, to find out the destined way to kill Jalandhar. He yielded to her charms and disclosed the secret. Vishnu then sent Shiva to the faithful wife of the giant in the form of her husband. He failed. At last, Vishnu himself appeared to her as a recluse or *sādhu* and succeeded. The moment this was done, gaint Jalandbar's head was severed by Indra and it fell in his wife's own hall. She cursed

Vishnu for the horrible deed he had committed and said that he would become a black stone. Vishnu retaliated and cursed her that she would become a shrub in the jungle. That is why the former has turned into a *shaligrām*, the ammonite found chiefly in the river Gandaki, and the latter *Ocimum sanctum*, the *tulsi* plant. But they have come to love each other so tenderly that they are married every year on the 11th day of the month of *Kārtik* (October-November). This ceremony marks the opening of the annual marriage season among high caste Hindus. It is said that he who performs this marriage ceremony assuming that *tulsi* is his daughter, gets all the credit due on the performance of a *Kanyādān* (giving away a daughter in marriage), a very meritorious act. There are people who devoutly repeat this episode every year, in the belief that a sure abode is reserved for them in Heaven. Tulsi has now become such a devoted wife of her ravager that she is supposed to rank higher than Rukmini, the married wife of Vishnu, in his eighth incarnation as Krishna.

In another account (Padma Purān), Jalandhar was produced from the fire from the brow of Shiva intended to burn Indra. Brahma had blessed him that he would be unconquerable to all except Rudra or Shiva. After the conquest by Jalandhar of Amaravati, Shiva, at the request of the Gods, took the side of Indra. Vrinda, the wife of Jalandhar, began, for the protection of her husband the worship of Vishnu. Before she had finished the *puja*, Vishnu appeared to her in her husband's garb, and Vrinda, finding her husband safe and sound (in Vishnu), did not complete the worship. This caused Jalandhar's death. When Vrinda was about to curse Vishnu for this wicked act, he said, you die a *sati*, from your ashes will arise, *Tulasi*, *Dhātri* (*Phillantus emblica*), *palas* (*Butea frondosa*), and *Asvatha* (*Ficus religiosa*). There was also a Rishi of the name of Jalandhar. According to the Brahmavaivarta Purān, "Tulsi," originally a "Gopika," was the wife of the demon Saukhachura. To cause the demon's death, as given above, Vishnn appeared to her in the form of Sankhachura.

Once upon a time Nārad, the celestial saint, went to Dwarka, the golden city, where Krishna was living with his 16,108 wives. When he went to Queen Satyabhāmā's (better known as Bhamā) palace, she requested him to advise her as to what she should do to secure Krishna for her husband in all her future births. He saw that an excellent opportunity to humiliate her and to pull her down from the high pedestal, as she thought she was supreme in Krishna's affections. He made up his mind to remove her illusion and devised a plan. He said that the law of Heaven is that whatever one wishes to have there, one should give away in charity to a good Brahman. Bhāma took the bait and worshipping Nārad offered him in charity her own husband Krishna. Krishna quietly yielded apparently to please her, but he was in secret league, with the cunning Brahman and wanted to enjoy the fun. Nārad commanded him as his disciple, for so he had now become, to take charge of his *Vina*, the stringed musical instrument, and to carry it for him. They started for Heaven. When the news of the loss of Krishna reached the other wives (except Rukmini), of that great man, they all rushed hurlyburly and stopped Nārad and Krishna. Nobody dared in those days incur the displeasure of the curse-armed Brahmans. They therefore prostrated themselves before him and asked him to wait until they could release their dear husband. Nārad stopped, and cunning Krishna winked at him. Then the host of wives ran up to Bhāma's house and demanded what right she alone could have to dispose of the common property of so many consorts. She had an uncomfortable half hour with these co-wives. At last, it was agreed that they should all go to Nārad again and beg of him to suggest some way out of the mess. He told them that 'no sin was more heinous than that of resuming a gift given to a Brahman." The only way they could get their husband back was to buy him, and he named his price. It was Krishna's own weight in gold and jewellery including pearls and precious stones. Proud Bhāma thought she was the richest woman in the world and chuckled. She offered her ornaments at once. A pair of scales were set up, Krishna was made to sit in one pan and Bhāma began emptying her coffers in the other. They literally proved but a feather in the scale. Then all the other wives except Rukmini followed Bhāma's example—after putting her to shame—for her arrogance in airing her riches. They showered jewels in head-loads but Krishna's pan of the scale could not be buoyed up. At last Nārad suggested that as Rukmini was the chief queen of Krishna (this was a thrust at Bhāma) she must be fabulously rich. She therefore should be induced to yield her treasure. All the co-wives thereupon asked Bhāma to go and call her. This was still more humiliating to the arrogant self-constituted chief queen. But she dare not refuse, and went to Rukmini's palace. That devoted woman was seen worshipping the *tulsi* plant in a plain dress. Seeing Bhāma approach her, she stood in reverence and received her most courteously. After the usual salutations she asked her to name her wishes so that they might be immediately complied with. Bhāma opened her heart and with tears in her eyes, described how foolishly she was about to lose their dear husband and how it was in Rukmini's power to release him by giving up her jewellery. "Very well," said Rukmini, "I do not possess jewels enough to counterpoise the Lord of the Universe, but I shall try." She returned to the *tulsi* plant, prayed unto her with folded hands and begged her to drop a gift with which she could weigh her Lord, for she—the plant—was his real first and most beloved wife and not herself (Rukhmini.) Tulsi dropped a leaf, Rukmini lifted it up and went with Bhāma to the place where the scales lay in the midst of a crushing crowd of wives, children and grand-children all struggling to get the last look of their beloved lord about to be hopelessly lost. On reaching the place, Rukmini stood suppliant, prayed, and bowed first unto Rishi Nārad and then unto her Lord. She then most reverently placed the *tulsi* leaf, in the pan, and lo! Krishna was high up in the sky and the other pan came down with a thud. Fearful was the struggle for the jewellery that titled out the scale and the question of identification of the thousands of claimants was too stiff for even the Chief Justice of Calcutta to solve. Nārad thanked Rukhmini for the treasure he secured in the shape of the sacred leaf which was a thousand times more valuable to him than the riches of the whole world. Rukhmini's reputation was established as the chief Queen but she never claimed that position. She transferred it to *tulsi* the *Ocimum sanctum* the ravished wife at first and then the widow of the demon Jalandhar, who is evey year married to her despoiler.

**Vāra Laxmi**—see Friday Fast for folklore.

**Vasant Panchami.** The Sri Panchami is the fifth day of *Māgh* (January-February). It is sacred to the Goddess Sarasvati. This Goddess has been compared, by Sir William Jones, to the unarmed Minerva, the Goddess of Wisdom of the Greeks and Romans. Sarasvati may also be compared to their nine Muses. Another name for Sarasvati is Vināpāni, so called from the instrument *Vina* which She holds in Her two hands. *Vina* is a kind of lute or lyre, formed of a flat piece of wood with strings, having a gourd at the end, and sometimes at both ends.

Vasant Panchami is also known as Shri panchami. In the best of health and spirits and in the best time of the year, spring. Bengal worships the Goddess for the highest of blessings—Knowledge.

Goddess Sarasvati is the daughter of Brahma. She is usually represented in Bengal as standing cross-legged on a lotus or water lily holding the *vina.* Her vehicle is the swan in Bengal, and peacock in Bombay.

Standing on white lotus, decked with white flowers, robed in white garment with a necklace of white beads, smeared with white sandal-paste, holding a white *vina,* lily-hued, wearing bright jewels, sung by the *Gandharvās,* worshipped by both the *Devās* and the *Asurās,* adored by the *Munis,* implored by the *Rishis*—such, in the *Padma Purana,* is the description of the Goddess, whose remembrance every day secures universal knowledge.

White and pure, no bloody sacrifice is made in her worship. On that day of worship, fish-eating Bengal abstains from fish. All the symbols of reading and writing are placed before the Goddess when children come out in gay saffron coloured dresses to make to Her floral offerings and the auspiciousness of the occasion is marked by Brahmacharya rather than indulgence.

The special flower for Her worship in *Basaka (Justicia gendarussa)* the floral decorations of the day are chiefly by *ganda* marigold (*Tagetes erecta*). During a grand celebration of the festival in years back, the house was literally covered with this flower leaving not a space which was not yellow with the leaves of this flower to represent the season—*Basanta* whose colour is yellow.

Poets invoke Sarasvati at the commencement of a play or poem, like the Muses.

In the Marhātta countries, She is sometimes called the wife of Ganesh and sometimes his attendant. At the name-giving ceremony, in marriage if a man's name for instance is Ganesh, his wife is named Sarasvati, just as a Rāmchandra's wife is named Sita, or Krishna's wife is named after His spouse Rukhmini.

She is called Brahmi, the daughter of Brahma just as Jānaki is called after her father Janak, As Brahmi She is considered the Goddess of Science, and as Bhārati the Goddess of History.

In the Bombay Presidency at the beginning of the theatrical performances She appears on the stage on a peacock and dances before Ganesh at whose command the Manager of the stage has called her to grace the stage with her presence. She asks him to name the blessing he wishes to be favoured with, and he says that the actors may be blessed with the power of speaking well. She says that they will speak like Brihaspati the learned *Guru* of the Gods and then disappears. For the first time, in the history of the Bombay stage (1866-67), a Poona theatrical company omitted this introductory portion and introduced Vishnu. Curiously enough that night there was a row with the Policeman on duty and the performance was stopped for nearly an hour. Everybody attributed this obstruction to that omission. Recently however, the Sarasvati prelude has gone out of fashion altogether. Sarasvati is among the deities especially propitiated in the marriage ceremonies of the Brahmans and Prabhus of Bombay.

Sarasvati is worshipped in the Bombay Presidency on the Dasara day. All family records, and impliments of writing are arranged on a carpet and worshipped as the symbol of learning, but this day it is believed, is specially sacred for writing important documents. A letter addressed to a friend or relation or a grant from the Rāja of the state is written on a country made paper. It contains the mention of a gift or an honorarium from His Highness. On the Dasara day young children are ceremoniously initiated in the alphabets. In Bombay on the Sri Panchami day a grand Darbār is held in the Native States and solution of saffron sprinkled over the dressess of the *Sardārs* and officials followed by *attar*, *gulāb*, and *pān*. Young children are given new dresses in every Marātha family.

They are sprinkled with the saffron solution. This day marks the beginning of the spring.

**Vaikunth 14th.** The fourteenth day of the first half of *Kārtik* (October-November) is sacred to Vishnu the Lord of Vaikunth. It is said that on this day in *Krita Yuga* Vishnu went to Benares. He bathed himself in the Ganges at the Manakarnika *Ghāt*, worshipped Shiva, and offered 999 lotus flowers to the emblem of that God repeating a fresh name as he placed each flower. The thousandth lotus was missing! As one thousand lotuses alone could complete the *puja* Vishnu took out one of the balls of his eyes and offered it. Shiva was pleased and gave him *Sudarshan* the enchanted and invincible weapon which Vishnu possesses ever since. Since then devotees of Vishnu offer him a thousand lotuses every year on this sacred day.

**Varāha-Jayanti.** The day of the third incarnation *Varāha* or boar of Vishnu. It is said that at the great deluge, Vishnu held up the earth on his tusk to keep it dry.

**Varsha-pratipada.** See Gudichāpādva new year's day.

**Vasu Bāras.** It is the 12th of *Ashwin* (September-October). It is observed in Bengal. There lived an old woman in a city. She had many cows and buffaloes in her farmyard. One day, on the 12th of the month of *Ashwin* she had to go to her fields. She gave instructions to her daughter-in-law to cook some vegetable food; but the girl misunderstood her and killed some calves! She cooked the veal and served it as food to her people! They were horrified at the sight. The old woman left her plate and went to her family idols, sat in front of them and prayed. She begged that the poor ignorant girl might be excused for the sin she committed unguardedly. She added that if the slaughtered calf did not come to life again she would kill herself. God granted the prayer. When the cows returned home in the evening the calf came to life and jumped up! The old woman was right glad and the daughter-in-law felt eternally grateful to her. They both worshipped a cow and a heifer, and offered them good food. Every one was glad.

**Vāman 12th.** When the 12th day of the bright half of *Bhadrapad* (August Semtember) falls in the *Shravan (Brachium absorptum)* constellation it is considered specially sacred. It is said that the Vāman or Dwarf incarnation of Vishnu was born on such a day of astronomical combinations, and as he ultimately granted the Kingdom of Indra the Emperor of the Gods, to Bali, a similar boon is promised to those who observe it as a fast, after a bath at the confluence of any two rivers. On that day every such spot becomes as sacred as the water of the Ganges. Before breaking the fast on the 13th, devotees should again bathe at the confluence and worship the gold image of Vāman. It should be wrapped in a cloth. A new earthen pot should at first be placed on the spot selected for the worship. Round it, should be placed new yellow silk cloths. A gold sacrificial cup should be held in the hand and the *puja* performed in the prescribed fashion. The gold image of Vāman fully decorated with ornaments and clothes should be given to *the priest.* The *mantra* is so interesting that it may be given here :—"I am Vāman, Vāman accepts, I offer the image of Vāman to the priest who is also Vāman," cows, umbrellas, shoes, gold, clothes, and bulls should also be given to Brahmans. The origin of the *puja* is thus given in the *Bhabishottar Purān* :—

To the West of the Dashārna country, there lies the large rainless sandy tract of Maruta (Mārwad). This province is very hot and fosters big snakes. The trees have hardly any foliage. They are covered with monkeys. Grass does not grow on the soil and mirages are often visible. There is no water and no rain. Birds are very scarce indeed, and if any migratory denizons come there with their young ones, they die of thirst.

In such a desert, there came a Bania named Hari Datta leaving his itinerant companions on the way. He saw there, a dirty, lean, and ferocious looking set of people. He was so distressed that he began brooding over his house, his country, and his relations. He did not know what to do and whither to turn. At night-fall he saw some ghosts. They looked like moving skeletons. They were running wild! The Bania was terrified. He followed them. They went to and sat under a large shady Indian fig tree *(Ficus Indica)*. He also sat at one corner. He then saw a big ghost carried on his shoulder by another and followed or surrounded by a group of other evil spirits. The chief ghost went to where the Bania was sitting, and asked him how he happened to come to that dreadful and desolate tract. He explained that he had lost his way, and that he was very thirsty, and very hungry. The chief ghost, who was now his host, asked him to wait under an adjoining *punnāg* tree *(Mesua ferrea)*. At mid-night from that tree issued a spring of fresh water, some cooked rice and sour milk. The Chief ghost sat in front of the tree and fed the Bania. He then fed his followers. At last, he fed himself. The Bania asked his host how he could get food and water in the desert, how the ghosts became so obedient to him, and why the food-supply disappeared as soon as he partook only of a mouthful. He also wondered how a single mouthful could satisfy his hunger. The ghostly host said :—"Listen to my history. I was a wicked Bania in the city of Sharal. I became an atheist. I did not feed Brahmans or the poor. There was a pious Brahman merchant in the same city. He was my friend. He took me to the banks of the river Tapti on the 12th of the month of *Bhādrapad* (August-September) when the moon was at the *Shravan* Constellation. At the confluence of the Tapti with the Chandrabhāga, my friend bathed himself on that day and fasted. He gave to a Brahman priest a pot full of that sacred water with an umbrella, a pair of shoes, clothes and the gold image of Vāman. I imitated my friend. When

I died, I became a ghost owing to my sin in leading the life of an atheist, but the good I did in merely imitating my friend (even without faith) has done me good and supplies me with the food and drink you just saw. I retain the history of my previous birth in my memory. That also is due to the *puja.* All these evil spirits have become my slaves owing to that single good act." He then added that the hospitality he could show to the guest has released him from the ghost form and that he was going to Heaven, but before leaving him, he advised him to take charge of the book he carried under his arm. It was the register of the ghost-army. He requested the Bania to go to Gaya and to perform the obsequies of each of the poor ghosts. He then described to him the spot on the Himalayas where he would get a treasure-trove to meet the expenses of the ceremonies. The chief ghost then ascended to Heaven in a *Vimān*—or celestial palanquin. The Bania guest followed his instructions and released one by one all the sufferers of the ghost world registered in the book. On another 12th day of the month of *Bhādrapad* at the conjunction of the *Shravan* constellation the Bania performed another *puja* of Vāman. He continued doing so all along his life and ultimately became the Emperor of the Gods, that is Indra. His Kingdom is said to contain trees which yield wished for fruits, the rivers contain milk and sugar. It has in it many beautiful tanks full of lotus and other flowers. There are fairies to enjoy. Kings Sagar, Kukkutha, Dhandhumar, Gādhi and others had performed this *puja.*

All those, therefore, who on the 12th day of *Bhādrapad* at the conjunction of the *Sravan* constellation will perform this *puja* will become in turn the Emperors of the gods—the Indras of Heaven.

**Varna Sathi.** It is the 6th *Shrāvan* (July August). There lived in a city a Brahman. He had seven daughters. Like King Lear he asked them through whose good fortune they lived happily. The elder six said that it was his good luck that made them happy. The seventh, the youngest said, that she depended on her own good or bad luck. The father was offended. He got his first six daughters married to rich men—young and good looking, and gave the youngest one to a leper simply out of spite! Poor girl! She served her husband faithfully but the disease was incurable and he died in distress. When his body was removed to the cremation ground, the wife insisted on being left alone with it. She would not allow people to burn it. All went home. She sat alone with the head of the corpse in her lap. She cried, she put into the mouth of the deceased husband a seed of the *Lablab vulgari* (or *Vāl*) each time reciting the name of God. At mid-night Shiva and Pārvati were passing the place in a celestial vehicle. Pārvati heard the cry of the girl and induced Shiva to get down to see who it was. They asked why she was crying and on being told of the history of the unfortunate marriage, they advised her to go to her maternal aunt at once and ask her to give her her accumulated religious merit for having fasted on the *Varna Sathi* day. She did so, brought the merit with her and poured it down the throat of the corpse in the shape of water! They both went to the house of the aunt. She received them well. She explained to her niece how the *Vrat* was to be performed. It was this:—

On the 6th of *Shrāvan* (July August), take a handful of rice on a plantain leaf, and on another the seeds of the *Lablab vulgari*, place a coin over the latter, and offer a spoonful of water saying "Shiva bathes, and Gauri dances, this is my offering to them on the *Varna Sathi* day." The rice, the *vāl* seed, and the money should then be handed over to a priest. This should be repeated every year. It grants escape from evils, fulfilment of desires, children, and wealth.

She did all that, went to her father's house and

reminded him that although he had deserted her, God or her Luck did not! All were happy.

**Vata Sāvitri.** The *Sāvitri-vrata* is a fast kept by Hindu women on the last three days, or the last day of the bright half of Jeshta (June) to avert widowhood.

In order that the reader may appreciate the Nature-myth of Sāvitri, which underlies the symbolism, and the ceremonies proper to the occasion, I will quote the Pauranic story:—She was the daughter of the king Ashvapati. When she had reached a marriageable age, her father asked her to go in search of a husband and make her choice herself. She returned and announced to her father that she had chosen Satyavat, the son of an old king, who, after being dethroned, was then living in the jungle with his wife. At this time Nārad, the all-knowing saint, who happened to be present, told her and her father that it would be choosing grief and misery, because Satyavat was fated to die within a year. But the high-minded maiden could on no account be persuaded to change her mind. They were therefore married. Sāvitri discarded her princely jewels and dresses, and followed her husband in the coarse raiment of the hermit. During the last three days of his life she vowed to fast. On the fated day, as her husband has gone out to collect fagots or to fell trees, she accompanied him. Fatigued by his work, Satyavān rested his head upon his wife's lap and fell asleep. At this point there are variants in the story. Some authors say that a branch of the tree fell on his head, while others proclaim that he was bitten by a snake. Anyhow the fact remains that he rested his head on the lap of his wife—Mother Earth, as will be shown further on. At that moment Yama, as the Marāthas call him, or Jama as the Bengalis say, snatched his soul out of his body in the presence of his devoted wife and moved towards the South. Sāvitri closely followed the God of Death, and as she was a *Sati*, even the hard-hearted Yama dared not interfere with her. At last,

Love conquered Death, and at her earnest solicitation, Yama restored to life the prostrate body of her Lord, and blessed her with gifts. Among them were—the restoration of the lost eye-sight, youth, and crown of her father-in-law, and the birth of a hundred sons to the now happy pair.

Sāvitri is therefore regarded as the highest type of conjugal fidelity, and her example is held out to every daughter of high-class India for imitation. Here the *Purān* ends, but Ethnology does not discard all mythological records as mere stories. Carlyle tells us that behind literature there is a great deal of the history of the evolution of religion handed down by tradition. Traditions are still recorded in India by symbols or in heiroglyphic or pictographic writings, and with my wife's help I have been able to get a copy of some traditional drawings lately made with sandal-wood paste on a wall. I have not interfered with her original production (Plate attached), as I prefer it to any of the embellishments of modern artists, who would introduce the ghost-like shadow of death in servile imitation of Watt's celebrated painting of Love and Death, and murder or mutilate the chaste symbolism of the past, *vide* modern chromolithographs sold in the *bazārs*.

The first impression produced by the picture is that it is a marriage scene. The priest (fig. 36) and the group of musicians (figs. 37, 38, 39) tell us that. But let us look at the Sun (fig. 1) and the Moon (fig. 5). They are the two eyes of the Mahāpurusa or the Great Person, the common source of life, the highest manifestations of fructifying force. Emerson tells us that it is the vivifying morning sun, which, rising, awakens the sleeping world and gives life to men and plants. The Sun* and the Moon signify

* Note by the Honourable Mr. R. Burn, I.C.S. The Sun and the Moon almost invariably occur on *Sati*-pillars in Bundelkhand, and are usually interpreted as symbols of chastity, thus implying the everlasting union of the faithful wife with her husband.

beatific life, and in their conjunction were emblems of blessedness. On the elaborate Shield of Achilles, Homer is careful to describe a representation of the Moon in full, together with the disc of the Sun. In Egypt the Sun is Osiris, the Good Being, the vivifying eye of Hor. In the harvest-scenes of the Mexican gods in the *Codex Tarono*, the lives of the seeds are shown to exist to immortal fruitage in the country of the Sun, and in that Blessed Isle, the garden of Ialon, even the soul of the man awaits the touch of the solar fire to kindle again and bloom into the familiar and coveted form of man. It is a boon which the Egyptian seeks in his appeal to Osiris that the Sun should shine upon his sarcophagus. The Persian symbol of the divinity resembles one drawn in India. Emerson adds that they are considered to be anthropomorphic beings, and are in both the countries represented with human faces. In India, the Moon is called *Oshadhipati* or Lord of the Vegetable Kingdom, and the brother of the Sun. In Egypt again, the Moon is the presiding genius of the Thunder Bird, the giver of rain. In Chaldæa, as well as in Mexico, the Moon is not always distinguishable from the earth-goddess, Coltine.

Figs. 2, 3 and 4 are hanging lamps. May it be that they represent stars or constellations? Fig 3 is called *ākāsha-dipa*, sky-lamp, and is exhibited on a pole at the time of the Divāli Festival, to guide, according to the Marāthās, the gods who are expected to grace the festival with their presence. In Bengal they are supposed to guide the departed souls of the people.

Fig. 6 is the *ārti*, or one of the floating frames for lamps which are launched on the Ganges in Benares and other places, reflecting in the limpid water a scene all ablaze. *Arti*, in some shape or other, is necessary in all *pujas*. The other articles required for a *puja*, as well as for a marriage ceremony, are also in evidence. Fig. 16 is the cylindri cal box for keeping *kunkum*, the red powder applied by married (excepting widows) or unmarried Hindu women to their foreheads. Fig. 17 is the box which contains a preparation of bees'-wax, the adhesive medium for the red powder. Fig. 18 is the *tabak* or tray for holding flowers, moistened rice, and sandal-wood paste. Fig. 19 is the *panchpāle*, or five-partite box, for keeping turmeric powder, *kunkum*, scented *abhir*, brown *gulāl*, and red *sendur*. Fig. 20 is the *tāmbya* or *lota* to hold water and to represent Varuna, the God of Rain. Fig. 21 illustrates the water-cup and the sacrificial spoon. Fig. 24 is the comb. Fig. 25 the looking-glass. There are the toilette requisites of a bride, and are not symbols, except in so far as they indicate the happy married state of the main figure.

Fig. 23 is, however, an exceptional group of five coils, with a double significance. In this place they represent the bamboo-trays, in which a bride's requisites are put together and distributed among married women. But when considered with the winnowing-basket trays, shaped like a horse-shoe, similarly used during the Gauri or Harvest Festival, they lead one to think of the coil—the symbol of the celestial serpent—the emblem of the awakened forces of the Spring, as will be seen further on. Fig. 7 is the serpent or *nāg*, represented in Hindu mythology by the Sesha, or thousand-headed cobra, who supports the Earth, and by Vāsuki, the snake that coils itself round Shiva. In Egypt, it symbolizes lightning. The North Indians attribute to this symbol the power of giving life in their shamanistic rites, and the medicine-man uses it to secure resurrection and preservation. The Mexican sun-snakes were marked with disks on their heads, and, says Emerson, would appear to refer to the awakened forces of Spring after the hybernating Winter (*vide* specimens in the Ethnological Museum of Berlin). The Indian rattlesnake is supposed to hold a *mani* or jewel in his head, which he puts out at night to guide himself with its bright light. This head jewel or *mani* is sometimes drawn above the head. The serpent hair of the Gorgonhead amulet of Athene's shield is a representation of the ærial serpent, seen to leap from the skies in forked lightning. The coils on the locks of the gods of Assyria and Chaldea, the waving locks of the Egyptian god Bes, and the serpent-locks of Ato-to-harto, the Indian demi-god, are all intended as signs of celestial approaches and domination. An idol in the Ethnographic Museum at Berlin has all the lineaments of its face composed of serpents, and is supposed to be a graphic, though barbaric, image of Immortal Reawakening Life, the God-head of Nature. The hybernating snake awakes with the approaching Summer. When the heat of the Sun descends in vast waves upon the Earth, and vegetation springs up, the serpent throws off his old garments and comes forth in burnished splendour, the symbol of bright Athene's celestial array. Thus then the serpentine coil suggests the joys of the vernal epoch of resurrection. Demeter, the goddess of maize, was once adorned with serpentine locks. It was she whom the Greeks believed to be in attendance within the tomb with the maize in her hand.

Fig. 8 is a peacock, closely associated, like the stormy petrel, with the approach of the monsoon. At that time the peacock puts on his annual new plumage. Sanskrit literature is full of references to the joy which the approach of a cloud produces in the peacock. Fig. 9 is called *jālindraphul*, which may mean fret-work, but the lotus-design deserves notice. Fig. 10 is called *chendu* a ball. I am unable to explain what it means and why it comes in here. Fig. 11, *seshācha-palang* or 'bed of the thousand-headed cobra.' Vishnu sleeps on it, but the name Vishnu literally means 'he who pervades the universe.' Fig. 12 is the sacred *tulsi* plant, the consort of Vishnu, itself an emblem of resurrection as well as chastity. Fig. 13 is a *kamal* or lotus, the seat of Brahma, the Creator, and of Lakshmi, the Goddess of Wealth. Fig. 14 is the fylefoot* cross, the *Svastik*, the symbol of the four quarters of the globe, as well as of the winds and the emblem of good-luck. Fig. 15 is the *Ficus indica*, the Indian fig-tree, with association like the Golden Bough of the West. It never dies, its aerial roots support its new branches and it goes on growing for ages, as the historical *kabir bar* has been. Fig. 22 is called Vata-Sāvitri after this gigantic tree, the king of the forest. It represents the chief deity :—Mother Earth, the daughter of the Sun. She holds a twig of the *Ficus religiosa* in one hand, and the aerial root of the *Ficus indica* in the other, and has growing over her head an off-shoot of the *vata*. She is the bride whose marriage is celebrated every year, with the revived Fructifying Force personified in Satyavān or Satyavat, who is seen climbing the eternal, evergreen fig-tree (fig. 40) in the presence of, and side by side with, a snake, the emblem of resurrection. Figs. 27 and 31 are sparrows, the harbingers of a crop. Fig. 28 is a mango-hawker, the mango being the first-fruit of June. Fig. 29 is the mango-tree. Its leaves are strung into wreaths to make festoons for marriage-bowers : its inflorescence is sacred to Madan, the God of Love ; its fruit is offered to gods. Fig. 30 is the *bel (Ægle marmelos)*. Its trifoliate leaf is sacred to Siva, the emblem of procreative power, as seen in the phallus. Figs. 32, 33, 34 and 35 are the usual associates of a river. All primitive colonies were established on the banks of the rivers. Fig. 36 is the priest reading his text, and figs. 37, 38 and 39 represent a group of musicians, so essential to a marriage ceremony.

One important feature remains to be noticed: the altar on which the two fig-trees and the central figure are depicted (see figs. 15, 22, 26). The square altar represents the

* The ring-topped cross or *crux ansata* of Egypt, Asia Minor, and Chaldea, the guarded cross, the gammadion or *svastika*, of Scandinavia, Central Europe, the Caucasus, India, Tibet, China, and Japan, is held to be lucky, Sir James Campbell, in his *Notes on Spirit Basis of Belief and Custom*, p. 53.

Earth in Egyptian hieroglyphics, the stepped altar indicates the verb 'to be' or 'to make.'* The Egyptian Isis bears upon her head a stepped altar or throne and kneels deploring the dealth Osiris, in a sculpture in the British Museum.† The Greeks used stepped altars, and to the lesser gods they built altars of two steps, as is the case in this pictograph.

From all these symbols and from the time at which the Sāvitri fast is observed, the conclusion forced on us is that it is a Nature-myth. Dr. Tylor ‡ tells us that the close and deep analogies between the life of Nature and the life of man have been for ages dwelt upon, and poets and philosophers have, in simile or in argument, told us of light and darkness, of calm and tempest, of birth, growth, change, decay, dissolution, renewal. The natural phenomena of the seasons due to the relation of the Earth with the Sun have given rise to many myths. The Sun is Savitur§ in Sanskrit, and Sāvitri means the daughter of the Sun, just as Jānaki and Bhimaki means the daughters of Janaka and Bhimaka respectively. Sāvitri is also the name of the wife of Brahma, the Creator (Nature), and the heroine of the legend is supposed to be her *avatār* or incarnation. The Sāvitrivrata‖ is therefore the annual celebration of Mother Earth's marriage with Nature, the Creative Power, Satyavān (lit., truth incarnate , or Nature) just reviving after the first few showers of the monsoon. It is the marriage (not rape) of Persiphone. It is Odysseus returning to his mourning constant Penelope.

A few points from the Sanskrit text called *Sāvitri-puja* in the *Skanda Purāna* deserve notice. The original Sāvitri

* MS. *Mexicaine Bibliotheque Nationale Paris, Codex Telleriano.*

† *Champolion, Gr. Egyptienne,* p. 454.

‡ *Primitive Culture,* Vol. I, p. 318.

§ *Tat Savitur Varenyam,* etc., *Hindu Sandhya.*

‖ Savitri is Gayatri, and Gayatri or Cow is the form in which Mother Earth appeared before Indra, whenever in distress through drought.

of the story is called the wife of Brahma, the Creator. When she appeared before "the king" she held *aksha sutra* in one hand, and a water-jug in the other. *Aksha sutra* means terrestrial latitude from *aksha*, to reach or to pervade, and it may mean the root of a tree when it reaches the earth and spreads itself. The king is called Dyumatsena, but *dyu* is sky and *dyumat* is brilliant. Satyavat or Satyavān, the husband of Sāvitri, who has mythologically been called his son, is also called Chitrāshva, which means a wonderful horse-player, which is the name of Aruna, the Charioteer of the Sun, who manages the seven-faced horses of the Sun, and these wonderful horses represent the Saptrishis or the Constellation *Ursa Major* of the Northern Pole. Further on, there occurs the expression *glānischa mahatija*, a great swoon. Can it be the state of hybernation? The God of Death is called Vaivasvat, Southern Yama. May it not mean the Southern blast of wind which destroys tender shoots?

One more interesting quotation, though not directly connected with this myth, gives strong corroborative evidenc of the belief in the little man (soul) in the body of the living big man, described by Fraser in his *Golden Bough*. It is said in the text that Yama forcibly took out an image of a man of the size of the thumb from the mortal frame of Satyavat. This quotation serves to confirm the conclusions ethnologists have arrived at regarding primitive belief about " life as distinct from the body."

**Vatsa-dvādashi.** See Vasubāras.

**Vijayā-dashmi.** See Dasara, under Navarātra.

**Vināyaki-chaturthi.** The fourth day of the light half of month. See Ganesh for folkfore.

**Wednesday and Thursday Worships.** On Wednesday or Budhvār planet *Budh* or Mercury is worshipped, and on Thursday Guruvār, alias Brihaspativār, Guru alias Brihaspati known in Europe as Jupiter is worshipped during the month of *Shrāvan* (July-August). The folkfore runs:—

There was a city in which there lived a king. He had seven sons and an equal number of daughters-in-law. To his palace, there came daily two Brahmans to beg. One was the nephew of the other. The conceited daughters-in-law always told them that they were very busy and that their hands were not "unoccupied" enough to offer them alms. The result was poverty. The family became poor and their hands free. But the six elder daughters-in-law still said to the Brahmans that their hands were empty and they could offer nothing. The youngest girl noticed that these very Brahmans were turned out during their palmy days on one ground, and that they are now being sent away on another. She came forward, she bowed to the Brahmans and said that it was a great sin to refuse alms while they were rich. She expressed regret at the blunder, and begged to be advised as to the way to regain their former position and wealth. The Brahmans advised, that during the month of Shrāvan a Brahman should be asked to dine. *Budh* (Mercury) and *Guru* (Jupiter) should be worshipped. If a woman's husband has gone out of town, she should draw two human figures behind the door-ways of her house and he will return soon. If she desires wealth, she should draw them on her box. If she wants grain she should do the same on the corn-bin. After worshipping the deities or planets thus drawn, she should feed the invited Brahman to the full. She did so. One day she dreamt that she was pouring *ghi* on their plates with a silver pot. She related her dream to her sisters-in-law, but they ridiculed her. What followed is very interesting. Her husband had gone to another town in search of work. The King of that town died. But, under the rule, his body could not be cremated before a new king was announced for "The King never dies." He had no son or heir and the Council of State decided that a cow-elephant be let loose with a wreath of flowers in her trunk. This was done, the whole city assembled to see the spectacle. Our traveller was among them. The cow-elephant with the wreath approached him and put the latter round his neck. Hurrah! He was the king elect in a minute. But the Council of State wanted to be sure of the divine selection thus made evident through the sagacity of the brute. They tried again; and again did the animal put the wreath round the neck of the same man. A third time was the experiment tried with the same result. He was therefore declared the King and enthroned. He had left his house in distress in search of work, and after he was gone all the members of his family had also left the town and wandered in search of employment. He sent messengers all over the country, but could get no news of his family. At last he opened extensive work for providing his capital with a suitable tank. Among the coolies collected there, he discovered and recognized his own kith and kin. He brought them home. His wife told him how devoutly she worshipped Mercury and Jupiter, how she dreamt of the feed she gave to Brahmans, how she held a silver pot (silver-spoon was too small) for pouring out the *ghi*, and how her sisters-in-law laughed at her. The next day, the new King gave a banquet to hundreds of Brahmans and the new Queen was given a silver-*lota* to serve out the *ghi*. The dream was thus realised, the sisters-in-law thence forward had the greatest respect for the new Queen. They prospered and lived happily all the days of their lives. Such is the power of the worship of the planets that preside over Wednesday and Thursday.

FINIS

# INDEX AND GLOSSARY

C

## H

## WORKS BY THE SAME AUTHOR.

### A. (PUBLISHED BY GOVERNMENT).

1. The Industrial Arts of Poona, Thana, and Nasik published in the Bombay Gazetteer, compiled by Sir James Campbell.
2. List of Art Manufactures, exclusive of Textiles of the Bombay Presidency, printed under Government Orders, 1885.
3. List of Raw Products of the Bombay Presidency forwarded to the Paris International Exhibition, 1878.
4. Descriptive catalogue of the Victoria and Albert Museum, Bombay.
5. Descriptive catalogue of the School of Art Museum, Bombay.
6. Descriptive catalogue of the Art-ware contributions of the Bombay Court of the Calcutta International Exhibition, 1883-84.
7. Descriptive catalogue of the Bombay Manufacture's Court at the Calcutta International Exhibition, 1883-84.
8. Manila Hemp.
9. Jute and Malachra Fibres.
10. Descriptive catalogue of the Ethnological Collection of the Bombay Court, Calcutta Exhibition, 1883-84.
11. Anthropometric data of Bombay.
12. Anthropometric data of Beluchistan.
13. Anthropometric data of Burma.

14. Prabhu Marriage.

15. Position of Women among Hindus, Musalmans, Buddhists and Jains.

16. General Indefinite Characteristics of the Tribes of Burma.

17 General Indefinite Characteristics of the Tribes of Baluchistan.

18. Craniological data from the Indian Museum.

19. Glossary of Indian Castes and Tribes.

20. Descriptive catalogue of Pictures at the Victoria Memorial Exhibition.

21. Descriptive catalogue of Arms and Armour at the Victoria Memorial Exhibition.

22. Descriptive catalogue of Sculptures at the Victoria Memorial Exhibition.

23. Descriptive catalogue of Medals at the Victoria Memorial Exhibition.

24. Descriptive catalogue of original Documents, Manuscripts and Books at the Victoria Memorial Exhibition.

25. Index of Pictures at the Victoria Memorial Exhibition.

26. Bibliography of Ethnography.

27. Agricultural Chemistry and Geology in Marathi (sanctioned prize book in schools).

28. Principle of Practical Geometry, a text-book for the Sir J. J. School of Art, Bombay (Marathi).

29. Practical Geometry, a text-book for the Sir J. J. School of Art, Bombay (Marathi).

B. OTHERS.

30. Prevention of Famines. Distributed by Government among officers of the Forest Department, Bombay

Presidency. This is a translation of Dr. Wellington Gray's "Tree Planting and Water Supply of the Decan." (Marathi).

31. Annoted Edition of Grant Duff's History of the Marathas.

32. Life of General Sakhāram Hari Gupte.

33. Life of Vithalrāv Devāji.

34. Rāoji Appāji and Bābāji Appāji, Ministers of Baroda.

35. Materials for the History of the Kayasth Prabhus. 12 issues.

36. Drink sanctified.

37. Industrial Arts of Western India Gujerathi).

38. Industrial Arts of India (Marathi).

39. Guide to the Poona Exhibition, 1888.

40. Bardic Songs of the Indore State (Marathi).

41. Revenue Hand-Book of the Indore State. (State Publication).

42. Police Hand-Book of the Indore State. (State Publication.

43. List of places in the Indore State. (State Publication.)

44. Indore from Jubilee to Jubilee.

45. The other side of the Indore Question.

46. Indian Dyers and the Art of Dyeing (Gujerathi).

47. Souvenir, Poona Exhibition, 1888.

48. Souvenir, Reay Workshops, 1889.

49. Six issues of the Journal of Indian Art published during the Colonial and Indian Exhibition (edited by Sir George Birdwood) 1886.

50. Traditions of the Indore State (Marathi).

51. Traditions of the Salsettes Guptes (Marathi).

52. Jivantik (Health Scraps, Marathi).

53. The Cultivation of Memory (Marathi).
54. The Modi Script (Marathi).
55. Jains and Jainism (Marathi).
56. The Kāyasth Prabhus of Bombay, Baroda and Central Provinces.

# PLATE No. 1

**Aditya, the Sun.**

See Aditdora for folklore, page 1.

The original design of the Sun is seen on the cover. Instead of one seven headed horse, there are 7 different horses shown in this design which is based on one found in the Sculpture at the Bhārat tope. See page xxxi for the origin of the seven-headed horse, from the *Ursa Major*.

Aditya-the Sun.

Manoranjan Press,

## PLATE No. 2

ADIT-DORA.

The mystic charm worn by high caste Hindu ladies, and the symbols of the Sun described at page 4.

Adit Dora

Adit Dora the charm and symbols of the Sun.

## PLATE No. 3

ANANT, the Endless.

It is the accepted picture of (1) Vishnu, who is supposed to be the Sun, (2) of Lakshmi, the Earth, and of (3) Brahma, the refraction of the Sun. See page xxxi.

Anant— the Endless

# PLATE No. 4

**DATTATREYA.**

For the origin of the myth-see Trimurti at page 221, and plate No. 13. For folklore see page 32.

श्रीगुरुदत्त.

## PLATE No. 5

DIVALI.

This is the hieroglyphic description of a myth based on the death and resurrection of the season. For folklore see page 35.

## DIVĀLI.

*Del. Mrs. Guptē.* C.S.P.

## PLATE No. 6

GANESH or GAJANAN.

See page 55 for myths, and page xxxi for its origin from the Cancer, the fourth sign of the Zodiac. It is also possible that the death and resurrection of the season (the *Bhādvi* crop) has much to do with the elaboration.

Gajanan.

## PLATE No. 7

GANESH as SIDDHI VINAYAK, or GOD OF SUCCESS.

See page 58 for the folklore.

Ganesh and the eight Goddesses of success.

# PLATE No. 8

GANESH and GAURI SYMBOLS.

See under Ganesh, page 55; and Gauri page 77, for description.

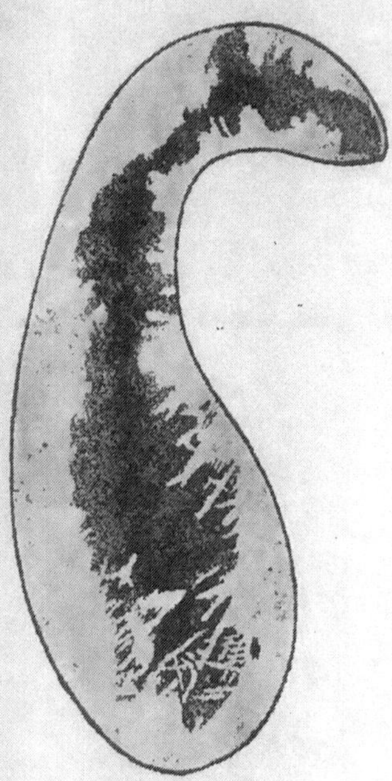

Foot prints of Gauri as produced with the hand.

Swastik.

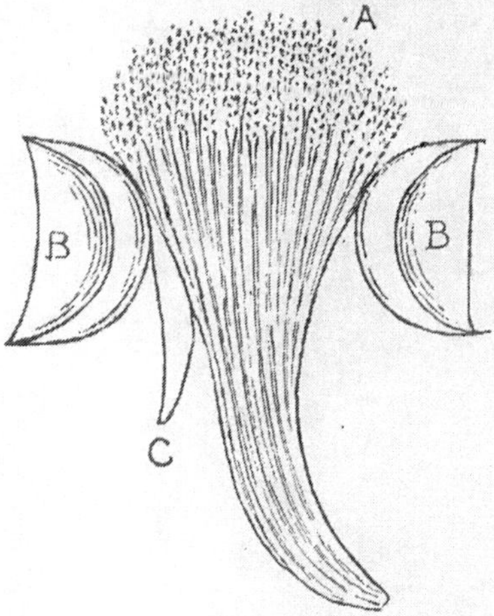


A Bundle of sheaf with a ploughshare and two winowing baskets.

## PLATE No. 9

LIAXM or LAKSHMI

The goddess ot wealth, see page 121 for description.

Luxmi.

## PLATE No. 10

MARTAND or SHRI KHANDERAV.

A representation of the Sun, destroying the demon of darkness. For folklore see Champa Shasthi, page 19.

Shri Khanderao.

## PLATE No. 11

SARASWATI.

The goddess of learning, see page 95 for the folklore.

Sarasvati.

## PLATE No. 12

SHIVARATRI.

The origin of the myth is traced to the second, third, and fifth sign of the Zodiac. See page 208 for the story.

*Mirga-Sirsha the Constellation Shivaratri.*

No. 1. Saggitarius.

No. 2. Capricornus

No. 4. Mirga-Sirsha.

LEO. SINGH.

GEMINI. MITHUN.

TAURUS. Vrishabha.

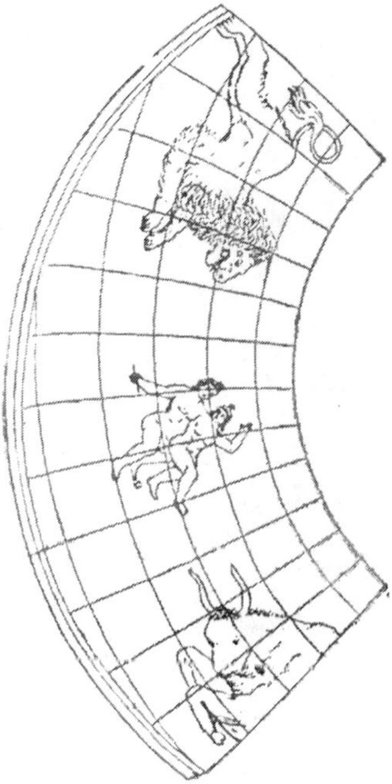

No. 5 Zodiac.

No. 3. Dhanu.

## PLATE No. 13

TORTOISE INCARNATION.

See page 220 for description and origin of the myth. It is based on the eclipse of the Sun which took place on the 25th of October 945 B.C. For the fourteen gems see pages xxxii and 226.

TORTOISE INCARNATION

## PLATE No. 14

TRIMURTI.

The origin of the myth of the three-headed god Trimurti (page 221) alias Datt or Dattātreya, is traced to the Orion in this plate. See also Datta Jayanti, pape 32.

PUNARVASU
(A House)
(Tauri)
ORION
(Mriga)
ARDRA
(A gem)
C.S.P.

## PLATE No. 15

VAT SAVITRI.

See page 238 for folklore. This is the original hieroplyphic description of the myth based on the death and resurrection of the season.

## VATA - SĀVITRI.

*Del. Mrs. Gupte* C.S.F

## PLATE No. 16

THE ANCIENT ZODIAC OF EGYPT.

The first six signs of this Zodiac suggest the origin of the Kokila Vrat, for its folklore see pages 104 and 106.

HASTA and CHITRA.

These two asterisms together with the cycle of Jupiter suggest the origin of the myth of the Kapilā Shasthi, see page 96 for the story.

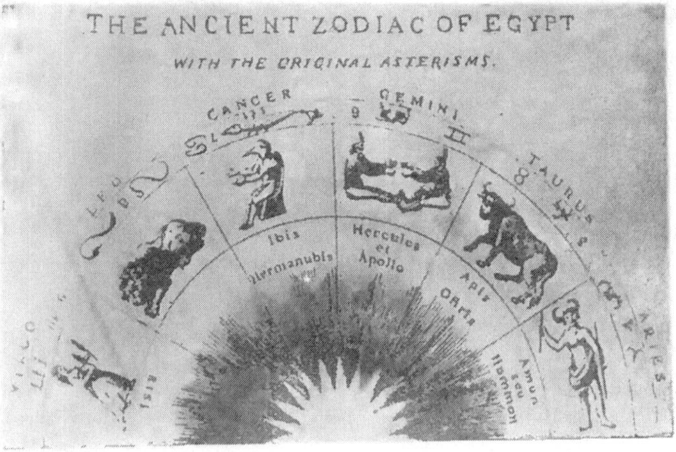


See page 106, Kokila Vrat.

Hasta

Rohini

See page 96, Kapila Shasthi.